YACHTING
MONTHLY

the **atlantic**
sailor's
handbook

YACHTING
MONTHLY

the atlantic sailor's handbook

Alastair Buchan

Adlard Coles Nautical
London

This book is dedicated to Gracie Mae Thurm
and one day she will understand why.

Acknowledgements

This is the work of a great team. Publisher, Janet Murphy, provided the encouragement when inspiration flagged. Editor, Carole Edwards, drew my attention to any gaps, contradictions and inconsistencies and waved her wand of blue pencil to make them readable. Designer, Susan McIntyre, took my mix of text, photos and drawings and put it together into a form which not only looks good but also makes you want to keep the pages turning.

At home, nothing would have happened without support from Liz who found the time to read what I have written and made sure that I did not transgress too many grammatical laws.

I owe them all unstinting thanks. What errors and omissions remain are mine and mine alone.

Published by Adlard Coles Nautical
an imprint of A & C Black (Publishers) Ltd
36 Soho Square London W1D 3QY
www.adlardcoles.com

Copyright © Alastair Buchan 2002, 2009
First published as *Sailing an Atlantic Circuit*
in 2002

ISBN 978-1-4081-0011-0

A CIP catalogue record for this book is available from the British Library.

This book is produced using paper that is made from wood grown in managed, sustainable forests. It is natural, renewable and recyclable. The logging and manufacturing processes conform to the environmental regulations of the country of origin.

Typeset in 10 on 11.5 pt Minion
Book design by Susan McIntyre
Cover design by Sutchinda Thompson

Printed and bound in China by WKT Co Ltd

Contents

Introduction

'*Proper planning and preparation prevents pretty poor performance.*'

(An age-old piece of military advice which has been forgotten by too many generals)

You have thought about it, dreamt about it, done it a thousand times in your imagination but too often prior engagements and pressing commitments conspire against following the sun south to warm seas and amenable winds. For years, your hopes of bluewater cruising are little more than a comfort blanket to snuggle under when reading accounts of far-flung cruises that become the bedrock to a fine stock of armchair opinions. Then, opportunity presents itself and you start to think that the dream could become reality. It is my aim in this book to give you some help and encouragement for your first Atlantic crossing.

The Atlantic finds new challenges for each generation. Long before Columbus arrived in the Bahamas, seamen from Phoenicia, Wales, Ireland, Norway and Portugal, the English west country and Galicia had ventured west. Statius Sevosus, a Roman historian, claimed that sailing westwards from the Gorgones (perhaps the Canaries or Cape Verde Islands) for 40 days brought travellers to a golden land called Hesperides. In the early 6th century St Brendan left Ireland on a two-way Atlantic crossing in a leather boat and returned with tales of ice palaces and lands of fire. In 1969, anticipating Tim Severins's better-known voyage, Bill Verity from Long Island built a 20-foot replica of St Brendan's boat and sailed it from Ireland to San Salvador in the Bahamas.

The Vikings pioneered the cold northern route to Greenland and by 1000 AD they had established settlements as far south as L'Anse aux Meadows in Newfoundland where they left evidence of voyages still further south. Breton fishermen visited impossibly rich fishing grounds somewhere far to the west. By August 1492, when Columbus left Pálos de La Frontera in southern Spain, he had a fair-sized body of knowledge to draw on about what the ancients called the Sea of Darkness, and according to one legend, Columbus sailed with a well-thumbed copy of the second edition of the Atlantic Pilot.

Today, the challenge of sailing across the Atlantic is not one of exploration, or proving that a particular type of vessel can cross, or make a record breaking voyage, or claim a 'first'. It has all been done. The challenge is personal, the fulfilment of a lifelong ambition, a rite of passage and a voyage of self-discovery.

Before setting out it is sound practice to have some idea how you intend to get to the other side. It is one thing to prop up the yacht club bar talking knowledgeably about crossing the Atlantic. Giving your ambition a public voice moves it to a newer, higher level. If there is a time to quit then it is before any emotional or financial commitment is made and that depends upon answers to three questions:

First, can you cross the Atlantic in your present boat? If not, then what modifications or additional equipment would be necessary to make her suitable? If your boat cannot be made suitable then what type of boat do you need and what would be required to make it ocean-worthy?

Second, how long will it take? Most of us can reel off crossing times like football scores but the published figures are for one-way passages. How long would it take to prepare a boat and then sail across the Atlantic and back? A single Atlantic circuit adds up to a programme

THE PIONEERS

The first yacht to cross the Atlantic was the 83-foot *Cleopatra's Barge* sailing from west to east in 1817. It was a mega-yacht of its day and ended its time as a commercial packet ship. In 1856 the 43-foot *Charter Oak*, similar in size to many modern blue-water cruisers, sailed from America to Europe.

The first small yacht to attempt the passage was the 24-foot *Vision*. She sailed for Europe on 24 June 1864. Given three masts and rigged as a brigantine with three square sails on the foremast (!) she had a crew of three and a dog. Apart from a brief sighting two days out from New York, she was never heard of again. Two years later the 26-foot *Red White and Blue*, a prototype lifeboat built in galvanised steel, sailed from New York on 9 July 1866 and arrived in Deal, Kent 35 days later. This was a very respectable performance for, like the *Vision*, she too had three masts and was square-rigged on all three. A square sail has much to commend itself on trade wind passages but on a west-to-east passage, square sails on so small a yacht must have been a sore trial. But the *Red White and Blue* showed that small boats could cross the Atlantic safely and thereafter one or two crept across each year, mostly from America to Europe. In 1870 the 20-foot *City of Ragusa* with a crew of two plus a dog became the first small yacht to cross from east to west and then sailed back to Europe to complete the first small-ship Atlantic circuit. Six years later, the 20-foot *Centennial* made the first single-handed passage.

Small yachts, canoes, inflatables (including RIBs), rafts, rowing boats, pedal boats, windsurfers and a jeep have all made it across. There is a fine distinction between making a seamanlike crossing in a small yacht, and putting to sea in a freak craft. Where this line is drawn is a matter of individual judgement. Is a yacht under 15–16 foot LOA freakish? Perhaps, but it is imprudent to be dogmatic. Robert Manry who crossed in the 13-foot *Tinkerbelle* in 1965, or Gerry Spiess in his 10-foot *Yankee Girl* in 1979, or Tom McClean in the 9-foot 9-inch *Giltspur* and 9-foot *Will's Way* or Eric Peters who in 1982 sailed the 5 foot 10½ inch barrel-shaped (!) *Tonkiy Nou* from the Canaries to Guadeloupe are examples to us all, and a reminder that seamanship and seaworthiness are not in direct proportion to overall length.

The pioneers made their voyages in the days of wooden ships, canvas sails, and hemp ropes. By modern yardsticks their vessels were ill-equipped. Most would be classed as estuary cruisers and some seen as fit only for inland waters. Slocum did not have a stove until he reached Gibraltar. We not only have stoves, we have all the comforts of home. Above deck we have roller-reefing headsails and mainsails, self-steering, solar panels and wind generators. To keep in touch and tell us where we are we have GPS, plotters, satellite telephones and radios. By the pioneers' standards we have it easy.

stretching over a year to 15 months with another six to nine months spent refitting before setting out – say two years in total. Corners can be – and are cut. Prune refitting time to three or four months, and it is possible to leave in April, sail to the Caribbean, turn round and sail straight back home again to arrive in August (it has been done) but this is a lot of sailing for very little fun.

Thirdly, can the family piggy bank stand the strain? There is little point starting work only to run out of money before you actually set sail. Assessing an accurate figure for costs is difficult. Writing out lists of work and equipment and placing estimated costs against each item helps, but these lists are always incomplete. Well-camouflaged unforeseen costs lie in ambush for the over-enthusiastic.

How much you spend depends partly on your boat and partly on how much work you decide is necessary to make it ready. Small is beautiful: buying a winch or a new sail for a 20-foot yacht may hurt but not as much as buying one for a 40-foot yacht. Most folk can expect that about half the preparation costs will go on safety equipment.

It is a delusion that any expenditure is recoverable. The shiny new equipment you buy for the trip adds little to the value of your yacht. It might just be possible to recoup some cash on your return by selling individual items such as wind generators, self-steering units and HF radios but this should not be relied upon. Sailing equipment, especially electronics, dates quickly and becomes almost worthless when you are the seller rather than the buyer. The only sure way to reduce capital costs is to delete items from your list and do without.

These are three very simple questions to ask but if the answer to any one of them is 'No' then all bets are off and it is back to the pontoon.

Planning and preparation are the loneliest of times. Your knowledge and understanding of what you are attempting is entirely theoretical or second-hand and much of what you are told stresses bad weather, danger and hardships. It is likely that you are extrapolating coastal and offshore experience further than common

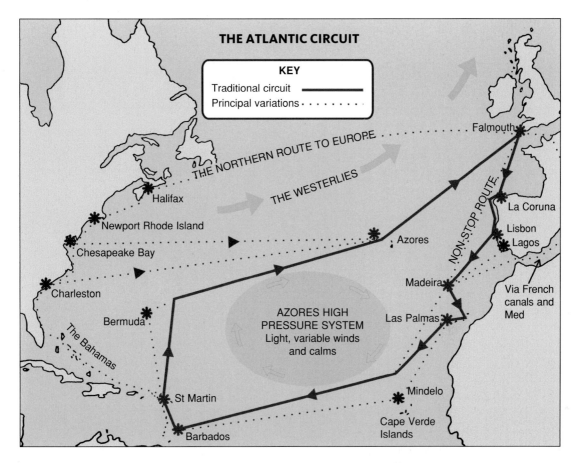

THE ATLANTIC CIRCUIT

KEY

Traditional circuit ————

Principal variations · · · · · · · ·

THE NORTHERN ROUTE TO EUROPE · · · · · · · · · · Falmouth

THE WESTERLIES

NON-STOP ROUTE

Halifax

La Coruna

Newport Rhode Island

Lisbon
Lagos

Chesapeake Bay

Azores

Charleston

Madeira

Via French canals and Med

Bermuda

Las Palmas

AZORES HIGH PRESSURE SYSTEM
Light, variable winds and calms

The Bahamas

St Martin

Mindelo

Barbados

Cape Verde Islands

sense suggests. As a result you are beset by doubts and unanswered questions and have no one to turn to for reassurance.

You are on a steep learning curve and know that you are not the first, but it comes as a surprise to learn that you are part of an annual migration. In a thousand harbours, anchorages, marinas and boatyards scattered across Europe and America others are struggling to find their own answers to the same questions, facing the same dilemmas and suffering the same highs and lows. They are reading the same books, searching the same catalogues, counting their pennies and doing the same sums. Every spring those who find the answers sniff the air, turn towards the sun, raise their sails and head south. Their tracks merge and cross and merge again. As the miles mount, nationality becomes irrelevant. You become part of an international community, known by your boat's name, not its flag, and membership is sufficient introduction to discuss plans, and swap information so that finding advice and support is no problem.

But that is the future. First it will be solitary hard work with little obvious progress. There are associations like the OCC (Ocean Cruising Club) for those who have made an ocean passage but there is no club for potential ocean cruisers. At this stage you are isolated dreamers.

I have tried in this book to include all the information, hints and tips I would like to have known before I sailed. I do not expect everyone to agree with everything I say (no one ever has) but I hope that this book will give you some useful advice based on practical experience that will help to see you safely and happily across the Atlantic.

The small harbour of Ribeiras in Pico island, Azores.

part one **planning and preparation**

chapter 1 When should I go?

Pioneers often sailed at unusual times of the year. In 1577 when he left Plymouth on his circumnavigation, Drake sailed on 15 November and ran into a gale that dismasted his ship and blew another ashore. Three centuries later, the first transatlantic race between the *Henrietta*, *Vesta* and *Fleetwing* was held in December 1866.

Departures often took place in late June and July when there was (and still is) a real risk of meeting a hurricane. In his book *Half Safe* Ben Carlin describes being caught in a tropical storm between the Azores and Madeira in December 1950. The Carlins had left Halifax late in July and were probably lucky not to have met one earlier. David Johnstone and John Hoare in the rowing dory *Puffin* were lost in Hurricane Faith some time in September 1966 as they raced Ridgway and Blyth across the Atlantic. They had left Virginia Beach, Norfolk on 21 May. In the last week of June 1968, entrants in the Single-Handed Transatlantic Race from Plymouth to Newport RI were heading towards Hurricane Brenda (the second of the season!) which was travelling east more or less along the latitude of the Azores.

Why sail when there is a risk of hurricanes? Or, for that matter, why sail when the odds favour bad weather? Re-reading accounts of transatlantic passages, I saw that one factor stood out. Those who sailed late in the season had met unforeseen problems and delays in their preparations and fallen behind schedule. They had to choose between sailing with their preparations incomplete, leaving much later than planned or delaying their voyage until the next season.

The lesson is clear. If you wish to sail with your preparations complete then the clock starts earlier than you first thought. At the very latest it begins ticking the autumn before you sail but if your boat needs major surgery then give up a season's sailing to be sure that the work is finished on time. Better still, double the estimated timescale for your preparations and then add half as much again as a cushion against unexpected problems. Initially, preparations are done in the evenings and weekends but for the last month or so when you are stocking the boat and catching up on all those tasks that have fallen behind schedule they become a full time task.

Even then be wary of a firm commitment to leave on a particular day. Naming a departure date concentrates the mind but it can be a rod for your own back. If a few days' delay would see the forepeak decently stowed, last-minute stores delivered and vital work properly completed and tested then it is time well lost.

Donald Crowhurst on *Teignmouth Electron* was caught both ways in this trap. He had too little time for preparation and a firmly fixed departure date. Committed emotionally,

RALLIES

Joining an organised rally can remove the fear of the unknown and provide support when it is most needed. It means meeting the standards the organisers lay down for safety gear carried, minimum crew numbers and training. Most rallies offer a range of seminars and training courses to help prepare those taking part. There is usually either a minimum, and sometimes maximum, size for participating yachts or a requirement to meet a minimum average speed.

THE PROS	THE CONS
Help with preparation, usually through seminars.	You sail to the rally's timetable. For slower yachts this can mean no time to explore intermediate ports of call and little time in official ports of call.
Advice and help on safety concerns including a system for reporting passage position to keep track of yachts en route.	Opportunities for variations in the route are few and sometimes not allowed.
Support teams at the major ports of call which, besides having good facilities for socialising and sightseeing, are selected to provide good transport links for crew joining or leaving and maintenance facilities.	Sometimes the numbers taking part can overwhelm the facilities of the ports of call. The number of yachts in the harbours and marinas can attract thieves.
Logistic support for repairs and supplies.	The organisers may claim rights over film, videotape and audio-visual material taken during the rally.

financially and publicly he started the 1968 Golden Globe Round the World Race with his boat unfinished, gear unstowed and generally unready to sail. It is impossible to avoid speculating what part his hasty start played in the subsequent tragedy. When Francis Chichester sailed *Gipsy Moth IV* round the world he stuck to his self imposed departure deadline despite the problems that plagued (and still afflict) his boat, even though another year of work and sea trials could have resolved his difficulties.

Good weather can never be guaranteed, especially at the margins of a season. It is wise to aim for the middle of each weather window where comfort and lazy sailing are most likely to be found. This tactic also provides an easily varied start date, a euphemism for 'delayed', without ever cutting it too fine.

Unless taking to the French canals and approaching the Canaries via the Mediterranean it is best to wait for the end of the spring gales before crossing the Bay of Biscay. This window closes when the equinoctial gales blow in from the Atlantic, by which time you ought to be somewhere close to Madeira or the Azores. Both Madeira, which the square-riggers called 'The Island', and the Azores are a two- to three-week sail from the European mainland; if you decide to sail direct to them from Europe it places the latest sensible departure in the middle of August.

Once in the Canaries, the next weather window opens at the end of November with the closing performances of the hurricane season. This is the earliest reasonable time for leaving the Canaries for the Caribbean although other factors come into play. Boats in the Atlantic Rally for Cruisers (ARC) leave Las Palmas on the last Sunday in November so as to have a fair chance of arriving in St Lucia in time for the Christmas parties. It is also possible to spend Christmas and New Year in the Canaries and still have time to sail to the Caribbean, or sail south in December to the Cape Verde Islands and celebrate there.

Most yachts arrive in the Caribbean in late December or early January. This gives five months of warm, bluewater cruising before the next hurricane season. If the plan includes returning to Europe, it is necessary to be at a suitable departure port in the Caribbean or the eastern seaboard of the USA and sail clear of the hurricane zone before the season's first storm arrives. A useful rule of thumb is to be in the Azores before the end of June. This leaves a few weeks to explore the Azores before sailing back to Europe in time to avoid the start of the autumn gales. Working backwards, it means leaving the USA or the Caribbean around the middle to end of May. If you decide to remain in the Caribbean then during late April or early May you should implement your chosen hurricane season strategy.

Popular rallies for an Atlantic Circuit are organised by:

- **World Cruising Club Ltd** (www.worldcruising.com/arc/) organises the Atlantic Rally for Cruisers (ARC) which leaves every year from Las Palmas in the last week of November for St Lucia.

- **Blue Water Rallies** (www.worldrallies.co.uk) organises round-the-world cruises starting in October from Gibraltar aiming to arrive in Antigua by December and, in July each year, the Biscay Triangle starting from Torquay. Boats can join and leave rallies as best suits their programme.

- **Offshore Passage Opportunities** has been organising the NARC Rally from Newport RI to St Martin via Bermuda since at least 1999. The rally leaves in the last week of October each year. Contact Offshore Passage Opportunities at PO Box 260 Halesite, New York or call 800-472-7724.

- **Cruising Rally Association** (www.carib1500.com) has been organising cruises to and from the Caribbean since 1990.

- **The Bermuda Race** or **Newport Bermuda Race** This is not a rally but a biennial yacht race for serious racers from Newport, Rhode Island to Bermuda. (www.bermudarace.com)

TIMINGS FOR AN ATLANTIC LOOP

KEY	
Shorebased activities	
Day sailing	
Passages under 1000nm	
Passages over 1000nm	

NOTE: It is possible to cruise the Madeiras and the Canaries all year round. With care, or by sailing south out of the hurricane zone, it is possible to sail all year round in the Caribbean.

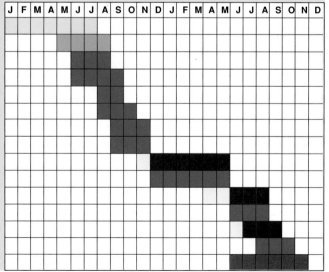

Action	J	F	M	A	M	J	J	A	S	O	N	D	J	F	M	A	M	J	J	A	S	O	N	D
• Refit. Probably begun previous Oct/Nov	▓	▓	▓																					
• Outward cruise: British and N European coasts				▓	▓																			
• Passage to north-west Spain					▓																			
• Cruise northern Spanish and Portuguese coasts						▓	▓																	
• Passage to the Madeiras: boats from the Med join here							▓																	
• Cruise Madeira								▓																
• Passage to the Canaries								▓																
• Cruise the Canaries									▓	▓														
• Passage to the Caribbean											▓	▓												
• Cruise the Caribbean inc Bahamas and E coast USA												▓	▓	▓	▓	▓	▓							
• Passage to the Azores																	▓	▓						
• Cruise Azores																		▓						
• Passage to British and N European coasts																		▓	▓					
• Homeward cruise: British and N European coasts																				▓	▓			
• HURRICANE SEASON																		▓	▓	▓	▓	▓	▓	

chapter 2 What will it cost?

Pre-sail refit

One of the most costly elements of your budget for the Atlantic circuit will be the pre-sail refit; it is difficult to accurately estimate the exact costs. You may wish to fit additional water and fuel tanks or buy a purpose-made awning. You will almost certainly want to purchase equipment such as self-steering, solar panels, wind generators, water makers, liferafts, EPRIBs, satellite phones and HF radio transceivers. If you need to cut costs then concentrate on the essentials. You can live without an HF transceiver, a satellite phone or watermaker but safety equipment, self-steering and some way of generating electrical power, which is independent of the engine, are non-optional. AIS radar and radar detectors to warn of approaching shipping are close to, but probably not quite, essential.

All sails should be checked and valeted. Some may require replacing. Standing rigging must be carefully inspected and running rigging renewed. A second bower anchor is essential and a third 'thank-God' anchor stowed in the bilge could be a prudent investment. Some sort of drogue or parachute sea-anchor might be useful in really heavy weather. All need their own anchor rode.

You will need spares and consumables for every item of equipment aboard (the more obvious examples are fuel and oil filters and engine fan belts) as well as sufficient paint for several coats of anti-fouling.

Insurance

Insurance is not a legal requirement but having adequate cover is comforting. Premiums are split into boat insurance and personal insurance. Insuring a boat for an ocean passage is not cheap. Probably less than four months of an Atlantic circuit is actually spent ocean voyaging. The remainder of the time is given over to partying in harbour or making short hops between ports. So you may believe that you only have to pay for offshore sailing with an additional premium for a few weeks ocean cruising.

Sadly, many insurance companies are reluctant to insure yachts making ocean passages. Some refuse point blank and those that do offer cover frequently impose restrictions. They may only insure vessels above a certain size or value. Insurers may insist on a minimum crew; three is a popular number. The skipper, and perhaps the mate may be required to hold an internationally recognised qualification such as an RYA Yachtmaster Ocean™ certificate. Insurance companies will almost certainly exclude cruising in hurricane areas during the hurricane season and ask for a much higher than normal deductible (excess), usually well into four figures. Such conditions and charges are sometimes justified on the grounds that if you call for assistance in mid-ocean then rescuers will save you but not your boat, leaving the insurance company to pay out.

If comprehensive cover is too expensive, think about taking out third party cover for the entire voyage and arrange separate cover for coastal and offshore areas. Ocean passages are then at your own risk but when you arrive in Spain, the Canaries or the Caribbean you will be insured for coastal and offshore waters.

Anything not bolted to the deck or hull counts as personal belongings and equipment and is not covered by the boat insurance. Cameras and laptops, even if used for navigation, are obvious examples of personal possessions, less so are binoculars and hand-held radios and

GPS units. On a long cruise you will carry far more personal belongings than usual and it is prudent take out a separate personal, all risks insurance policy. Your crew should be aware of this and encouraged to take out their own insurance cover.

Emergency fund

No plan survives contact with reality. The emergency fund consists of cash that you must find very quickly to meet any unexpected problem or emergency. This may be flying home to deal with some crisis, gear failure or the theft of some vital piece of kit that can only be replaced by having it flown in from Europe or the USA. At the very least the fund should cover the cost of flying everyone home from the remotest and most expensive (in travel terms) area of your trip. This includes the cost of laying your boat up somewhere safe for the duration of your time away. With luck this money will be spent celebrating your return as planned.

Day to day costs

How much you spend on day-to-day living depends on how high on the hog you choose to live. If you insist on gourmet dinners then your figure will be fatter and your costs higher than those who boil rice and open a can of tuna. If, in port, you eat in the best restaurants, hire cars and take every sightseeing trip as though on a two-week package holiday then your daily living costs will be high.

For shore transport in, say, the Canaries, a folding cycle beats walking and is cheaper than taxis. In the Caribbean, road conditions, longer distances and a good cheap public transport network make cycling more demanding and less attractive. An often unforeseen extra

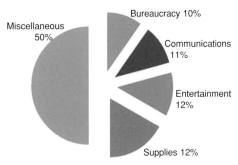

Annual personal costs

Bureaucracy 10%
Communications 11%
Entertainment 12%
Supplies 12%
Miscellaneous 50%

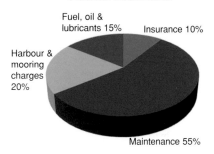

Annual boat costs

Fuel, oil & lubricants 15%
Insurance 10%
Harbour & mooring charges 20%
Maintenance 55%

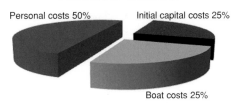

Atlantic circuit costs

Personal costs 50%
Initial capital costs 25%
Boat costs 25%

is paying to enter, and sometimes to leave, Caribbean countries. Most charge a fee for each crew member, and ask for more cash before issuing a cruising permit. Some countries demand that you have a visa and a few occasionally arrange matters so that you pay overtime charges when you check in or out. Although most yachts rarely enter a harbour, and navigation lights throughout the Caribbean are spectacularly unreliable, it is usual to pay harbour and lights dues. The average cost of clearing into each country is between $25–100; more if you have a large crew. There are over 30 countries in the Caribbean Basin.

Boat costs

Boat costs include the obvious like fuel, oil and lubricants. The near absence of berthing charges comes as a pleasant surprise. Away from European waters, anchoring is the rule, and for the most part it is free. For those who cannot break the habit there are marinas. Prices vary from 50 cents to around $5–6 per foot per night with power and cable TV adding around 10 per cent to the bill. Local taxes are added to reach a final figure. In the Caribbean, water is also extra and in some marinas, water charges based on LOA are added automatically to the price whether you use their water or not.

Without power, TV or water charges, and based on a totally unrepresentative sample, the average charge for a 38-foot yacht is probably between $1.25–1.50 per foot per night, say $50–60 per night. For a short summer cruise these costs are bearable but over a year or more they will devour your budget. Discounts are available for longer stays but at the height of the sailing season, when marinas are at their busiest, their charges reflect the increased demand and boats frequently book ahead days or weeks in advance. This is particularly true if a recent hurricane has damaged marinas and taken berths out of use. This is also the time when staying in marinas means living with the hassle of rebuilding work. In the Virgin Islands there is the practice of laying moorings in the more popular anchorages. Anchoring is almost impossible and charges for using a mooring are close to those of a marina berth.

Refitting during the cruise

In the course of an Atlantic circuit, you sail further than most folk manage in ten seasons. Maintenance is inevitable not because your boat is falling apart but because living aboard encourages constant daily maintenance. Everybody is always working on their boat.

There is no set refit time in your cruise programme. You should start out with an adequate supply of consumables like fan belts, impellors, fuel, oil and water filters. They may be difficult to source en route and you can save cash by buying compatible rather than branded items. One way or another, you probably end up spending as much on maintenance as you would during any annual refit.

Fixing the budget

Faced with a long list of unknowns and wild guesstimates for your day-to-day budget, it is best to decide upon a daily or weekly figure you can afford and try to stick to it. For a variety of reasons this is not always possible: when provisioning for a long passage there is a tendency to buy more than you will ever eat, and a few days partying or two or three extra trips will make a mockery of any budget, but at least you know when you are being extravagant and, in the end, the daily or weekly figure will not be wildly adrift.

Creative accounting helps. Ashore or afloat you still have to pay out day-to-day living costs and if you include annual marina fees (about half your annual costs of keeping your boat at home are marina charges), insurance costs, lift out charges, annual refit expenses and the usual season's fuel budget you have a respectable figure to set against your daily cruising budget to make it look affordable.

If you have a car laid up for the duration of your cruise then its running costs can be set against the day-to-day costs and if you are leaving a house or a flat unoccupied while you are sailing for a year or more, then a popular way of raising some income is to rent it out.

You might even show a profit if you have a crew of friends (as opposed to family) for the costs of provisioning, harbour dues and entry fees can be shared. Be warned that most insurance policies exclude commercial operations and it may be prudent to check with your insurance company where they draw the line between friends sharing costs and paying passengers.

No two boats will have the same budget. Amongst variables to be taken into account are:

- Lifestyle and personal circumstances
- DIY skills to keep maintenance costs down
- Number of crew
- Size and type of vessel

How you factor these points into your equations will determine your final budget. It will never be enough.

chapter 3 Finding the right boat

Refitting for a year-long cruise is as much a journey into the unknown as crossing an ocean. The Atlantic circuit involves sailing 10,000 miles in 15 months, about the same distance most yachtsmen sail in 10 to 15 years of normal cruising. How do you prepare a yacht for 10 years' wear and tear in just over a single year?

The lazy man's refit is to buy the ideal boat. With luck, most of the cost would be recouped by selling it on your return. However, what makes the ideal bluewater cruiser is a debate without an end. Everyone has their opinion and they are probably right. If the yardstick is 'Can it cross an ocean?' then yachts of all sizes, hull shapes, and rigs meet it. They have been built of wood, GRP, concrete, steel, aluminium, canvas and rubber. Once, Bernard Moitessier contemplated building a boat out of paper and sailing it back to France.

There have been big yachts and small yachts, yachts with single-chine hulls, multi-chine hulls, and round hulls, and of course, multihulls. The first multihull to cross the Atlantic was the 42-foot *Ananda* that sailed from France to Martinique in 1947. They have been rigged as sloops, cutters, ketches, schooners, brigantines, and ships. They have been powered by Bermudan rigs, gaff rigs, freedom rigs, junk rigs, kites and rigid-computer-controlled wing sails. They have had aft cockpits, centre cockpits, and in the case of yachts like *Jester*, no cockpit. They have had full keels, fin keels, lifting keels, wing keels and twin keels. They have been given diesel engines, petrol engines, outboard engines and no engine. The list includes production boats, one-off designs and 'innovative' designs as well as standard production boats, old boats, home-built boats, and conversions too modest to mention either their age or antecedents.

This list is not culled from reference books. Visit the Muelle Deportivo in Las Palmas in the Canaries around November and you will see various permutations of all these types making ready to cross the Atlantic. Every owner believes their craft is ideal and they have all sailed well over a thousand miles off soundings to prove it. On that evidence alone it would be silly to claim one type of vessel or design, method of construction, hull form or building material is better suited than another. Some boats may sail faster, others may be more comfortable but all will make the voyage.

Liveability

Discomfort, fatigue and adversity may be character-building but they do not bring out the best in people. As the voyage progresses, a person's ability to ignore small irritants gradually disappears. Trivial disagreements fester and poison relationships until the only cure is amputation. Yachts have arrived in the Caribbean with skippers issuing orders to their crew in writing, and once happily married couples speaking only through their solicitors. The absence of liveability has turned the dream voyage of a lifetime into a passage to hell.

Liveability is difficult to define. At its simplest it is enjoying a comfortable, relaxed, civilized lifestyle. Crossing an ocean is adventure enough without seeking out unnecessary hardship. Liveability in harbour is different from liveability at sea but somehow you must find a balance that resolves their differing demands. What form this compromise takes varies with personal preference, pocket and inclination but it includes: a sea kindly boat, adequate personal space, ample social space, good onboard facilities.

Bear in mind that for a year or more the boat will be your home. Small yachts lack standing headroom. Once in the tropics, where the cockpit is the principal living area, this is not much of a problem but sitting headroom is usually associated with a lack of living space below decks and a lifestyle on passage resembling the squalid conditions of a small, wet, mountain tent. Such an existence is neither romantic nor challenging.

Everyone aboard must have at least one space below deck to call their own. A berth is more than a bed. It is where you hide from the rest of the crew and find personal peace and quiet. Hot bunking is out, so too is a saloon that spends half its life pretending to be a bedroom. The size of your boat is dictated more by the number in the crew than by its performance. Most bluewater sailors have a marked preference for beamy yachts with a high internal volume. A typical 32-foot LOA cruising yacht with a nominal six berths will provide comfortable accommodation for two, three at a pinch and four if they are very, very good friends. The average size of yachts crossing the Atlantic has risen to 40–45 feet LOA: most have crews of three or four.

Windward performance is not a high priority. Most bluewater sailing is either reaching or running. This makes a hull form with good lateral stability desirable. Given a preference for a high internal volume to maximise living space, it adds up to a broad-beamed bathtub. Do not scoff. This is a fair description of Columbus' caravels and his best time for the crossing was 21 days. In 1573 on his voyage home from the Caribbean, Drake is supposed to have sailed back to Plymouth in 23 days.

An easily-handled rig is important. Best of all is a rig where you do not have to leave the cockpit to set or reef sails. Most headsails are fitted to some form of roller-reefing system with the control lines led back to the cockpit. Over the years, headsail roller-reefing systems have proved very reliable, though on the rare occasions when they do fail it is always spectacularly inconvenient.

A mainsail that needs one person on the helm, and a second handling the sail, places a considerable strain on the crew, especially during night watches when reefing means rousing someone from their bunk. In such cases, sail changes are often left to a change each watch, which still shortens someone's rest, or a reef is taken in before dark, regardless of wind conditions, which slows the boat down. Single-handed mainsail handling options include in-mast or in-boom reefing systems or single line slab reefing systems with jackstays to catch the sail as it is lowered. All have their supporters and detractors, none are cheap and most require either modifying your existing mainsail or buying a new sail. Some insist on modifications to the mast or a new boom. Lateral solutions include opting for a junk rig or a wing sail.

Off the wind, ketches and schooners can throw up between-mast staysails, the lazy man's spinnaker, and romp away. Twin masts break the sail plan into small chunks managed easily by one person and for that reason were popular before modern sail-handling systems eroded their advantage.

The ideal boat

It is possible that the perfect boat could be the one that you have now, even though you may believe that it is too small. Nowadays the average bluewater cruiser is probably between 40–50 foot LOA but up to the 1960s/70s this figure was nearer 25–32 foot LOA. Size alone is not a measure of seaworthiness. It is safer going to sea in a small, well-equipped, well-maintained yacht than a much larger ill-equipped, poorly maintained boat.

You know your present boat's good and bad points and, just as important, it knows you. She has carried you safely for many thousands of miles and the pair of you have long since come to an understanding. She does the sailing and you do as you are told. You know every

▲ Felix *is a home-built steel yacht constructed on a very tight budget (look at the mast step) but it sailed across the Atlantic and also carried on to India.*

◀ *This is a home-build cat boat designed by Phil Bolger around standard plywood sheets and without the traditional pointy bow.*

▼ *This boat is not only home-built, she was also home-designed. Apparently, her skipper learned to sail on the way from Sweden to Falmouth before setting out across the Bay of Biscay.*

▲ This is a Wharram-designed catamaran with
most of the living space in the hulls. Catamarans
offer lots of accommodation compared to
monohulls of the same length and are fast off
the wind.

▶ TOP Ever since Jester, ease of handling has made
the junk rig a popular choice on small, bluewater
yachts. After sailing to the Caribbean and back,
this junk went on to explore the Mediterranean,
the Black Sea and the Lofoten Islands.

▶ If catamarans have a downside it is their tendency
to slam in a seaway and if they capsize then they
do not come back up. Running in strong winds
and big seas it is important to slow the boat
down to remove any possibility of pitch-poling
or broaching.

▶ FAR RIGHT On this computer-controlled wing sail,
reefing is achieved by varying the angle of attack
to the wind. If the computer works this is done
automatically; if it does not then it can be
cranked manually.

Size is not the main criteria to apply when choosing a
bluewater cruiser. All three of these boats crossed the Atlantic.

A typical bluewater ketch with hank-on foresails, boomed
staysail, and small main; all designed to make sail handling as
easy as possible.

creak and squeak she makes, how close she lies to the wind in different conditions, how much sail she happily carries in any given wind strength and sea state. You know the best place to stow everything and can put your hand on anything, day or night, good weather and bad. These are important advantages which should not be lightly given up. She may have her faults but like a loving partner in any long-lasting relationship you have learned to live with them.

Over the years you have made many small modifications to make her more suitable for your type of sailing. Nothing major, just one or two small improvements at each winter lay-up. Those that had not worked had either been re-thought and redone or ripped out. The end result has been a huge amount of work that has been tried and tested but always in small increments. If this is the case with you, then think long and hard before investing in a new boat and then falling into the trap of believing your preparations are complete. There are few, new or second-hand, sail-away, bluewater cruisers on the market and all will need some work to make them suit you. Any reasonably thorough inspection will produce a list of tasks longer than expected and as work progresses, unforeseen defects and deficiencies will be discovered. Nor will the work be limited to straightforward replacement and upgrading. It is almost certain that a number of modifications will recommend themselves to you. They may seem desirable, even sensible, but you will not know how they will work until you take them to sea, and if experience proves them unsuitable then time for remedial work is limited.

Be wary of switching from a monohull to multihull or family cruiser to ocean racer. You may have powerful arguments that the change is to a much more suitable boat but whether brand-new or second-hand and new to you, not only will a huge amount of work be needed before you are happy with it, you will need a lot of sea miles before you know your new boat.

chapter 4 Preparing your boat for ocean cruising

Refit above deck

A good refitting programme falls into two phases: servicing the existing fittings and equipment and then making modifications. The division is not clear-cut but it is useful for planning purposes and at the top of everyone's list is keeping the sea out and the cabin dry.

Seas pouring over the deck are more spectacular than dangerous but every hole in the hull and deck is a potential leak. None are likely to be life-threatening but all carry the certain promise of misery. If any water finds its way below, you will be astounded how little it takes to ruin the contents of lockers, soak bunks and reduce life to damp, humid, discomfort. Keeping below decks dry is important to morale as well as comfort. Before you sail, check that every hole through the deck and hull is watertight. Watertight is absolute. Left unchecked the smallest drip soaks everything it touches and in time it touches everything.

Leaking hatches

The easiest way to check if a hatch is waterproof is to close it and attack it with a power washer. If it leaks then its seals need replacing. On smaller yachts it is often only possible to open the forehatch on sunny days in harbour. At sea, they leak and the argument that they provide an alternative way out to the main hatch is nonsense. Give some thought to sealing the forehatch permanently shut.

Main hatches often have washboards of plywood dropped into a length of rebated wood fastened to the side of the hatchway by wood screws. This arrangement creates visions of sitting in the cabin, holding the washboards and wondering why you are knee deep in water. The easy solution is to bolt a strip of ¾ in (5mm) stainless steel to the inside of the hatchway. A more elaborate but stronger answer is to make new runners out of stainless steel that bolt to the front of the hatchway.

The hatches to cockpit lockers and lazarettes should have good seals and be capable of being locked shut. Self-adhesive neoprene tape makes good seals. Many yachts have a hatch in the cockpit floor opening onto the engine space. It gives excellent access to the engine but sometimes it is held in place by two hinges on its forward edge and secured by a hasp and staple aft. Without a padlock, the hasp and staple are useless and you may discover that the hinges are held on by self-tapping screws into GRP. Try to find some arrangement which bolts it down and makes it waterproof.

If there is a hatch you do not need, then think about sealing it down permanently. Otherwise check its seals and replace any that are suspect. If possible, install fittings for strongbacks so that in heavy weather the chance of a hatch being forced open by a sea is much reduced.

Deckhouse windows

After hatches, windows are the biggest holes in the deck and hull. Use the power washer to check if they leak. If they do then the cure depends on the type of window. On newer boats windows are sometimes attached using structural adhesives. In theory they should be leakproof and last the lifetime of the boat. Other window frames have rubber or plastic seals

ABOVE DECK REFIT TIPS

Helming

Self-steering	Some form of self-steering is essential. Windvanes are more expensive than electronic systems but they are more powerful, do not require any battery power and are silent in operation.

Safety

Anchor points for safety harnesses	It must be possible to clip in before leaving the cabin for the cockpit and remain clipped in until you return to the cabin. Make sure that there are enough anchor points for everyone to have their own.
Jackstays	Jackstays normally run down the sidedecks but it is better if you can arrange for a single jackstay on the centreline as this reduces the chances of anyone falling into the water.
Grab rails	Upgrade grab rails so that they can take serious abuse.
Granny bars at mast	If you have to work at the mast and if deck space allows, granny bars give some extra security.
Non-slip deck	A deck with alternate patches of patterned non-slip and glossy gelcoat is a real danger in heavy weather. Make sure that wherever you put a foot down on deck it stays there and if you slip, you leave your shoes behind.
Boarding loops	Fit boarding loops at intervals round the deck so that if anyone does fall overboard they can get their weight onto their feet as soon as possible.

Power

Wind generators	These require a location which makes it impossible for anyone to come into contact with the blades.
Towed generators	These require no deck space but can slow the boat down.
Solar panels	These need deck space which is not normally walked upon. On top of a doghouse is good.

Comfort

Pramhood/doghouse and dodgers	In good weather, a pramhood or doghouse backed up by dodgers provides shade and shelter in bad weather.

Rig

Roller reefing headsail(s)	Essential.
Mainsail reefing	Must be a one-man job and preferably done from the cockpit. Reefing means that the wind is picking up and the deck of a small boat is a hazardous workspace in heavy weather.
Halyard/topping lifts/ guy arrangements	Leading all lines aft to the cockpit sounds great but it may be better to leave some on the mast. Experiment before you sail to find the best arrangement.

Cockpit instruments

Visibility	Day or night cockpit instruments should be easy to read. Instruments on bulkheads tend to be obscured by people sitting in front of them.

Equipment to refit above decks

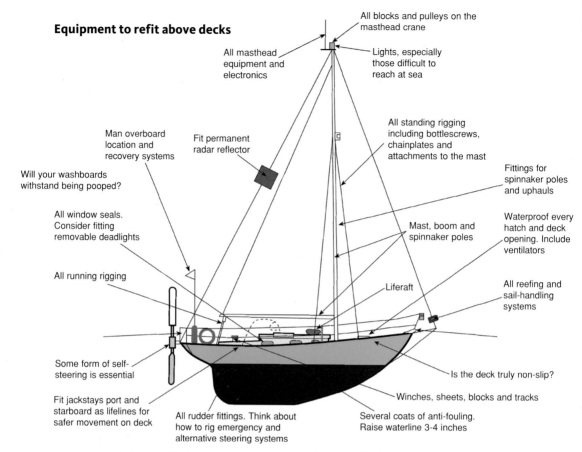

All blocks and pulleys on the masthead crane

All masthead equipment and electronics

Lights, especially those difficult to reach at sea

Man overboard location and recovery systems

Fit permanent radar reflector

All standing rigging including bottlescrews, chainplates and attachments to the mast

Will your washboards withstand being pooped?

Fittings for spinnaker poles and uphauls

All window seals. Consider fitting removable deadlights

Mast, boom and spinnaker poles

Waterproof every hatch and deck opening. Include ventilators

All running rigging

Liferaft

All reefing and sail-handling systems

Some form of self-steering is essential

Is the deck truly non-slip?

Fit jackstays port and starboard as lifelines for safer movement on deck

All rudder fittings. Think about how to rig emergency and alternative steering systems

Several coats of anti-fouling. Raise waterline 3-4 inches

Winches, sheets, blocks and tracks

in metal frames. Unless the seals are new, they should be replaced, for the tropical sun shortens their life dramatically. The seals and fastening mechanism of any opening windows, especially inward-opening windows, should be checked very carefully; if there is any doubt about their integrity they should be replaced. On older boats it is possible that replacement rubber seals are unavailable. If so, consider fitting new frames and windows.

A mix of aluminium frames and stainless steel screws or bolts may cause the frame to corrode. Drilling out the holes to take larger bolts may be the easiest method of cutting out the corrosion. If so, remember to fit suitable insulation between the new bolts and the aluminium to prevent a reoccurrence of the corrosion. If this does not work it may be necessary to replace the frame. If you cannot find frames to fit the existing holes then think about fitting oversized windows bolted directly to the coachroof

The windows on some yachts are Perspex bolted over holes cut in the sides of the coachroof. In some cases, self-tapping screws are used to hold the windows in place. Given a decent thickness of Perspex, a liberal application of sealant and bolts instead of screws, then this arrangement produces a strong and secure window.

In the sun Perspex becomes brittle and a fine mesh of crazing is a warning sign that they are ready to shatter if given a good whack and should be replaced. DIY windows of this type are not difficult to make but Perspex does not like being cut or drilled. All can go well until the last inch is sawn or the final hole is drilled when there is a crack and the sheet splits from side to side. The answer, and it does not always work, is to use sharp tools; saw slowly to keep the blade cool and, wherever possible, to drill holes slowly using a bench drill.

It is tempting to replace Perspex windows with a polycarbonate like Lexan. This is much friendlier to work with and far less likely to split but, despite claims to be resistant to ultraviolet, after a couple of years polycarbonate windows go smoky.

If it is possible for a wave to push the windows into the cabin then consider fitting storm boards. These are wooden boards, of at least half-inch plywood, that are bolted over the outside of the windows to protect them from seas. One or two small 'portholes' cut in the board will allow light to enter the cabin.

Grabrails

The traditional wooden grabrail running along the coachroof is usually a length of hardwood with handholds cut out and held on by woodscrews coming up through the coachroof. Alternatively, a flat strip of timber is screwed down onto GRP pillars moulded into the coachroof. This timber is often sawn across the grain to follow the curve of the coachroof. If you are happy with either arrangement then all grabrails should be removed, cleaned up, rebedded and refixed. If you have any concerns about their condition then they should be replaced. If you have a mental image of going overboard hanging on to the grabrail for dear life then fit a type of grabrail which will keep you safely on board.

As you leave the cockpit to go forward to work on deck it is instinctive to treat the pramhood as a grabrail. Sometimes the pramhood is no more than a framework of canvas and light aluminium tubing held to the coachroof by a couple of small bolts. This is fine for holding it up but raises visions of you going over the side and taking the whole arrangement with you.

Traditional grabrail

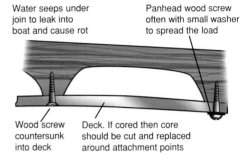

Water seeps under join to leak into boat and cause rot

Panhead wood screw often with small washer to spread the load

Wood screw countersunk into deck

Deck. If cored then core should be cut and replaced around attachment points

Pillar and strip grabrail

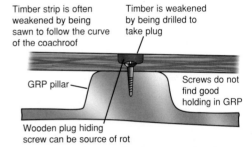

Timber strip is often weakened by being sawn to follow the curve of the coachroof

Timber is weakened by being drilled to take plug

GRP pillar

Screws do not find good holding in GRP

Wooden plug hiding screw can be source of rot

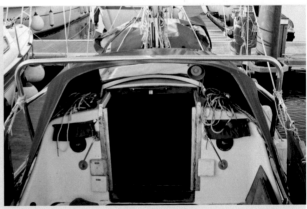

Roll bars and grabrails should provide a decent grip and be strong enough to hold a couple of frightened crew. Try to arrange them so that they can be grasped without having to bend down. This keeps your weight vertical and makes you more secure.

Better quality pramhoods use stainless steel tubing for the frame with cut-outs in the canvas so the frame can be used as a hand-hold. This is a vast improvement but if you opt for this then do check how it is fastened to the coachroof.

A stainless steel roll bar running over the top of the sprayhood makes a splendid handhold and can double as a boom crutch. To prevent it wobbling fore and aft it is necessary to have a support running forward on either side. This presents an opportunity to remove any wooden grabrails that run along the top of the coachroof and use the supports of the roll bar as grabrails. In a further refinement, if these supports are higher than the original rails then as you step out of the cockpit your hand would naturally drop onto them without having to bend down.

Bow rollers

Your boat spends days alone at anchor while you explore ashore. The entire anchoring system from the anchor through to fastening the anchor rode to the boat must be sturdy enough for this duty. Should any part fail then Murphy's Law states that:

a) you will not be onboard to retrieve the situation, or
b) you will be aboard, but fast asleep.

Bow rollers on many production yachts are frequently more ornamental than useful and off-the-shelf replacements are often pretty looking aluminium things that any respectable forestay fitting would eat in a season's sailing. The bow roller needs to withstand the loads imposed by pitching and yawing 24 hours a day and the cleat or samson post taking the anchor rode must be large enough for the rode and be securely fastened down onto the largest possible backing pad.

One answer is to have a new bow roller made out of ⅜in (5mm) stainless steel plate using 4in (10cm) diameter stainless steel rod for the rollers spinning round a 1in (25mm) pin. Pin diameter is important, not because the greater its diameter the stronger it is, but because it is easier for the rollers to rotate under load.

Take a hard look at your bow roller and foredeck cleats. If necessary fit bigger and stronger versions.

If metal working is beyond you and welding a mystery then when you want a one-off, tailor-made item, hunt down a small machine shop that can do the work. Explain to them what you want without nautical jargon. Simple drawings, giving dimensions and mock-ups in plywood, are a tremendous help. Perhaps because this type of work is out of their ordinary run of business, these small workshops take great pains to produce a first class job.

If the bow roller is also the anchor point for the forestay check it is in good condition. In some bow rollers, particularly those made of aluminium, the clevis pin holding the forestay to the bow roller begins chewing its way through the bow roller. If this is happening then either drill a new hole or replace the bow roller.

Deck fittings

Deck fittings are notorious for leaking. It is tedious but sensible to remove every deck fitting, clean it and also clean where it fits on deck. Wipe both areas with a solvent to degrease them and then refit them bedded on a generous layer of sealant; if the fitting does not have a large backing pad on the underside of the deck then take this opportunity to fit the largest possible. Every deck fitting comes under load and backing pads reduce the possibility of a leak.

Deck fitting

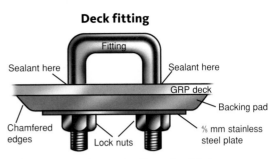

Apply more sealant between backing pad and deck

Stanchions are a special case. They tend to be grabbed and used as levers as you climb in and out of the dinghy. The probability of them leaking is high. Examine every stanchion closely. It is not unknown for their bases to deform from misuse or for the wire of the guardrail to slice through the stanchion. Replace any stanchion that shows signs of damage.

Standing and running rigging

The standing and running rigging should be carefully checked. Rod rigging is particularly treacherous because it can develop invisible hairline cracks that only an electronic inspection can detect. If the standing rigging is close to the end of its safe working life (about 8–10 years) then it and the bottlescrews (turnbuckles) ought to be replaced. This will be a major expense and the only comfort is that replacement now is both easier and cheaper than a broken mast later. When renewing the standing rigging, a few pennies more pays for upgrading to the next size of wire and buys extra peace of mind. If you are considering installing an HF marine radio then this is the time to fit the insulators to the backstay and, when your yacht is out of the water, is also the time to install a suitable ground plate for your HF radio.

When the mast is down, it is a good opportunity to replace the bulbs in spreader lights, steaming light and masthead tri-colour light. If the old ones are not burned out they can be kept as spares. At the same time, all pulleys and blocks on the mast should be checked, serviced or replaced as necessary. Unless running rigging is reasonably new then it will not last the entire trip. A spare halyard or two is a useful insurance. If a halyard breaks then you can rehoist the sail instantly without the drama of first climbing the mast to reeve a new halyard. If you have only internal halyards then fit some external halyards.

Chainplates

Chainplates carry enormous loads and often leak. It is not always possible, but if you can, check how each chainplate is attached to the hull. Ideally they should be fixed either to a bulkhead or some structural hull member but sometimes this is not the case. If they are simply through-bolted to the coachroof or the hull then, in the time available to you, all you can realistically do is explore ways of fitting the largest possible backing pads so that the load is spread over the greatest possible area.

Jackstays

Jackstays are port and starboard lines running the length of the boat. If you are going to work on the foredeck then you should clip into this line before leaving the cockpit and remain clipped in until you have returned. The idea is that should you fall overboard then you remain attached to the boat and only (!) have the problem of climbing back aboard.

Jackstays must be led outside of all obstacles. Their anchor points must be as strong as possible and have large backing pads. The jackstay can be wire or rope. As a wire jackstay

THE SAIL WARDROBE

A huge wardrobe of brand new sails is nice but not essential. On the traditional Atlantic circuit most of the sailing is off the wind. Unless your sails are showing their age then they will probably survive the trip. If you buy new sails then have them triple stitched. A spare genoa is useful, and if you wish, add a cruising chute, gennaker or spinnaker. Some yachts also carry a heavy duty storm jib and a trysail but few use them. Reefing copes with most conditions. By the time the weather is bad enough to justify fitting storm jibs and trysails it is time to take all sail down and live under bare poles.

Early reefing reduces wear and tear. Sails die from chafe and sunlight. Avoid chafe by keeping the sails clear of the spreaders, topping lifts, jackstays, and sheets lying across a sail. Stitch or tape every tear, however insignificant, the instant you spot it. The only protection against UV is to cover sails the moment you arrive in an anchorage.

A second spinnaker pole is useful in the Trades when it is usual to sail under twin jibs.

If the price of buying a second pole shocks, then beg, borrow or scrounge a couple of end fittings and visit your local aluminium distributor. Somewhere in the depths of his shed he will have a length of thick-walled, aluminium tubing that is exactly what you need and a few minutes with a drill and a pop-riveter will produce a serviceable spinnaker pole.

Twin-boomed jibs.

▶ *Twin-roller headsails.*

rolls back and forwards across the deck the noise it makes inside the cabin starts as an irritation and ends up as a torture. Rope 10–12mm in diameter is much quieter and still strong enough to hold a fall. It needs to be checked regularly for chafe and replaced at least once a year.

Self-steering

Unless there is a need to keep the crew gainfully employed some form of self-steering is essential. The tyranny of steering a compass course takes all the fun out of sailing. It can be done but it is better to fit a self-steering unit. Of all the additions and alterations made during the refit, installing a reliable self-steering system is one of the most important. The initial

Slab-reefing.

Early versions of in-mast reefing systems had a foil riveted to the existing mast making it bulky and heavy.

In-boom reefing is a modern twist on roller reefing. One drawback to old-fashioned roller reefing is that as you roll away the mainsail, the boom tends to drop. This was solved by stuffing a sailbag into the end of the boom as the sail was rolled away. Check that your in-boom system does not have this fault.

choice is between a powered autohelm or a windvane and some multihulls may give you no option but a powered autohelm.

Powered autohelms

Any deviation from the desired compass course is detected and an electric motor pulls or pushes a rod or pumps hydraulic fluid which moves the rudder about until the boat returns to the chosen course. Most units can be fitted with a small windvane transducer that allows a course to be steered relative to the wind. Autohelms can also be integrated with the ship's instruments so that it will make any necessary course corrections without being told.

Manufacturers do not have ocean passages in mind when preparing their recommendations on which of their machines is best for different sizes of boat. If you follow their

Some form of windvane self-steering is an essential on most yachts. This is a Monitor self-steering system which is based upon the world-famous Aries gear.

advice you may work the autohelm to death or discover in heavy weather it is simply not man enough to do the job. Choosing the right autohelm for your yacht and the type of sailing you are planning to do is simple: regardless of the size of your boat, install the most powerful unit you can afford.

Reliability is all important. If your system cannot be trusted to steer a course in all wind and sea conditions, then life will be disagreeable. If it breaks down through overwork, then its electronic innards are beyond the capabilities of most yachtsmen to repair. When it is working it devours a great chunk of your energy budget, typically between three and five amps an hour, varying with factors such as sea conditions, sail trim and the amount of weather helm.

Windvane self-steering

Windvanes always steer a course relative to the wind. While this makes for lazy sail trimming it does mean that if the wind direction changes then you follow the wind. It is not unknown to come on deck and find the boat steering the reciprocal of the desired course. This is a small penalty to pay for a system that imposes no drain on your battery. Windvane systems first appeared in the early 1900s and attracted most interest from model yachtsmen. Half a century later Francis Chichester developed his Miranda self-steering gear for the first OSTAR by watching model yachts race across a pond. That race introduced windvanes to the sailing public and soon any yacht with pretensions to long-distance sailing had one hanging from its stern. This is one of the differences between windvanes and autohelms; windvanes are big, obvious. Fitting one can be a challenge to your ingenuity and depends not only on the shape of your vessel's stern but on what is already hanging there in the form of mizzen booms, boarding ladders, swim platforms, rudders and davits.

The vane may be horizontally or vertically mounted. A vertical vane weathercocks like the windvane on a church steeple, a horizontal vane falls over to one side or the other and is reckoned to be more sensitive and powerful. Once a change in relative wind is detected, that information is used to deliver the power to steer a yacht. Windvanes work best with a balanced sail plan and their efficiency falls off as weather (or lee) helm grows. This means reefing early and upright sailing, which increases the comfort factor but will not win races. On a run, wind passing over the vane is reduced by the boat speed and, again, efficiency falls off.

The simplest systems use the movement of the vane to pull lines attached directly to the tiller. They lack power and work only in a gale or when approached in a threatening manner with a hammer. A trim tab linked to the vane can be attached to a transom-hung rudder. This is a much more powerful arrangement which avoids separate steering lines to the tiller and is a useful system if you have a centre cockpit that would otherwise require extremely long steering lines. An alternative for centre cockpit yachts without a transom-hung rudder is to fit a system which includes an auxiliary rudder. This steers the yacht while the main rudder is used to reduce weather helm. These systems work well but reversing under engine with the auxiliary rudder in place can be exciting.

A popular form of windvane is the servopendulum system which traces its ancestry to the first models designed by Blondie Hasler for *Jester*. The vane turns a paddle and the water rushing across the paddle causes it to swing to one side or another, pulling on a line attached to the tiller or wheel until the vessel is back on course. This type of vane is very powerful and extremely reliable.

Windvanes are simple. Generally they can be repaired on board but they work only if there is a wind. If you wish to motor through calms then an autohelm is necessary. With a little ingenuity one of the push-rod type autohelms can be rigged so that it is linked to the windvane and pushes it from side to side instead of the tiller. This reduces the loads and power consumption of the autohelm.

The choice between autohelm or windvane is not straightforward. Every system has its adherents who swear on a stack of almanacs that their particular arrangement is the only sensible option. In practice it appears that the more powerful a system (autohelm or windvane) is then the better it works. The price of a good windvane system will buy two or three autohelms and some argue that it is cheaper and wiser to buy two autohelms and have 100 per cent redundancy, for two-thirds of the cost, than to rely upon one windvane system. It is worth considering but if you opt for this, then you place a premium on the capacity of the ship's batteries and reliability of your battery-charging systems.

Awnings

In the tropics lounging in the cockpit adds a touch of gracious living but only if there is an awning to shade you from the sun. This can be anything from a simple boom tent to a sophisticated combination of fold-away bimini with an awning fitted with opening windows and electric lights.

A sailmaker-made boom tent can be expensive. A heavy duty (so called) mail-order tarpaulin at a twentieth of the price thrown over the boom as a simple A-tent covering the cockpit works just as well. Alternatively it can be hung underneath the boom, fastened to the backstay or the A-frame on the stern and shrouds. A tendency to flap in the wind is reduced by lashing lengths of plastic water piping across the ends as spreaders. A plastic skin fitting in its centre can take a hose that leads to the water tank. When it rains slacken off the awning to create a hollow and allow water to run to the tank. It is amazing how much water can be gathered in a single tropical downpour but living in the cockpit with a hose dangling down is a nuisance. Place the skin fitting at one end.

If you have the space, then fit an awning that can remain in place when underway. It will need to be taken down in strong winds but at all other times it will be much appreciated by all on board.

An awning is essential in the tropics. Best of all is one that can be put up when you are underway but make sure that it does not create blind spots to hamper visibility for the helm.

Pramhoods

A pramhood is essential. It provides shelter in heavy weather and protects the cabin from spray when you open the hatch to take a look around. Plastic windows in pramhoods become smoky in the sun. Think about replacing the canvas pramhood with a version in GRP. This allows you to fit toughened glass or perspex windows which will improve forward visibility and the space underneath the pramhood can be used as a home for instruments protected from the worst of the weather.

'Goalposts'

The competition for deck space to fit radars, antennas, wind generators and solar panels is intense. One solution is to fit an A-frame or 'goalposts' on the stern. This is a U-shaped arrangement of stainless steel (it could also be made in aluminium) that carries equipment that would otherwise clutter the deck or mast. It also provides room for a spare tri-colour light (if the masthead light failed then you do not have to climb the mast at sea to repair it) and a strobe light. Using a

Consider fitting 'goalposts' on the stern to carry such items as antennas and lights.

strobe light as a steaming light is wrong but there are times when being seen at night rates above being legal. Besides, fishermen have been using strobes for years to mark their nets and single-handed record breakers usually have one banging away.

Refit below deck

On a bluewater cruise, a boat is not just a place to eat, sleep and sail, it is where you entertain and socialise or find a quiet corner to call your own and curl up reading a book, watching a DVD, listening to music or the radio. It is where you party, celebrate anniversaries, birthdays, Christmas, Easter and Thanksgiving. Lockers are not just stowage for cruising gear but for the personal bits and pieces that make up your life. You are going to live aboard for a long time so make it feel like home. Finding out how to make life below decks civilized begins by asking:

- Are there enough comfy bunks?
- Is the living area adequate for eating, relaxing, personal hobbies and chartwork?
- Is the galley up to the cook's specifications?
- Are the water tanks sufficient for an Atlantic crossing?
- Is there enough locker space for clothes, food, books and personal possessions?
- Are the ablution facilities up to scratch for a long passage?
- Is the lighting and ventilation adequate?
- Will the below-deck areas be safe during a blow?

Top priority is a comfortable bunk where you can stretch out and sleep, warm, safe and secure regardless of the weather. The first requirement is good, thick bunk cushions. Four inches of foam is adequate but six inches is better especially if the top two or three inches are self-conforming memory foam that moulds itself to your body shape. You must be able to stay in your bunk without hanging on for dear life. Quarter berths are good but not the whole answer, for the top half of your body can slip out. Lee cloths or lee-boards along the length of the bunk which are deep enough to prevent you from being thrown out are best. Lee cloths are more comfortable than lee-boards, and form a cuddly, secure cocoon. They must be strongly made. The usual eyelet in the corner of a hem is fine for a static load but if you are thrown against them the eyelets will pop out and the cloth will tear. The corners should have a strong resemblance to a storm jib clew. The lines holding the lee cloth in position must be

Small yacht below-deck layout

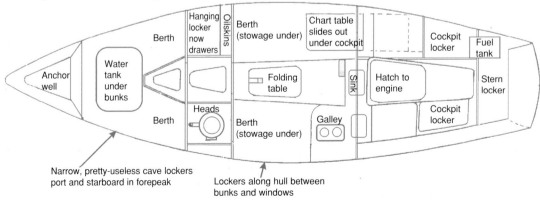

Narrow, pretty-useless cave lockers
port and starboard in forepeak

Lockers along hull between
bunks and windows

fitted with some form of quick release to allow you to escape from your bunk and dash to the cockpit. For the same reason a duvet is preferable to a sleeping bag.

Lacking anyone else to blame, single-handers are best placed to endure cramped living conditions. Otherwise you need a reasonable amount of well-planned, adaptable space if the crossing is going to be enjoyable. Homes have different rooms for different functions and as far as possible, aim for a similar arrangement below decks. You will probably find one solution in harbour and another at sea but expecting everyone to eat, sleep, work and play in one area is asking for trouble. Try, as far as possible, to keep sleeping and living areas separate and ensure that

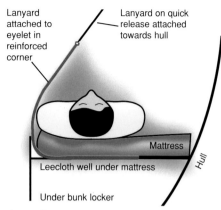

people have their own space. You may find that you opt for different arrangements at different times: for example a couple may use the forepeak as a bedroom in harbour, leaving the saloon for socialising, while sleeping on the saloon settee berths at sea. A family needs separate cabins for parents and children whether at sea or in harbour. Think ahead to what everyone's needs will be during weeks afloat and how you can best meet them.

Safety below

Careful consideration should be given to movement below decks:

- Do people have to climb round the cook or navigator?
- Does a table in the saloon cause gridlock?
- Are there enough grab handles below deck so you can move around safely?
- If you are thrown across the cabin by a rogue wave, what will you hit? Hard, sharp corners and edges break ribs, backs and fracture skulls.
- Is the cabin sole non-slip, especially when wet?
- Will lockers fly open and saucepans become missiles?
- Are you sitting comfortably? Francis Chichester sailed with a gimballed chair to guarantee a comfy seat (he needed it on *Gipsy Moth IV*) but on most yachts the choice is between sitting to windward, feet braced, or in the depths of a leeward settee. Finding everyone a snug, secure seat with sufficient space to eat or read is no problem in harbour but what about at sea?

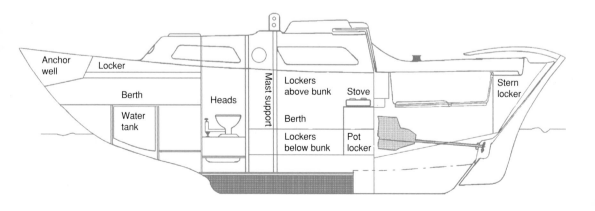

Stowage

This is when you begin your quest to find the perfect stowage system. Every ocean cruiser has twice as much kit as locker space. Entire cabins have circled the Atlantic filled with equipment waiting to be stowed 'one day'. The ideal solution is to throw away any you do not need and stow everything else by numbers, but few folk are that organised.

Try fitting doors to those open lockers that line the inside of the hull on many yachts. Not only will this prevent their contents flying around the cabin but also they will hold more and make the cabin look tidier. Do not stow anything in the bilges that you are not prepared to see soaked and for the same reason, items stowed in lockers under bunks should be protected against wet. You will have lots of charts. Roll them up and stow in lengths of plastic drain pipe bought from your local builders' merchant. At the same time buy caps to go over the ends of each length so your charts are safe from damp. Make compartments in large lockers with plastic boxes of the type found in most DIY stores. They come in different sizes and colours that can be used to colour-code their contents. Fit netting to deckheads. If you do not use nets for stowing fruit and vegetables they are good for keeping odds and ends out of the way.

Lighting

Lighting below decks is either general lighting for an entire cabin or local lighting for a work area such as the chart table or galley or for individual bunks. Standardise your lighting units so that you need only carry one or two different kinds of bulbs. Although they give a kinder light, paraffin lamps are mostly restricted to the cockpit when at anchor. Fluorescent strip lights give good general illumination below decks and small tungsten lights provide individual lighting for bunks, galley or chart table. However, fluorescent lights do interfere with MF and HF radio reception so must be switched off when you listen to the weather forecast.

Bright, white LEDs are now available and are excellent for providing either general, low-level cabin lighting or spot lighting over chart tables and bunks. They also make superb compass lights. They can be self-contained and run off their own batteries; battery life is usually measured in 10s of hours or from the ship's power supply. If necessary you can make up your own LEDs for pennies.

Ventilation

It is easy to provide enough fresh air below decks at sea, but in harbour it is a different tale. Within minutes of anchoring in the tropics, the cabin will become an airless hotbox. If you do not have air conditioning, then the first step is to spread an awning which will cover as much of the deck and cockpit as possible. This not only keeps the sun off the deck but drives cool air between the awning and the deck. Next, open the hatches and, if necessary, fit wind-sails to push air through the boat. This should make life bearable. You can also buy a couple of the 12 volt fans that car owners mount on the dash board of their cars to direct a stream of cool air wherever you wish.

LEDS AT SEA

What is a LED?

A LED is a diode which glows. Like all diodes it passes current only in one direction and is polarity sensitive. Wire the positive side of a diode (the cathode) to the negative side of the supply line and nothing happens. Wire positive to positive and you have light.

Unlike filament lamps, the output from a LED is directional, with its light concentrated into a narrow cone. The angle varies but is typically around 20°–30°. This makes it difficult to draw brightness comparisons with a filament bulb but LEDs are very bright, and staring into the latest generation of ultra-bright LEDs could damage eyes.

If you want an omni-directional LED you must use a diffuser but if you want a bright light shining over a predetermined arc then you have this without the complications of reflectors and lenses.

LEDs are tolerant of low voltages. The LEDs in this project are designed to work at 12.5v but they will still light up, though not so brightly, at 10.0v when your battery is not so much dead as buried at sea. If you need a light in an emergency this could be important.

Too much voltage is another matter. It is myth that LEDs run cold. Much above 16.0v they begin running hot. Continue increasing the current and they burn out just like a filament bulb. To prevent this, the current reaching the LED must be limited by adding a resistor to the cathode.

Resistance and Ohm's Law

Resistance is measured in units called Ohms and the value of the resistor you need varies with the voltage and the type and number of LEDs used. If you like doing your own sums you must apply Ohm's Law (right).

LEDs at sea

The uses of LEDs onboard is limited only by your imagination. Domestic lights, anchor lights, navigation lights, compass lights, instrument lights all follow the same DIY principles. The circuits are very simple and anyone who is happy wielding a soldering iron should not have any problems putting them together.

Epoxy encapsulated dome. This is usually clear and the colour of the light comes from the LED, not the dome. Keep different coloured LEDs in separate, labelled boxes.

Light emitting diode (LED)

Flat indicating cathode

The anode is the longer leg. THE ANODE IS POSITIVE

The cathode is the shorter leg. THE CATHODE IS NEGATIVE

OHM'S LAW

Ohm's Law describes the relationship between voltage (volts), current (amps) and resistance (ohms). Know two of these three and you can calculate the value of the third. For resistance the equation is:

$$R = v/I$$

Where R = Ohms (Ω)
v = volts (v)
I = current = amps (A)

There is a catch. There is a voltage drop across a LED. The exact figure is in the LED's technical specification but it is typically 3.0v for white and green LEDs and 1.8v for red LEDs. The 'v' in the equation is the battery voltage (usually 12.0v) minus the voltage drop across the LED. For white and green LEDs the 'v' in the equation is 9.0v and for red LEDs it is 10.2v. This means that red LEDs need a different value resistor to white and green LEDs.

When LEDs are wired in series the voltage drops are added together and then applied to the equation. With four white or green LEDs in the same circuit you do not need a resistor.

If you are wiring the LEDs together in parallel then each LED becomes one LED circuit and needs its own limiting resistor but unless you have different coloured LEDs in the same circuit, this is an unnecessary complication.

Galley

After sleep, the next priority is food. It is important that, regardless of sea conditions, you are able to prepare decent hot food and drink. Ideally, the stove should be gimballed. Some vessels have fixed stoves and rely on fiddle rails or pan holders to keep pots in place but on most yachts at sea, the motion is so lively that unless single burner stoves and very deep pots are used, this arrangement would see the food on the cabin sole. Even a well-gimballed stove needs good fiddle rails or pan holders.

When working in the galley you must be able to devote both hands to cooking and not to hanging on for dear life. Ever tried peeling a potato one handed? It is easiest and safest to work in the galley sitting down. A strap across the galley, against which the cook can lean, is good; you could also install the stove and work surfaces at a level which allows the cook to sit down on a settee.

On small to medium-sized yachts a stove, sink and small workspace pass for a galley but bigger boats are as well-equipped as any shoreside kitchen. Fridges and freezers are commonplace and microwave cookers, some running at 12 volts DC and others on mains voltage using rectifiers, are appearing on more and more yachts; some yachts even have a washing machine. Check how efficient your fridge and freezer are at keeping the cold in and the heat out. In the tropics the difference between the temperature inside a fridge and the outside air is much greater than in European waters. Everything works harder and the drain on your battery increases. It might be possible to uprate the insulation or to change to top-opening rather than side-opening fridge and freezer to prevent cold air escaping each time the fridge is used.

The value of a sink on small boats is debatable. They are very useful in harbour or at anchor where throwing a bucket of dirty water over the side is regarded as anti-social behaviour. If you have a sink then it should be as deep as possible to hold a fair amount of water when heeled. On smaller yachts it is unlikely that the sink outlet will be above the waterline on both tacks unless it is on the centreline of the boat. This means the most likely place for the sink is on the steps to the main hatch which leads to much broken crockery and wet feet. If the sink is placed to port or starboard then it is necessary to fit a pump to prevent it flooding the boat as seawater siphons back into the sink. Pumps do not like kitchen waste and many an unhappy and messy hour can be spent unblocking them. Buckets are much simpler and are one hole less in the hull.

Cooking fuels

Despite a tendency to flare up during the ignition stage, paraffin stoves avoid the problems associated with using gas. Paraffin may smell if you spill it but it will not blow up the boat. Alcohol stoves are an alternative. They are safe, but in Europe finding fuel in sufficient quantities is difficult, and also alcohol or paraffin stoves with an oven are rare. If you wish to bake or roast then it is necessary to use a metal box that sits on the top of the stove. This glows in the night and brands anyone who falls against it. Against all expectations they work quite well.

Once away from the European mainland, gas bottle exchange is rare. When your bottles are refilled in the Caribbean you will usually receive either propane, or butane or occasionally an LPG cocktail called 'cooking gas'. Cylinders are tested at regular intervals and the next test date appears on the aluminium tare disk that comes with every cylinder. Before leaving Europe be sure that your cylinders are in good condition and that they will not need testing before your return. Suppliers may refuse to refill scruffy or out-of date-cylinders.

There is normally little choice in the matter but cylinders should never be completely filled. In Europe a 'full' cylinder is 80 per cent full but in the tropics it is safer to reduce this figure to 70 per cent. Propane is stored at a much higher pressure than butane and while a propane

Typical LPG installation

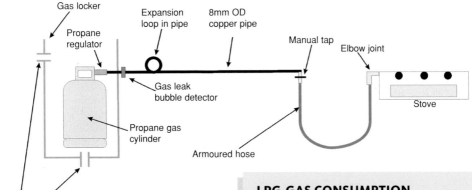

Two-bottle installation

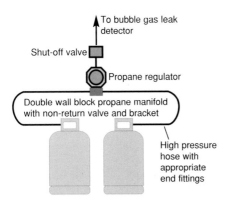

LPG GAS CONSUMPTION

Set to 'high' a single gas burner will use about 170gm (6 oz) of gas per hour. At this rate a kilogram of gas lasts a shade under six hours. The exact figure is 5 hours 54 minutes but expecting such accuracy is unwise, for burners are rarely set to high all the time and different burners use fuel at different rates. An oven or grill probably uses twice as much as a single burner. Check what weight of gas one of your bottles holds when full and calculate how long it should last. It is unlikely that you will start a passage with all gas bottles completely full. It is good practice to have three bottles on board, one in use and two in reserve. There is the temptation to install the biggest bottles possible but remember you will have to take them ashore and carry them around when they need to be refilled.

regulator may not like butane gas it will handle it safely, but a butane regulator will throw a wobbly if fed propane. Butane has a higher calorific value than propane and burns with a hotter flame. If your stove is not rated for butane (modern stoves can usually handle either fuel) then this may warp the unit, buckle oven doors or burn out the burners. If rigged for propane carry a butane regulator just in case.

European yachts are generally fitted with a butane gas supply, but in the USA butane is almost unknown. Many production yachts come with built-in gas lockers that meet the regulations on gas safety and are sized round a standard Camping Gaz bottle. Once in the Caribbean, Camping Gaz is only readily available in French possessions like Martinique. Elsewhere, finding Camping Gaz is a problem.

You can refill Camping Gaz bottles but it is not easy as the fittings in most filling stations are for propane bottles. But there is a way round this. Remove the insides from a Camping Gaz regulator so that gas can flow into the bottle and on the outlet (now the inlet) side attach a short length of hose with a propane adaptor on the end. This allows the Camping Gaz bottle to be filled with propane but this is a technique which would have any gas engineer expressing his disapproval from behind a distant, sandbagged, blast-proof shelter.

A safer solution is to buy a propane bottle and regulator. Now your problem is that standard propane bottles will not fit into the smaller Camping Gaz locker. In some American yachting magazines custom-made propane bottles are advertised but they are expensive. Other options are to modify the existing locker, build a new locker, or carry a propane cylinder on deck and run a new gas line to the stove.

Propane and butane have different fittings to attach the regulator to the bottle. Propane cylinder valves have a female 'POL' connection with a ⅝in BSP female left-hand thread. Butane cylinders have a ⅝in BSP male left-hand thread. But there are also differences between different suppliers in different countries. It is important to always use the right connector between the regulator and the gas bottle and if you expect to change to a different type of bottle en route then it may be best to use some variation on the two-bottle LPG installation and all you will need to change is the connector to the bottle. American yachtsmen heading towards Europe should give this serious consideration for the near complete absence of bottle refill schemes and the prevalence of Camping Gaz in Mediterranean areas means that their easiest solution may be to enter the bottle exchange scheme while in European waters, and then trade in the European bottle before leaving for home.

The chart table

A full-sized chart table is a major selling point of many cruising yachts. Yet the first requirement of any modern navigation area is wall space to hang an ever growing array of instruments. Some screens display information from more than one instrument but it still adds up to a fair impersonation of the *Starship Enterprise*.

Ocean navigation is a part-time activity and cannot justify the exclusive use of space that could be put to better use. In the days when positions were fixed using a sextant, the sum of the daily navigational duties consisted of taking one sight in the morning, another in the afternoon (or noon), sitting down to work out both sights and running the morning sight forward until it crossed with the afternoon sight to give a position. This takes about half an hour. Occasionally star sights would be taken and another half-hour or so spent doing simple arithmetic and plotting. It adds up to a total of an hour a day spent navigating – a fraction of the time spent working in the galley or lying in your bunk – and yet many chart tables occupy a quarter of the main cabin, holy ground that may not be put to any other use.

The box on the wall will, if asked nicely, tell you where you are, where you are going, what course to steer and when you will arrive. Who needs a chart table or a navigator? It is nice to spread charts out on a table and see where you are going but any table will do the job. It does not have to be a dedicated chart table.

Radar

In busy waters in poor visibility, most yachtsmen would sell their grandmother for the radar set that they had ruled out either on the grounds of cost or that they did not carry enough batteries to power it up long enough to be useful. Since the mid 1990s radar sets have been reducing both their price and power demands. In sleep or standby mode they make two or three sweeps at predetermined intervals and only power up if they see a target. The remaining argument against them is that, once in the Caribbean, fog is unknown but heavy tropical rain can give a very good imitation of fog, and when night sailing, it is common to meet unlit local boats. If you must make a landfall in the islands at night, then a radar set is a pearl without price, provided the screen is where it can be seen by those on watch.

Radar detectors

Radar detectors work on milliamps and can be left on all the time. They give a warning bleep every time their antenna is hit by another vessel's radar beam and their display gives a good idea of the vessel's relative bearing. With some practice it is possible to make a fair guess as to the target's course and whether or not it is approaching or moving away. In mid-ocean, where traffic is scarce, it is splendid and gives early warning of any approaching vessel.

Radar detectors have their drawbacks. They rely on other vessels switching on their radar set. Not all do this. Secondly, there is no indication of range. Their absolute range depends on the height of the detector and power of the transmitted signal but even if a radar detector shows the relative strength of the radar signal, there is no way of telling if it is a distant high-powered radar or a nearby low-powered radar. High-power military radars light up radar detectors from miles over the horizon and look as if they are about to run you down. A small fishing boat may only trigger the alarm when it is about to run you down. Thirdly, when there is a lot of traffic, even if the radar detector is not confused by multiple signals then you are.

A radar detector and radar set is a great power-saving combination. In normal conditions you can rely on the radar detector to tell you if there is a vessel nearby and only power up the radar set if in doubt.

AIS
All ships over 300 tons are required to transmit by VHF their name, MMSI number, position, course and speed. This is known as AIS (Automatic Identification System) and the information can be received on some plotters or a dedicated AIS receiver which, like a radar set, allows you to set a guard zone which triggers an alarm. The disadvantage of relying on AIS is that it does not include vessels under 300 tons or warships, who often prefer anonymity.

Engines
Engines are mainly used for entering and leaving harbour and keeping batteries charged. Motoring through calms or motor sailing in light winds is now common and many yachts carry fuel for a range of over 1000 miles under power.

Outboards Only the smaller yachts use outboards as main engines. They may be in a cockpit well or hang off the stern. If the latter, then they should not interfere with the operation of the windvane self-steering. Outboards are greedy for petrol, and fuel storage is a problem both from the space demanded and the danger of spillages and fumes. Petrol may be less readily available in marinas. Also, outboards rarely produce enough power for recharging batteries, perhaps just enough to run an auto-helm, but insufficient to keep the batteries charged. You are almost entirely dependent on solar power or wind generators for electricity. The greatest advantage of outboards is that if the prop is fouled, it is simple to raise the engine and clear the obstruction.

Diesel engines Diesel engines are more economical and their fuel is less volatile than petrol. The propeller is normally deeper in the water and therefore more efficient and they have an alternator which will charge the batteries.

Diesel engines come either as saildrives or with a prop shaft emerging through the sternpost via a stuffing box and bearing to the propeller. Fitting a warp cutter to the prop shaft could prove useful. Modern diesels are very reliable. Provided you observe the recommended engine servicing schedules the most likely source of engine problems will be in the fuel system, starter motor or alternator. Good pre-voyage servicing with special attention being given to hoses and drive belts is essential. These items should be checked, replaced if necessary, and an adequate supply of oil and fuel filters along with pump impellers and other consumables like fan belts and hoses should be carried.

WATERMAKERS

Watermakers turn seawater into pure, fresh drinking water. All work on the principle of reverse osmosis. Pressurised sea water is pushed along a rolled-up semi-permeable membrane. Some seawater is forced through the membrane emerging as fresh water and is collected in the water tank. The rest is discharged over the side. Some watermakers are computer controlled but the combination of watermaker, electronics and seawater may create problems that cannot be resolved at sea. It may be wiser, and cheaper, to opt for a non-computerised model.

Powering a watermaker

Watermakers are powered by:

Mains electrical power or mains power from a generator delivering at least 5kW. These take up a lot of space which makes this option more suitable for the larger yacht. It is also possible to obtain mains electrical power from the ship's batteries via a suitable rectifier but this option places a premium on keeping the batteries charged.

DC electrical power drawn directly from the ship's battery bank. There are two basic types of DC powered water-makers: those employing energy recovery systems to minimise demands on the battery bank and those that do not. The latter are cheaper, simpler to install and last longer, although these claims will be disputed by supporters of the energy recovery systems.

Belt driven systems where the pump on the watermaker is driven by a belt taken off the engine in the same way as that powering the alternator. Finding space around the engine to fit the pump may be a problem but if these can be overcome it is possibly the simplest and easiest option, especially if a regulating valve is fitted to provide a constant pressure regardless of engine revs.

Consider fitting an extra fuel tank with its own fuel lines and filters. This reduces the problems of fuel transfer and if there is a problem with one fuel line then the engine can be kept running using the second tank while the first is repaired. Use a siphon or electric pump when transferring fuel from cans to tank and make it a rule to always filter the fuel and treat with additives to prevent algae growth. Otherwise there is a real danger of a sludge growing in your fuel which will be sucked into fuel lines, filters and injectors causing the engine to stop.

Skin fittings

Skin fittings have a very low failure rate and are taken for granted. Before sailing they should all be taken off, checked and refitted. Every skin fitting, even those above the waterline, should have a valve, which allows it to be shut, instantly and without fuss. Sometimes the wheel on a gate valve spins lock-to-lock and does nothing. You may think it is working perfectly but the valve is either permanently open or shut. The pretty red wheel handles are only painted mild steel, and rust until they crumble in your hand. If you like gate valves then carry a selection of spare handles. A suitably-sized wooden plug should be taped to the line leading to every valve so that should the valve fail then you can quickly reduce the inflow of water to manageable proportions.

Consider fitting a valve to the engine exhaust fitting. On a long passage under sail, with the waves constantly slapping the stern, it has been known for water to be forced through the siphon and into the engine.

The stern gland on the prop shaft internal engines should be checked and if it is of the traditional type, replace the packing. Carry a spare bearing and if you do not know how to fit it, then learn.

Rudders and rudder tubes

Rudders hanging on gudgeons and pintles are easily checked and serviced. Through-hull rudders are more of a challenge. There will be a rudder tube with a thrust pad in the hull to carry the load, and bearings to ensure the rudder shaft turns smoothly. Check and replace the bearings as necessary. Carry spare bearings.

Ideally, the rudder tube should be made of stainless steel tubing. Sometimes galvanised tubing is used. This can rust secretly from the inside out until one day it begins to leak. At sea this is frightening because a good bang could snap the tube, leaving a hole that is impossible to seal off.

When you are happy with the rudder tube, check how the rudder shaft is attached to the tiller or steering quadrant. Satisfy yourself there is no way this could become loose and allow the rudder to drop out.

Fresh water tanks

Carrying the fresh water required for a three-week voyage in a single, large tank is not good practice. If the tank develops a leak, or the water is contaminated then you lose the lot. If you carry your water in several tanks, losing one or two tanks will be inconvenient but not disastrous. Secondly, you can monitor your water consumption and make sure you are not exceeding your daily ration.

When adding extra tanks, it is tempting to fit collapsible water tanks. They are convenient and easy to install but, although they are made of very tough material, no matter how well they are fastened down they will chafe and eventually leak. A rigid tank, even with all the problems of fitting it into the space available, is better.

A water maker that meets your daily ration and keeps the tank topped up is an alternative to fitting extra tanks. It is more expensive but takes up less room.

Once away from the Channel coast, marinas and harbours have water points but not hoses. A long hose with a selection (this grows as you go) of different tap (faucet) fittings is essential if you wish to fill your tanks without fuss. A hose that rolls flat takes up less room but it is a nuisance to use. It must always be fully unrolled before use and, when finished, rolling up must be done carefully if it is to fit on its holder.

At anchor in the Caribbean, tanks are either filled from a water barge that comes alongside or by ferrying plastic jerry cans to and from the shore. Water is not free and not always potable so always ask before you fill your cans. Even if it is potable it is a good idea to add about a teaspoon of chlorine (chlorine bleach will do) or iodine to every 40 gallons (180 litres) every time you fill up. A good in-line water filter should be fitted between the water tank and the taps. Remember they do not last forever and an out-of-date, dirty filter can contaminate the water supply. You should carry enough filters to see you through the entire cruise and be scrupulous about changing them before they reach the end of their useful life.

Tropical squalls can replenish water tanks by catching rain in an awning. This is easily done at anchor but less so underway. Canting up the boom and catching the run-off from the mainsail in a bucket is another possibility but it is necessary to let the rain rinse the salt off the sail before putting the water in the tank. The lazy sailor's option is to leave a couple of buckets in the cockpit for the rain to fill.

Antifouling

Antifouling is about the last task to do before launching. Be generous and use several coats for it will have to work hard in warm tropical seas. This is the time to raise the boot topping a few inches. Cruising yachts always sit low in the water. Just how low, you will discover by trial and error.

SPARES LIST

A comprehensive spares package is carried, not for use in harbour when anything needed can be borrowed or bought, but for use at sea for repairs or essential maintenance.

What spares are carried will depend upon your expertise, type of boat and equipment onboard. An electronics expert will carry the tools and spares to tackle the innards of autopilots and radios, a mechanic will have enough odds and ends to build a new engine. A wooden boat will carry caulking cotton, and a steel boat will have welding kit. Boats with refrigerators, watermakers, and petrol generators will need spares for these.

It helps to standardise the spares you need. Having one model of bilge pump or winch or sticking to one or two sizes of shackle, or the same sized rope for sheets and halyards, reduces the amount of spares you need to carry. What follows is a starting point to build up your own list.

Type of spare part or equipment	Comments
Alternators	
Replacement alternator	
Brushes	
Diodes	
Drive belts	
Inflatable dinghy	
Patches	Carry a good selection of different sizes
Adhesive	Check shelf life of adhesives
Valves	
Electrical	
Battery connectors	These fit on the battery terminals
Bulbs for all lights	Including domestic, deck and navigational
Cable ties	Various lengths
Co-ax cable	For antennas
Co-ax connectors	
Flashlight batteries	For every flashlight, radio, GPS etc Rechargeable batteries are best
Flashlight bulbs	
Fluorescent tubes	
Fuses/circuit breakers	Various ratings
Heavy duty cable	
Insulating/electrical tape	
Plugs	Various to fit sockets as necessary
Solder	

Terminals	Crimp and solder-on types
Wire	In various colours, lengths and gauges
Engines	
Air filters	
Drive belts	
Fuel filters	Plus additives to kill off bacteria
Oil filters	
Gasket sealant	
Gaskets	For everything that needs a gasket
Hoses	Complete set of engine hoses, including exhaust hose, plus a long straight length of hose and a good length of reinforced hose for bilge pumps.
Impellers	
Injectors	
Oil filters	
Stern gland packing	
Thermostat	
Gas supplies	
Spare regulator for cooking gas bottles	Outside the French islands, it can be difficult to refill Camping Gaz bottles
Burners for stove	
Hose	Enough for the longest run of hose
Burners and thermo-couples for stove	
General	
Service kits and hard-to-get spares for any specialist equipment you might have such as a watermaker or refrigerator	
Bolts – normal/self locking	In various sizes
Circlips	In various sizes
Clevis pins	In various sizes
Distilled water	
Epoxy filler	
Gaffer/duct tape	
Glues – wood/epoxy/rubber/neoprene	
Lengths of marine plywood	
Locktite	For locking nuts that might vibrate loose
Neoprene self adhesive tape	For sealing lockers etc
Nuts – Slot/hex/allen head	
Paint brushes	

Pop rivets and riveter

Rope	Various diameters and lengths
Sandpaper	
Screws – wood/ self-tapping/machine	In various sizes
Seizing wire	
Self-amalgamating tape	
Shock cord	
Split (cotter) pins	To fit clevis pins
Thimbles – plastic/steel	
Threaded rod	In various sizes and lengths, useful to make up bolts
Washers	Various
Wet and dry paper	
Whipping twine	
Wood	Various lengths

Heads

Service kit for the heads
Gaskets
O-rings
Valves

Hull

Antifouling	
GRP repair kit	Including the type that sets underwater
Paints	
Sealants	
Varnish	
Yacht paint	
Zincs	

Hydraulics

Filter	
Fluid	
Hose	Take enough for the longest run
Hose fittings	

Lubricants

Engine oil	
Gearbox oil	
Mineral oil	
Petroleum jelly (Vaseline)	
Silicone Spray	
Solvents – acetone/ white spirit	These represent a fire hazard.
Thinners	
Waterproof grease	

Pumps

Service kits for all bilge pumps including gaskets and diaphragms
Bearings
Gaskets

Hose	Various long lengths are useful

Jubilee clips
Seals
Valves

Rig

Blocks	To suit halyards
Bottlescrews	To fit spare rigging wire
Bulldog clamps	
Halyards	Or enough rope to make up new halyards
Norseman terminals	
Rigging wire	At least enough to make up the longest stay
Shackles	In various sizes
Sheets	Or enough rope to make up new sheets

Winch handles
Service kits for sheet and halyard winches
Winch pawls and spares

Sails

Length of sail cloth
Needles
Palm
Sail hanks/slides
Sail repair tape

Spare battens	At least two of the longest battens
Spare jib/genoa	Desirable
Spare mainsail	Desirable
Thread	
Wax	For the thread

Windvane

Spare vane
Spare paddle

Tools

Take enough tools to:

- Carry out all the maintenance you would do in a normal year's cruising and refit
- Fit all the spares you carry
- Make every repair within your capability

Make sure that you know how to use the tools you carry. All tools rust. Spray them with WD40 and stow them in a sealed container.

EMERGENCY NAVIGATION LIGHTS

You will need:

- 4 white LEDs
- 4 green LEDs
- 4 red LEDs
- One 180 ohm resistor
- Three LED holders
- Resin
- A piece of white card

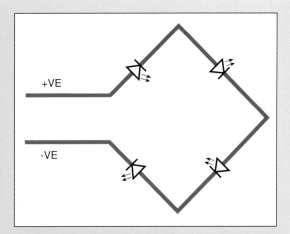

Don't be fooled into thinking the easy answer is putting white LEDs inside an old tri-colour housing. The colour spectrum of white LEDs is not continuous and when seen through the filters, the colours are wrong. To get the right colours, scrap the tri-colour housing and use red, white and green LEDs.

To assemble the lights, blocks of four LEDs are soldered together and fitted through holes spaced round the perimeter of a plastic cap from an old aerosol can. The power supply cable comes out of its side. The wiring is encapsulated using cheap polyester resin and after it has set, the excess plastic is trimmed off. This leaves a thin disk with the LEDs protruding through the plastic cap. Finally a hole for a mounting bolt is drilled through its centre.

The four LEDs in each disk cover the arc appropriate for its colour. To ensure that this is correct, draw a circle on a piece of card and mark the arcs on it. Tack the LEDs together as shown in the wiring diagram (above right) and place them in the centre of the circle so that they cover their sector. Their light will fan out across the card. Adjust the LED nearest the bow so that its beam just cuts the bow line. Mark the position of the LED on the card.

Emergency navigation lights. Aligning LEDs to cover their arc. The LEDs on the lines marking the arc are brought in slightly to keep the beam within the arc. The directional nature of LED light is clearly visible.

Now holding the bow LED steady, adjust the stern LED so that its beam just cuts the line marking the stern arc. Mark the position of that LED on the card.

Transfer the positions you have marked to the LED holder. Drill the holes for the LEDs with those of the other LEDs evenly spaced between the bow and stern LEDs.

Un-solder the LEDs and carefully insert them in the holes you have just drilled. Cut the anodes and cathodes as short as possible to keep the wiring tidy and uncluttered. Re-solder the anodes and cathodes together as shown in the wiring diagram.

Next encapsulate the wiring and cut the LED holders down. If you reckon that a single disk of each colour is not bright enough, then make two or even three disks for each colour and stack them one on top of another.

This is an emergency navigation light. It will not comply with the regulations but it is brighter than the usual flashlight with a coloured filter that does duty as an emergency navigation light.

chapter 5 **Power supplies**

Thirty years ago you could have sailed across the Atlantic with no more than a few gallons of paraffin for lights and cooking and a handful of throw-away, flashlight batteries. Today radios, radars, plotters, computers, autopilots, fridges, freezers, washing machines and micro-waves running all day, every day, take your energy budget far above demands of the normal summer cruise and you cannot depend upon shore-based power supplies to keep the ship's batteries topped up. Instead, you must rely on a combination of onboard battery charging systems. Batteries are the backbone of your electrical system. If they are not kept well fed then they die and everything stops.

Batteries

There are four basic types of battery:

- Car batteries
- Marine batteries
- Engine-start batteries
- Deep-discharge batteries

Marine batteries are more expensive and are supposedly more robust than car batteries. Both are constructed in the same way and sometimes the greatest difference is more in price than quality. Engine-start batteries deliver a blast of power which is quickly replaced from the engine alternator. Deep-discharge (or deep-cycle) batteries give steady power for modest (compared to the demands of starting an engine) loads for long periods between charges.

Battery capacity

A typical 12-volt battery is made up of six separate cells and, when fully charged, a healthy battery has a voltage of around 12.6 volts when not under load and between 13–14 volts when being correctly charged, although it may go as high as 15 volts if it is being heavily charged.

Battery size or capacity is measured in ampere (amp) hours. A 100-amp hour battery can pump out one amp for a hundred hours or 100 amps for one hour or any ratio of amps and hours as long as the answer does not exceed 100. The usual 25-watt masthead tri-colour bulb draws just over 2 amps so a 100-amp hour battery will keep it shining for about 50 hours. The higher the amp hour figure, the more power the battery contains, the bigger it will be and the more it will cost.

It is usual to have separate engine and domestic batteries and a switching system that allows you to use the deep discharge battery solely for domestic use and yet still charge it from the engine alternator when it is running.

If a battery shows a low charge and is slow or impossible to recharge then there may be one or more bad cells. Normally, resurrection is impossible: the battery is dead. The charge remaining in a battery can be checked in two ways. Firstly, the probes of a multimeter set to the correct voltage range can be placed across the battery contacts and the battery voltage read. The higher the voltage, the more charge there is in the battery. Secondly, it can be checked by a hydrometer. Each 12-volt battery has six cells, each nominally of 2.1 volts when

BATTERY BANKS

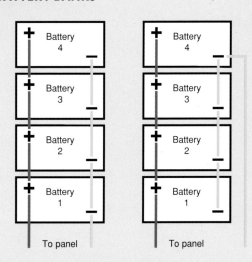

There is a natural tendency to link all the positive and negative terminals in a battery bank together in simple, straight lines (above left). This keeps cables short and reduces voltage drop, but power from Battery 4 has to pass through four sets of cables before it reaches the control panel and works twice as hard as Battery 1. On a load of 100 amps:

Battery One   provides 35.9 amps.

Battery Two   provides 26.2 amps.

Battery Three   provides 20.4 amps.

Battery Four   provides 17.8 amps.

Link the batteries as shown in the diagram above right and with the same 100 amp load:

Battery One   provides 26.7 amps.

Battery Two   provides 23.2 amps

Battery Three   provides 23.2 amp

Battery Four   provides 26.7 amps

fully charged. A hydrometer measures the specific gravity of the electrolyte in each cell. It is a glass tube with a narrow opening at one end and a rubber bulb at the other. Inside the tube is a small, weighted float graduated to read specific gravity; the higher the reading then the greater the charge.

Check the specific gravity cell-by-cell. Every cell should be about the same specific gravity but if one is 50 or more points lower than the rest then it is possibly a 'bad' cell. Sometimes plates buckle and touch or a build-up of sulphate can short out a cell. Usually there is little that can be done but it is nice to know where the fault lies.

If you have opted for sealed or gel batteries then using a hydrometer is out of the question as is carrying out a cell-by-cell check using a multimeter unless the battery has external straps connecting each cell to its neighbour on top of the battery case. Most batteries have internal straps.

Batteries need tender loving care. They should be fastened down in an easily accessible, well-ventilated battery box; their terminals kept clean, free of corrosion (a coating of petroleum jelly is good) and their charge checked daily. No battery, even deep cycle batteries, likes being run flat. They should be given a charge at least every couple of days. The usual advice includes keeping batteries horizontal (wry smile from most yachtsmen) to prevent electrolyte spilling out or flooding from one cell to another. Even sealed batteries can leak for they have vents to allow the charging gases to escape. All this is a counsel of perfection. Batteries are abused and continue working but the mistreatment they receive does shorten their useful working life.

Charging batteries

Do not confuse your energy budget with battery capacity. It is not a one-to-one relationship. Much depends on how often and how much you charge your batteries. Your charging regime should aim to keep your batteries at a minimum of 30–50 per cent charge, higher if you can manage it. There is a better chance of maintaining continuity of supply if you have two or more independent means of generating electricity to recharge your batteries. If you lose one then the other(s) continue charging the batteries.

Engine alternators

With an inboard diesel engine, uprating the alternator that recharges the batteries more quickly is a possibility but if for any reason the engine will not start then you will be unable to charge the batteries. Investing in a small petrol generator might be a better bet.

Wind generators

Wind generators are common on bluewater boats. They are usually stuck on a pole on the stern or by the spreaders on a mizzen mast. Wherever they are located it must be high enough above the deck so that no one can accidentally stick their face into the blades. If mounted on a pole then it must be stayed just like a miniature mizzen.

Wind generators come with a graph showing their output in watts for different wind speeds and at the higher end of the scale the figures appear to indicate that you could light up the town. You need this information in amps when calculating how much new life you are putting into the battery, and dividing the output in watts by 12 gives a much less impressive figure. After allowing for calms, where the blades do not turn and gales, where you might have to stop the blades, wind generators produce power for about 18 hours a day. Multiply the output in watts by 18 to find your estimated daily output.

THE ENERGY BUDGET

It is surprising how much power even small to medium-sized, modestly equipped yachts consume in a typical day at sea. To work out a yacht's energy budget, make a list of all electrical equipment aboard and note how much power (watts) each item takes to run. Next calculate how many amps it takes to work by using the formula:

Amps = watts divided by volts

Since most boats run on a 12-volt circuit this can be simplified to:

Amps = watts divided by 12

The answer to this sum is multiplied by the number of hours each item is used in a typical day. This gives the daily amp hours needed to run each item. Add all the amp hours together and add 20 per cent for inaccuracies and over-optimism. It is useful to prepare separate energy budgets for when on passage and at anchor. The maths involved can be reduced by putting it all onto a spreadsheet.

The energy budget for your boat will almost certainly be greater than you first thought, probably between 100–150 amp hours a day. Failure to meet your energy budget means turning equipment off to meet your reduced circumstances or accepting a return to a simpler age when your batteries run flat. Battery-charging on a motor vessel presents no difficulties. On a yacht you will probably need to run the engine for battery charging every day or so to supplement intermittent systems like wind generators or solar panels.

Water-towed generators

A close cousin to the wind generator is the water-towed generator which is thrown over the stern just like a taffrail log only this time the spinning line does not turn cogs to show speed but a generator hanging from the pushpit. They require a minimum speed of about three knots before they start working and are reckoned to reduce your speed by about half a knot. Some claim to produce five watts at five knots which means running them for 10–12 hours a day to keep a typical two-battery bank charged. This takes 12 miles from your daily run or, on a 3000 mile passage, adds around two days to your passage time. Some towed generators solve the problem of providing power in harbour or at anchor with a kit that allows you to temporarily convert it to a wind generator and hang it in the rigging.

Solar panels

Solar panels do not require a complicated mounting system or affect sailing performance but they do demand acres of flat space and on a small yacht free, never mind flat, space is in short supply.

Like wind generators, solar panels come in different sizes and are improving all the time. Each has a rated peak output and like wind generators this is advertised in watts rather than

BATTERY STATE

By open circuit voltage
(Using a multimeter)

Open circuit voltage	State of charge
Over 12.6 volts	Fully charged
12.4 to 12.59 volts	75–100%
12.2 to 12.39 volts	50–74%
12.0 to 12. 19 volts	25–49%
11.7 to 11.99 volts	0–25%
Under 11.7 volts	Dead

By specific gravity
(Using a hydrometer)

Specific gravity	State of charge
1.265	Fully charged
1.225	75%
1.190	50%
1.555	25%
1.120	Dead

Notes

1 All voltages are measured with no drain on the battery.

2 Use a good meter set to the right scale: there is only 0.9 volts between a fully charged and a dead battery.

3 Besides having a scale for specific gravity, most hydrometers have traffic light markings (red, yellow, green) to give an indication of battery charge.

4 The above figures are correct at 27°C (80°F). For every 5.6°C (10°F) above 27°C add 0.004 to your hydrometer reading and for every 5.6°C below 27°C subtract 0.004 from your hydrometer reading.

5 If checking after charging the battery wait 10–15 minutes before testing.

6 Hydrometers are normally sold in throwaway packaging and storing them safely is a problem. A length of plastic tubing wide enough to hold the hydrometer and capped at both ends is ideal. Stick one cap on permanently and mark the other 'TOP'.

amps. Figures for typical daily output of a solar panel normally assume 12 hours of useable daylight and that the panel is operating between a quarter to a third of its peak efficiency. Convert the wattage of your panel to amps and multiply by 12 to have some idea of how many amp hours you are putting back into your battery each day.

No solar panel likes the dark. They work best when pointed directly at the sun and on some yachts solar panels have been mounted on swinging arms or poles with universal joints to make sure the panel can always point at the sun.

Petrol generators
A petrol or diesel generator has the advantage that it puts out domestic mains voltage. This can be used to charge batteries or power electrical equipment requiring mains current. Their output is measured in watts and the higher the wattage, the bigger and heavier the generator.

Generators need to be securely fastened down so that there is no possibility of their going walkabout. A good ventilation system is essential so that poisonous exhaust fumes cannot build up in the cabin.

Battery management systems

You may wish to consider fitting a battery management system. There is a good selection, each slightly different from the other, but all aim to make your alternator recharge your batteries as quickly as possible and then to keep them charged.

Battery state meters
Most energy management systems include a battery-state meter which tells you how much charge is left in a battery. Some allow you to switch between batteries or banks of batteries. Their displays generally use a zener diode and resistor to measure the battery voltage. This information is then used to indicate the level of charge by a traffic light system of LEDs or

on an LCD display as a percentage of the total battery capacity or even amp hours remaining. If you have a voltmeter on the engine panel then switching between domestic and engine batteries will give you the voltage of each battery bank which tells you the overall battery state.

Inverters

At the same time as sorting out batteries and battery charging, think about an inverter. This will convert the battery's 12-volt direct current to domestic alternating current. In the UK this is 240 volts at 50Hz. This allows you to use domestic appliances and the type of domestic appliance you use determines the size of inverter you need. An inverter that will comfortably handle a laptop computer and printer will baulk at an electric drill. It is wise to buy an oversized inverter capable of handling several hundred watts or more.

Mains electricity alternates between positive and negative voltage and this switching back and forth follows a sine wave. Part of the task of an inverter is to recreate this sine wave from a battery's direct current. Some inverters produce a modified sine wave and others, at the top end of the market, a true sine wave identical to mains power. A modified sine wave inverter can be electronically noisy and the equipment it powers often hums to itself when in use. Some equipment like pumps, fridges and many power tools take an inductive load and may not work with a modified sine wave supply. A pure sine wave converter is about twice the price of a modified sine wave inverter. Some inverters can take the output from a solar panel or a wind generator and convert it directly to mains voltage.

Living with a power blackout

No system of power generating is ideal, they all have drawbacks, but there are two guiding principles to follow: first, over rather than under-estimate your power consumption, and second, two independent generating systems are good, three is even better. Not only will the advantages of one system cancel the draw-backs of the other(s) but it would be very bad luck to lose every system.

Murphy's law says this is still possible. If all electrical power were lost, could you continue sailing? Not long ago this would have been a ridiculous question. Not now. What about something as simple as navigation lights? The small dry-cell emergency navigation lights are a nod towards obeying the Collision Regulations and are invisible a few feet away. A paraffin lantern is great for giving a soft light in the cabin but no better at providing light for being seen. A paraffin pressure lantern like a Tilley lamp is great but it uses much more fuel. Besides, how many yachts carry a paraffin lantern or Tilley lamp? Battery-operated strobes running for hours on one battery are a better answer if you carry enough batteries or keep a night-time watch and switch it on whenever another vessel is seen.

The battery life of a handheld GPS unit is now over 20 hours and most yachts carry at least one handheld set as a back-up to the main GPS unit. On passage it is not necessary to run it continuously; once a day, at noon, is enough to see where you are and make any course corrections. One set of batteries should be enough for the entire trip.

There will be no log, no wind instrumentation, echo-sounder or radios but if you have made a point of charging the handheld VHF then you will be able to speak to other stations. Even if it is not switched on, the battery will slowly lose its charge. A small SSB receiver will run for between seven and ten hours on one set of dry cell batteries. This limits your listening to weather forecasts.

In reality you are more likely to have lost a single generating system. If you have not lost the engine or its alternator then the easiest way of making up the shortfall is by running the engine for longer each day, provided his does not increase fuel consumption beyond the amount carried.

If you have lost the engine or its alternator then you will have to rely on wind generators and solar panels. Increasing output from these is impossible. A typical wind generator produces 30–40 amp/hours per day and a decent-sized solar panel 10–20 amp/hours per day. Bearing in mind that a single navigation light uses around 25 amp/hours a day, you must reduce consumption so that it matches your generating capacity. This is achieved by some combination of switching off non-essential equipment, reducing the time equipment is switched on or using less power-hungry versions of the same equipment.

If you have been taking part in a daily radio net over the power-greedy HF transceiver you may need to make one last, brief broadcast telling everyone that you have electrical problems and will be off air until they are repaired. Do not just stop transmitting. People worry. The same holds good for satellite links.

If you are relying on a water maker or an electrically-pumped water system, without any form of manual back-up, then you have problems that can only be solved by having multiple, independent power-generating systems each capable of providing enough power to meet your minimum requirements.

Electrical modifications

Apart from adding one or more generating systems, a couple of extra batteries and buying a decent sized inverter, little needs to be done to the electrical system except to add more sockets. Cigarette lighter units with multiple sockets are best. Everyone will have cell phones, cameras, Ipods, MP3/4 players and laptops that they wish to recharge, usually at the same time.

part two **life aboard**

chapter 6 **The skipper and crew**

The skipper's responsibilities

Qualifications

Qualifications are not the same as experience and experience is more than the sum of sea miles or sea time. Whether or not you are ready to skipper an ocean passage is a matter of personal judgement.

Not very long ago an essential part of the skipper's preparations was learning the black art of astro-navigation. For most this involved acquiring an appropriate certificate such as the RYA Yachtmaster™ Ocean Skipper. The universal adoption of GPS and the widespread use of plotters have made the sextant history and learning how to use one unnecessary.

If you intend to use an HF transceiver then someone aboard must hold a Long Range Radio Certificate to operate it on the marine bands and if you wish to include the amateur bands, a Class A Ham Certificate is also required. While on the certificate trail add first aid and sea survival certificates.

Leadership

The only certainty about the forthcoming passage is nothing will be as imagined and little goes as planned. On good days, decisions are simple black and white no-brainers that anyone could make. Not so when difficulties arise. Ships are not democracies and not skippered by management committees. Everyone can (and should) offer honest advice and constructive criticism but the skipper makes the decisions and carries the can. They must persuade their crew to cheerfully implement any plan as though it was their own. This is astonishingly easy in theory and simple with hindsight, but in real time, when nothing is certain and much unclear, it is something else again. You are beset by doubts you dare not show and only too aware that you are responsible for keeping your crew alive. It is a scary responsibility.

Responsibilities towards your crew do not end when you reach harbour. As long as they are on the ship's papers, each and every one of them remains the skipper's responsibility. This is usually unimportant in home waters but further afield these responsibilities become very real and breaches carry heavy financial penalties. Immigration officers, for example, demand assurances that you will take your crew with you when you leave. The only acceptable excuses are crew members leaving to join another yacht (much paperwork is needed to prove this) or when they sign off your boat they produce a ticket home.

If they fall ill you may have to pay their medical bills and, until they leave, you are expected to cover their living costs. Nit-picking or not, the possible impact on your wallet makes it wise to insist that everyone on board has had their prophylactic jabs. Check that no one is suffering from any chronic illness or on medication and that everyone holds a valid, comprehensive medical insurance policy for several million pounds sterling (or its equivalent), including medical repatriation home. If they are making a one-way trip they must have either a ticket home or the cash to buy one. Insist that everyone hands over documentary evidence in the form of tickets, cash, insurance certificates and passports to the skipper for their safe keeping and his peace of mind.

Problem solving

There are two kinds of problems at sea. There are those that sink the boat in the next few minutes and those that do not. If you encounter the former, then all you can do is to arrange a rapid retreat to the liferaft taking with you as much as you possibly can to ensure your survival until rescued.

Abandoning ship in an orderly manner does not occur by chance. It happens only if you have prepared a plan and rehearsed the crew to the point where actions become instinctive. Your plans will be improved by taking a sea survival course where you discover the joys (and problems) of climbing into a liferaft in a home-made gale.

For all other problems there is time to make a cup of coffee and assess the situation. It helps to remember that no situation is as good or as bad as first reported. From your assessment you then produce a tailor-made plan. There is rarely an obvious 'tick the box' solution that everyone agrees upon, only a selection of grey answers of which any might work. One of the skills of leadership is selecting one of these possibilities … if necessary with a pin … and then persuade everyone to work together to put it into action. It may not be the right or best plan but it is your plan and a less than ideal option implemented with confidence, commitment and enthusiasm stands of far better chance of success than everyone sitting around exchanging opinions on the ideal solution. This is not an excuse to rush into action. There is a checklist to work through before announcing your choice of solution.

Crew management

The boat will only remain seaworthy and habitable if there is a daily regime of system checks and housekeeping. The boat must be cleaned, meals cooked, dishes washed, watches stood and a thousand and one checks made. All this can be put into a daily routine. If you have picked the right watch system, the tasks rotate so that everyone has their share of the good and the bad. Without a formal daily routine, willing horses either work themselves to death or into a state of self-righteous fury. With a daily routine the skipper is free to observe the ever-changing relationships between crew members and step in early and light-heartedly to defuse conflicts and disagreements long before they become critical.

The daily routine

The daily routine has as much to do with safety as it has with housekeeping. Start aft and work forward up the port side and back along the starboard side. Check the self-steering gear, the rudder, the tiller, and every shroud and bottlescrew. Make sure that the sails are not chafing and the sheets and halyards are running free. Inspect every sheet and halyard for chafe, delve into cockpit lockers to check that the gas bottles and piping are in good condition and secure. Gas alarms are great but a visual check is better. Give the batteries their health check; dip the fuel tank and ensure that the fuel cans are secure and not leaking. Inspect the water tank, the fresh fruit and vegetables. Re-stock the ready-to-use food stores.

PROBLEM SOLVING

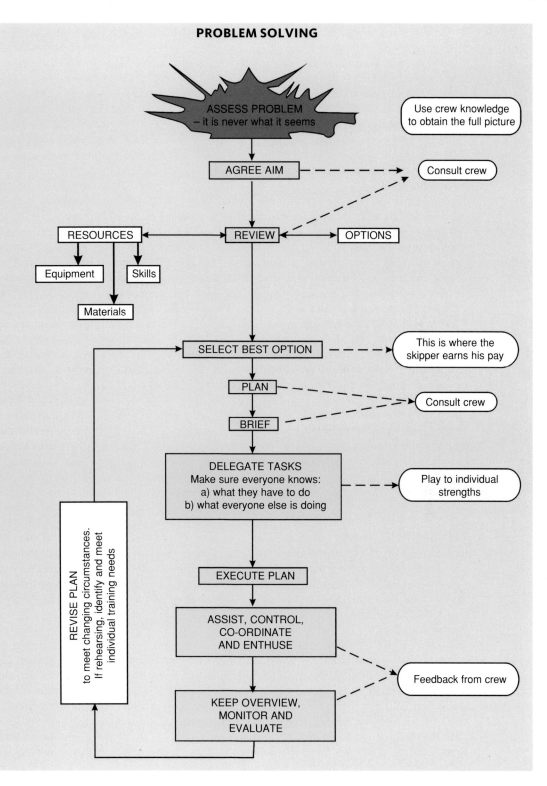

ASSESS PROBLEM
– it is never what it seems

Use crew knowledge
to obtain the full picture

AGREE AIM → → → Consult crew

RESOURCES ← REVIEW → OPTIONS

Equipment   Skills

Materials

SELECT BEST OPTION → → → This is where the skipper earns his pay

PLAN → → → Consult crew

BRIEF

DELEGATE TASKS
Make sure everyone knows:
a) what they have to do
b) what everyone else is doing

Play to individual strengths

EXECUTE PLAN

ASSIST, CONTROL,
CO-ORDINATE
AND ENTHUSE

Feedback from crew

KEEP OVERVIEW,
MONITOR AND
EVALUATE

REVISE PLAN
to meet changing circumstances.
If rehearsing, identify and meet
individual training needs

Check every hull fitting and turn on every seacock. Raise floorboards to expose the bilges and pump them to prove that the pump is working. Every boat should have at least two hand pumps of a size that allows a frightened man to throw several hundred gallons a minute overboard. One, at least, should be in the cabin and usable with the cabin secured against bad weather.

Carrying out these simple checks properly every day demands a high level of self-discipline. Heavy weather, for example, can see them disappear entirely from the agenda but they are important. A stitch in time saves nine is trite but very true. Inspections and the day-to-day maintenance that follows reduces the likelihood of an incident occurring, but should a problem arise, you know your boat's condition without wasting time finding out.

Delegation

With a crew, the work of checking the boat can be shared. This speeds the process and if the results are logged, a full history will be instantly available. When you allocate the daily checks out amongst the crew, play to their strengths. Make the radio ham responsible for the electrics and communications, the mechanic becomes the engineer, the accountant the purser. Delegation enhances an individual's status and self-confidence and a sense of playing an important role in the voyage.

Do not spend the free time this gives you playing back seat driver. Let them get on with their work but lay down limits where they must make you aware of problems. For the engineer this could be when fuel consumption exceeds its daily limit; for the purser when food is being eaten faster than expected, for the watch officer when another vessel is sighted and for the navigator the receipt of a gale warning or an unusually large cross-track error. It is sensible to include these limits in the ship's standing orders.

Captain's rounds

Leaving people to get on with their work is not the same as not knowing what is going on. Once a day go round the boat making your own informal checks, read the crew's reports in the log, chat to them about their work, and discover what they have found and how they are coping. If you have noticed a problem they have not or if they are letting standards slip, this provides an opportunity to bring the subject up in a friendly, informal, non-confrontational manner.

The crew

Signing on the right crew for a transatlantic cruise is never easy. You are embarking on a great adventure; fulfilling the ambition of a lifetime and wishing it to be fun and memorable for the right reasons but, as William Bligh discovered, poor relations with your crew ruins the voyage for everyone. There are four types of crew: single-handers, couples, friends, and families.

Singlehanders

Sailing single-handed evades the problems of choosing a crew but raises difficulties over watch keeping, sail handling and the question of who plays nurse if you fall ill. It would be wrong to make too much of the solitude that goes with solo sailing. An ocean voyage alone is so completely different from a short offshore passage that it is impossible to know if you can handle it until it is too late for second thoughts. The pros and cons of single-handed sailing is a debate that began before Joshua Slocum and its end is not in sight, but solo ocean passages have a long and honourable pedigree. Many of the great, pioneering voyages were small-boat passages made by single-handers, but it is not for everyone and only you will know if it is for you.

Couples

Couples have been sailing the Atlantic for fun ever since Mr and Mrs Crapo sailed across in their 20-foot *New Bedford* in 1877. Some younger couples take a sabbatical, older couples have the time to join the international tribe of sea gipsies, and some are joined by holidaying family and friends from time to time.

Family sailing

The questions that arise when sailing with young children are:

- How will they react to being away from their relations, friends, school and places they know?
- What are the health and safety issues for children?
- Will their education suffer?

There are no simple or straightforward answers. Kids appear to profit from the experience. There are no latchkey kids at sea but despite having their parents always to hand they are independent, self-confident, and play their part in sailing and living aboard. Irrespective of language problems they mix well and make friends easily with children from other boats and other lands.

The usual childhood illnesses appear to raise no more problems than if they were living ashore. Watching the children swarm about the rigging dispels fears for their safety and they learn to swim like fish. It would appear the greatest danger is the usual range of bumps, scrapes and broken bones that children attract as they grow up.

On the strength of a wholly unscientific survey, most liveaboard children are pre-teens. This may be because teenagers prefer the company of their peers to their parents or because the teenage years are when schooling takes on an importance that reverberates throughout their life, and the family swallows the anchor until those years are out of the way.

Schooling kids

The subject of home schooling has generated a considerable amount of information, both on paper and the internet, and distance learning and home schooling schemes are available to keep their formal education up with their stay-at-home contemporaries. *The Complete Home Schooling Source Book* by Rebecca Rupp, or *Home Schooling for Excellence* by David and Micki Colfax or *Home Schooling Handbook from Pre-School to High School: A Parents' Guide* may help. Or visit the Education Otherwise website. Other websites include www.netspace.org, which has details of educational on-line resources. In England the government's education department has its national curriculum and schemes of work on the internet. This is also true of other countries.

ENTERTAINMENT AT SEA

In heavy weather it is amazing how going below, crawling into your bunk and playing your favourite music can make misery of the day seem a distant memory. If you do not already have a stereo system then it is worth fitting one. The type used in cars with tape and CD decks is best. Second-hand models can sometimes be picked up from the small ads in the local paper or from firms who specialise in installing sound systems in cars. Be warned that the cost of the music centre rarely includes the speakers; buy speakers that will survive in salty air. It is important to install the system where it is least likely to become wet. This is not as easy as it sounds as such spots are scarce and there is other equipment, like VHF, HF radios and radar, claiming priority.

Encourage crew members to bring their own Ipod or MP3 player with earphones so that they can listen to music of their choice without disturbing anyone else. Laptops and MP4 players can show films; when you have played your film library to the point of complete tedium you can swap films with other boats. Onboard internet links are possible but are expensive. Make sure you have enough power outlets to keep the batteries of these gadgets fully charged. Finally, a goodshort wave receiver will bring in stations like BBC World Service to keep you up to date with the news of the outside world.

Distance learning schemes for children are available from the Calvert School, Maryland, USA or the World Educational Service in Britain. Calvert School, established in 1897, can provide a year's worth of textbooks, workbooks and lesson plans in a single package with free help a phone call or e-mail away. The World Educational Service started ten years earlier as the Parents' National Education Union. Its courses follow the English national curriculum.

A school visit before departure can help you to find the most suitable learning programme. It may be possible to keep in touch with the school through an internet link. Internet teaching schemes with video conferencing already exist and some schools use them to provide tuition for small numbers of pupils in subjects where the school lacks a specialist teacher. This may be a partial answer for some families.

Home schooling, ashore or afloat, places heavy demands on parental time. There will be at least 12–15 hours a week actual teaching with almost as much time again spent in lesson preparation and marking. Teaching kids, as every teacher knows, is very nearly a full time job.

Sailing as a family chooses your crew for you. With luck and good propaganda, bluewater cruising will be a family-wide ambition, and all that can be hoped is that the ups and downs of the voyage will be absorbed in the normal fluctuations of family life.

Sailing with friends

Cruising with friends makes onboard relationships both easier and harder. It is easier because, however inconvenient or difficult circumstances become, it is always possible to agree to differ, and go your separate ways. It is harder because friends will have contributed towards the running costs, helped prepare the yacht (what else are they for?), sought time off work or away from their family and made a huge emotional investment in the project. Friends will expect their views not just to be heard but also to be taken into account. It takes considerable maturity to accept that while everyone is sailing the dream, you may not share the same dream. It does not matter that you have sailed together for years and are survivors of a thousand Channel passages. An Atlantic crossing is so different that it is a useless yardstick to compatibility.

Advertising for crew

If having friends for crew is fraught with difficulties then advertising for crew magnifies them tenfold. Who are these strangers? What are their backgrounds, their interests, moods, habits and temperaments? Are they into recreational drugs? This makes no moral judgement. If the authorities find drugs aboard it can mean losing your boat and as skipper some of the blame will inevitably fall on you. Lots of people wish to sail across the Atlantic. At Las Palmas hopefuls leave copies of their CVs pinned anywhere they may be seen.

Many have, or claim to have, impressive sailing pedigrees but can you live with a stranger for four weeks? This sounds a silly question but a month can be no time at all or just short of the downside to eternity. Modern society does not travel slowly in small, self-contained groups making their own entertainment. It hurries crossing the Atlantic in eight hours. On a good day, life at sea moves at a brisk walk. Some days there is no progress. There is never any escape from the same faces, voices, ticks and quirks. With nothing better to think about, the small mannerisms of others rub blisters on otherwise placid temperaments. Slights fester, tempers flare, arguments erupt, and black spots are exchanged.

If you decide to advertise for crew, then a short familiarisation cruise as part of the interview may reveal the unsuitable applicants, but is not necessarily a sure guide to compatibility for it is much harder to put your best face forward for three or four weeks than for three or four days.

If you are confident of your yacht-handling ability, then rate crew compatibility far above competent crew. If, before you are committed to making the transatlantic crossing, there is a hint of incompatibility between you and any of your crew then look for ways to part as friends without either side losing face. Folk can be taught how to sail as they go but they cannot be taught how to live together in harmony.

Crew training

Every yacht has its own ways and it is sensible that you and your crew agree on what these are. This is an early step in team-building which is helped by trivia such as handing out T-shirts marked with the boat's name. Take time to practise reefing, tacking, anchoring and man overboard drills until they become second nature. Rehearse abandon ship drills so they can be done swiftly, in the dark, without lights and without anyone falling overboard. Encourage everyone to take a sea survival course. Knowing how things are done and who does what breeds confidence, not only in individual crew members but between crew members.

Everyone should be familiar with the care and use of all aspects of:

1 Safety equipment carried
2 Heavy weather procedures
3 Fire precautions and fire fighting equipment carried
4 Using radios

CREW JOINING OR LEAVING SHIP

If crew fly in to join then you will need to meet them at the airport with a letter from the port immigration officer confirming that they are joining you as crew. The airport immigration officers often admit them for one day, during which you are expected to take them to the port immigration office, sign them onto the ship's papers and pay an embarkation fee.

When the time comes for crew to leave it is necessary to return to the port immigration office with evidence that the departing crew member is leaving the country (an airline ticket is good) or joining another vessel. When the immigration officer is satisfied, he will sign the crew off your crew list in return for a fee.

If members of your crew are signing onto another vessel, even for a single passage, the skippers of both boats with the crew members involved must report to immigration with the ship's papers and passports, and complete the paperwork for signing off one boat and onto another.

Be careful about taking on strangers as crew. The skipper is responsible for their behaviour, health costs, and eventual departure from any country you visit. Check that they have a passport and that it is theirs. Confirm that their health insurance is valid and adequate. Make sure that they have all the visas they may require and sufficient cash or an air ticket to return home.

When you delegate tasks make sure the recipients of these have the necessary skills to carry them out. Everyone wishes to play their part in making the trip a success. This makes it hard for anyone to refuse when asked to accept an area of responsibility outside their comfort zone but their ignorance of what they have to do, besides placing the ship at hazard, puts them under unnecessary stress. If necessary, send your nominated mechanic on a diesel maintenance course and the medic on a first aid or captain's medical course. Training breeds confidence, gives status and creates a sense of professionalism amongst the crew.

Watchkeeping

You need to set up a watchkeeping system that all on board will understand and accept. Tied in with the daily routine, watch systems bring a sense of rhythm and order to each day. Try to avoid:

1 Changing watch systems during a passage. This is the equivalent of switching time zones. It leaves everyone exhausted and introducing a new watch system always starts by giving some unfortunate crew member a double shift.

2 Having only night time watches, say from 8.00pm to 8.00am, for when 4.00–8.00am watch comes to its end, who do those on watch call out? Because there are no daytime watches, no one feels obliged to turn out of their bunk. It can be 10.00am or later before anyone offers to stand watch.

THE SLEEP CYCLE

Sleep stage	Body state	Duration	Time
Stage 1	Transition state between wakefulness and sleep	About 2–5 per cent of total sleep time	2–6 minutes
Stage 2	Light sleep	50 per cent of total sleep time	45–55 minutes
Stages 3 and 4	Also called Slow Wave Sleep. There is evidence that Stage 3 and 4 sleep, the most common in the first few hours of sleep, serves the function of physical and mental restoration. The amount of Stage 3 and 4 Sleep increases after strenuous physical activity. Disturbances, such as loud noises, interrupt the deeper sleep stages and take the sleeper back to lighter sleep stages	About 20–25 per cent of total sleep time	18 to 28 minutes
Stage 5	Rapid Eye Movement (REM) sleep, where dreaming occurs	About 20–25 per cent of total sleep time	18 to 28 minutes

Windvanes and autohelms assist with the helming and leave those on watch free to carry out other tasks. It is usual to sail with only one person on watch to maximise everyone's off-watch time.

The aim of a watchkeeping system

The aim of any watchkeeping system is to ensure that the vessel is sailed in a safe and seamanlike manner. This is most easily achieved when the crew are fed, warm, dry and, above all, rested. Just what system suits you, and still achieves this aim, depends partly on the number on board but whichever system you choose, it must fit round the sleep cycle.

The sleep cycle

The nightly eight hours sleep enjoyed by landlubbers is made up of four or five separate cycles. Each lasts about 90 minutes. It is not necessary to take these cycles in a single lump. It is almost as effective to take them one or two at a time throughout the day. If you must wake someone up then do so in the light sleep phase otherwise even though their eyes are open, they are sleep-logged and take some minutes to become effective.

It is a common myth that anyone can miss a night's sleep and still function.

No one beats the clock. After a sleepless night your reactions and judgement are those of someone who is legally drunk. It is no coincidence that night shift workers have more than their fair share of accidents or that some of the world's most serious disasters occurred in the small hours; this is the time when your brain assumes your body is asleep and switches off.

Everyone must have sufficient time for at least one sleep cycle when they go off watch. Allowing for handing over the watch and the counting sheep rituals we all use before dropping off, then the shortest sensible time off-watch is three hours.

Circadian rhythm

Whether you are a night owl or day bird you are still subject to your circadian rhythm. During the day your body swings in and out of alertness. Early morning and afternoon it shuts down ready for sleep. You can push through these troughs but you will not be at your brightest or best. That is reserved for the peaks in your circadian rhythm. A wise skipper takes this into account when preparing his daily routine and avoids asking crew to carry out demanding tasks during troughs in the circadian rhythm.

Signs of fatigue

Fatigue is insidious. It can be difficult to notice in others and impossible to spot in yourself. A simple self-administered test is to pick an odd number between one and ten and add seven to it; repeat this for a minute. The more mistakes you make, the more tired you are. Another warning sign is 'micro sleeps', when you fall asleep for a moment or so and wake up wondering what you have missed.

Single-handed watchkeeping

The challenge for single-handers is finding an answer to the dilemma of keeping a lookout and still getting sufficient sleep. For passages lasting no more than about 48 hours, most single-handers live with the tyranny of an egg timer set for just less than the time they think it will take for a ship to come over the horizon and run them down. Everyone has their own answer to this calculation but it should not exceed 20 minutes, after which they move into deep sleep and can then sleep through the timer's alarm.

For longer passages, it is necessary to build in at least three or four complete sleep cycles each day. To do so with confidence means

CIRCADIAN RHYTHM

Time	Body state
0700–1300	Once through sleep inertia you are heading for a peak. Between 0900 and 1000 hours short-term memory and logical reasoning are at their best: Concentration is at its best between 1100–1200 hours: morning is a good time for daily checks: most people are at their most efficient during this period.
1300–1600	Minor trough or lull otherwise known as siesta time. A good time for a sleep cycle after a light lunch.
1600–2200	Between 1700–1800 hours the body is at its physical peak: a good time for physical tasks. Athletes often turn in their best performances in early evening events. Digestive system peaks around 1900–2000 hours
2200–0700	Trough which reaches its nadir in the small hours of the morning: people are at their least efficient. The body is at its lowest ebb between 0300–0400 hours. Many accidents happen when folk work through this period. No regular tasks should be scheduled during this period.

CAUSES OF FATIGUE

Sympton	Remarks
Lack of sleep	Monitor your total sleep debt including the day or so before departure.
Broken sleep	Too much cat napping without any proper sleep has a limited effect before you need to sleep for eight hours.
Adverse environmental conditions	Be careful about staying too long in wet, cold cockpits. If working on deck, then when finished, get into the cabin and have a warm drink.
Monotonous watch keeping or other activities	Sitting in the cockpit for the sake of it is not a good idea.
Poor or inadequate diet	Try to eat proper meals regularly.
Poor or inadequate fluid intake	If making a warm drink is too much effort, then drink fruit juice or water.
Strenuous physical work	After a session of hard work take a rest.
Prolonged but not necessarily strenuous physical work	Long hours of fairly light work are just as tiring as a short bout of very strenuous work
Heavy mental workload	Thinking is tiring and when you are tired you make mistakes.
Emotional strain	You may be worried about the weather, a landfall or what's happening at home. The result is the same ... you tire more easily.

either being so far off shipping lanes that the chance of meeting another vessel is negligible or that onboard electronic systems maintain an effective lookout.

The most obvious aid is radar. You can set a guard zone and any vessel entering it triggers an alarm that wakes you up in good time. There are also radar detectors and AIS receivers. Even in fairly busy waters, a combination of electronic systems will keep a pretty good lookout and allows the single-hander to sleep with confidence for a couple of hours.

Probably the best watchkeeping system for single-handers is to catnap on the egg timer whenever they have nothing better to do, then when there is time for a couple of hours' sleep, let the electronic gizmos take over. In this way it is possible to take three or four complete sleep cycles each day. If these can be taken early morning and afternoon in the troughs of the circadian rhythm then so much the better.

Two-man watch systems

With two crew onboard it is a case of working 'watch-and-watch'. Four hours on and four off is probably best but some folk prefer three one-hour watches. Including dogwatches is a good idea for they rotate the watches each day so that no-one is stuck with the dreaded midnight to four watch. Some vary this system by working four one-hour watches during the day and three hours at night. Short watches make sense only in heavy weather when those in the cockpit suffer. In his book *The Last Grain Race*, Eric Newby describes a watch-and-watch system using a mixture of four, five, and six-hour watches. It has much to recommend it.

Three-man watch systems

This enables you to use the traditional watch system of four hours on watch and eight off (with or without dogwatches) and a mother watch system where each day one person is taken off watch and is responsible for all

TRADITIONAL WATCHES

Bells	First watch	Middle watch	Morning watch	Forenoon watch	Afternoon watch	First dog	Last dog
8	2000	2400	0400	0800	1200	1600	
1	2030	0030	0430	0830	1230	1630	
2	2100	0100	0500	0900	1300	1700	
3	2130	0130	0530	0930	1330	1730	
4	2200	0200	0600	1000	1400		1800
5	2230	0230	0630	1030	1430		1830
6	2300	0300	0700	1100	1500		1900
7	2330	0330	0730	1130	1530		1930
8	2400	0400	0800	1200	1600		2000

Note:

1 Sometimes the First Dog Watch is called Lookout and the Last Dog Watch becomes the Dog watch.

2 Anchor watches were called 'quarter watches' because only a quarter of the crew were on watch.

cooking and the ship's housework but is (almost) guaranteed an unbroken night's sleep while the other two work watch-and-watch. The small print states that the 'mother' is on standby and will be the first to be called out if an extra hand is needed.

Four-man watch systems

With four people onboard you can run a mother watch, with the remaining three working four on and eight off. Or you can have two-man watches working watch-and-watch or everyone working four hours on and twelve hours off.

ERIC NEWBY'S SWEDISH WATCH SYSTEM

Time	Hours on watch	Day 1	Day 2
0000–0400	4	B	A
0400–0800	4	A	B
0800–1300	5	B	A
1300–1900	6	A	B
1900–2400	5	B	A

Rolling watch systems

Rolling watches see those in a watch as individuals, not team members. If you have three people, A, B and C on board A and B would be on watch. After an agreed interval, A would go off watch and C come on. Then B would go off watch and A would come back on. Proponents reckon this system widens your social life and suits odd-numbered crews. The problem is deciding the interval that folk go on and come off watch and still strike a sensible

This crew are on the alert as the skipper manoeuvres the yacht in harbour.

balance between work and rest. Unless you have a very large crew or are exceptionally cunning, rolling watches mean spending more time on watch than off. More importantly, there can be doubts about who is the watch officer in control of the boat.

Is your system suitable?

If you believe that a watch system that had served well on coastal and offshore passages will work for longer ocean passages then you may be asking too much of your crew. Be prepared to rethink. Almost any watch system can be made to work; a good system is one which sails the boat efficiently, plays to people's strengths, shares the workload fairly, minimises time on watch, maximises time off watch and has the willing support of the crew.

chapter 7 Communications

Communications, whether from yacht to yacht or between yacht and shore, is an area of fast moving change and when these changes will stop, or even slow down is anyone's guess.

Radio

VHF
Despite the introduction of GMDSS, Channel 16 still retains its role as the primary calling and distress channel, although in a number of anchorages some other channel, often 68, is used as a 'cruiser net' for ship-to-ship and ship-to-shore traffic. In some anchorages this is a completely informal arrangement, in others there is a regular morning net with a controller and half an hour or so given over to news, advice, weather and the nautical equivalent of garage sales. The cruiser net is where you call up the fuel barge, the water taxi, and the laundry, order a pizza and check when and where tonight's party is going to happen.

Having a couple of handheld VHF radios is useful when at anchor for it allows communications to be maintained between yacht and crew without the trouble or expense of using cellphones.

VHF in the Caribbean and USA
When you are listening to VHF channel 16 in the Caribbean you may hear the curious sounding demand 'switch to channel seven eight alpha.' The USA has its own system of VHF channels and they are not all compatible with the International channels used in Europe. Some VHF sets change between systems at the flick of a switch. If yours is one then you may find it convenient to switch your VHF set to US channels when in the Caribbean and USA but if this is not possible or too much trouble, do not worry. Using international channels creates few difficulties if you stick to the common channels. The common channels between the International and US systems are: 6, ... 8, 9, 10, 11, 12, 13, 14, 15, 16, 17, ... 20, 24, 25, 26, 27, 28, ... 61, 62, 63, 64, ... 67, 68, 69, 70, 71, 73, 74, ... 84, 85, 86, 87.

US VHF CHANNELS	
Use	**Channel**
Distress safety and calling	16
Intership safety	6
Coast Guard Communications Ship to ship or ship to coast	22A
Port operations	1, 5, 12, 14, 20, 63, 65A, 66A, 73, 74, 77
Navigational Intership and ship to coast	13, 67
Non-commercial Intership and ship to coast	9, 68, 69, 70, 71, 72, 78A
Commercial Intership and ship to coast	1, 7A, 8, 9, 10, 11, 18A, 19A, 63, 67, 77, 79A, 80A, 88A
Public correspondence Ship to coast radio station	24, 25, 26, 27, 28, 84, 85, 86, 87

INTERNATIONAL MARINE VHF CHANNEL CHART

CHL	Transmit	Receive	S/D	Channel assignment	Ship to ship	Ship to shore
1	156.05	160.65	o	Public correspondence, port operation	YES	YES
2	158.1	160.7	o	Public correspondence, port operation	YES	YES
3	156.15	160.75	D	Public correspondence, port operation	YES	YES
4	156.2	160.8	D	Public correspondence, port operation	YES	YES
5	156.25	160.85	D	Public correspondence	YES	YES
6	156.3	156.3	S	Safety (compulsory)	YES	NO
7	156.35	160.95	o	Public correspondence, port operation	YES	YES
8	156.4	156.4	S	Commercial, intership	YES	NO
9	156.45	156.45	S	Commercial/Non-commercial	YES	YES
10	156.5	156.5	S	Commercial	YES	YES
11	156.55	156.55	S	Commercial, VTS	YES	YES
12	156.6	156.6	S	Port operation, VTS	NO	YES
13	156.65	156.65	S	Bridge to bridge (IW) Navigational	YES	YES
14	156.7	156.7	S	Port operation, VTS	YES	YES
15	156.75	156.75	S	Receive only–coast to ship	YES	YES
16	156.8	156.8	S	Calling and safety, compulsory	YES	YES
17	156.85	156.85	S	State controlled ship to coast <1 Wt	YES	YES
18	156.9	161.6	o	Port operation	YES	YES
19	166.95	161.55	D	Port operation	NO	YES
20	157	161.6	D	Port operation	NO	YES
21	157.05	161.65	D	Public correspondence	NO	YES
22	157,100	161.7	D	Public correspondence	NO	YES
23	157.15	161.75	D	Public correspondence	NO	YES
24	157.2	161.8	D	Public correspondence		
25	157.25	161.85	D	Public correspondence		
26	157.3	161.9	D	Port operation,VTS		
27	157.35	161.95	D	Public correspondence, port operation		
28	157.4	162	o	Public correspondence, port operation		
80	156.025	160.625	D	Public correspondence, port operation		
61	156.075	160.675	D	Public correspondence, port operation		
62	156.125	160.725	D	Public correspondence, port operation		
63	156.175	160.775	D	Public correspondence, port operation		
64	156.225	160.825	D	Public correspondence, port operation		
65	156.276	160.875	o	Public correspondence, port operation,	YES	YES
66	156.325	160.525	o	Public correspondence, port operation	YES	YES
67	156.375	156.475	S	Non-commercial, VTS	YES	NO
68	156.425	156.425	S	Non-commercial	YES	YES
69	156.475	156.475	S	Non-commercial	YES	YES
70		156.525	S	DSC distress, urgency, safety and calling	YES	NO
71	156.575	156.575	S	Intership, port operation, or commercial	YES	YES

CHL	Transmit	Receive	S/D	Channel assignment	Ship to ship	Ship to shore
72	156.625	156.825	S	Non-commercial	YES	NO
73	156.675	156.675	S	Port operation, VTS	YES	YES
74	156.725	166.725	S	Port operation, VTS	YES	YES
77	156.875	156.875	S	Intership, port operation	YES	NO
78	156.925	161.525	D	Port operation, public correspondence	YES	YES
79	156.975	161.575	o	Port operation, public correspondence	YES	YES
80	157.025	161.625	D	Port operation, public correspondence	YES	YES
81	157.076	161.675	o	Port operation, public correspondence	YES	YES
82	157.125	161.725	D	Port operation, public correspondence	YES	YES
83	157.175	161.775	D	Port operation, public correspondence	YES	YES
84	157.225	161.825	D	Public correspondence	YES	YES
85	157.275	161.875	D	Public correspondence	NO	YES
86	167.325	161.925	D	Public correspondence	NO	YES
87	157.375	161.975	o	Public correspondence	NO	YES
88	157.425	162.025	o	Port operation, public correspondence	NO	YES

HF

Many yachts carry HF transceivers. This allows them to join the various radio nets and keep in touch with friends outside VHF range. A good HF transceiver requires as much attention, and sometimes expense, on installing the tuner, antenna and ground (earth) system as the set itself. An HF receiver is much easier to install. A simple long wire antenna gives good reception.

SSB and HF are often used as synonyms. Properly, the HF band is the part of the radio spectrum equating to the short-wave band and SSB a method of transmitting signals used in that band. For an HF signal to carry a voice or music signals then a band of audio signals is added to the carrier signal. This is called *modulation* and the oldest system of modulation is called *amplitude modulation* (AM). AM is cheap and cheerful and was used for marine communication until 1982 when it was abandoned because it transmitted the modulated signal on either side of the carrier signal. In effect, the same information was transmitted twice and so occupied twice as much of the radio spectrum as necessary. This makes AM a double sideband (DSB) or A3E signal.

Single sideband

Transmitting one sideband rather than two is more efficient and if the carrier wave is also suppressed along with one of the sideband signals, so much the better. The carrier requires two-thirds of the transmission power with the remaining third equally divided between the two sidebands. Simple arithmetic shows that in DSB (A3E) signals, only a sixth of the transmitting power is used to carry the information sent, and of the 100 watts used, less than 20 watts carry your words.

On an SSB radio the unwanted sideband and the carrier wave are filtered out before the signal is amplified and passed to the antenna. When the signal is picked up, the receiving radio reinserts the carrier to allow the sideband signal to be demodulated and changed back into an audio signal. This halves the amount of the radio spectrum used and makes almost all the transmitting power available for carrying information. This is a single sideband

USING MARINE HF FREQUENCY BANDS

Different HF bands are capable of communicating over different distances at different times of day. Selecting the best band to listen or transmit can make all the difference to reception or transmission. Take the ranges as a rough guide. Radio transmissions can be quirky and with multiple skip, transmissions can be made and received over considerable distances.

Band	Range by day	Likely max.	Range by night	Likely max.	Remarks
2MHz	50–60	100	150–200	300	Often called LF band
4MHz	150–200	300	800	1500	Dead by noon
6MHz	400		1000		
8MHz	300	500	1200	2000	At night stations closer than 500nm are in skip zone
12MHz	2000		1000	3000	
13MHz	2000		800		
16MHz	4000		unreliable		
17MHz	4000		unreliable		
22MHz					Daytime only worldwide band

Note: Onboard electrical equipment, especially inverters, can seriously degrade both radio reception and transmission and may need to be switched off when you are using the radio. Be alert for equipment like bilges pumps or refrigerators which may kick in during radio schedules.

suppressed carrier signal or J3E. DSB and SSB signals are not compatible although during the transition period when SSB was introduced, a signal that could be received by both DSB and SSB receivers was introduced. This is the H3E mode, and SSB sets would tune for the USB signal. H3E was mandatory for 2182MHz.

Buying a short-wave receiver capable only of picking up commercial stations is a mistake. With an SSB receiver you can listen to the transatlantic ham radio nets, eavesdrop on the weather forecasts from Herb on *Southbound 2*, and listen to Mechanical Mike, the voice of NOAA weather. With the right computer programme, and a demodulator plugged into a laptop, you can also receive weatherfaxes.

Weatherfax and weather information bulletins are transmitted on regular schedules by about 80 stations worldwide. If you do not have a dedicated weatherfax (WEFAX) receiver, you need an SSB receiver, a computer and a demodulator that turns the analogue radio signal into a digital signal that the computer will understand. Your computer audio card may do this for you. You will also need a program for the computer to transform the signal into pictures or words. Weatherfax charts are either an analysis of actual conditions or a forecast of future weather. Each chart takes between 8–10 minutes to receive and in remote areas they may be amongst your best, possibly the only, source of weather forecasting.

Most weatherfax programmes also handle Navtex broadcasts but if you do not wish to run a computer all the time, inexpensive dedicated Navtex receivers are available. In theory, Navtex broadcasts have a maximum range of 300–400 miles. There are those who claim to have regularly received Navtex broadcasts in mid-ocean but this has probably been from sky wave signals at night.

Earthing and antennas for HF

Installing an HF transceiver requires a good ground plane (also called *counterpoise*). This means it must be earthed. An external keel or encapsulated solid keel can be used but best of all is a special, and expensive, external earthing plate fitted to the hull during the pre-cruise refit. If you are laying up your own boat then a copper mesh can be laid up between fibreglass layers to make a good ground plane or the mesh of a ferroconcrete hull can be used. It is also a good idea to ground all electrical equipment using the same wide copper tape used for the antenna. This will reduce the possibility of onboard interference to your signal.

Ideally there should be a separate antenna for each frequency band. Instead it is usual to trick the backstay into behaving as if it is the correct length by fitting an automatic tuning unit (ATU). This is sometimes referred to as an antenna coupler. The best are automatic and cover all frequencies but some meant for ham use, or older models, may only cover a limited number of frequencies and must be manually tuned.

If you are buying a second-hand set-up, check that the ATU covers all the frequencies you are likely to use. You may be told that it will 'broadband' on frequencies it does not cover. This sounds good but you are still putting out a lousy signal. If you have your HF transceiver professionally installed then, when the work is finished, ask the technician to make a radio check with a station at least 1000 miles away. His wattmeter may show 100 watts of power going out and his VSWR meter (Voltage to Standing Wave Ratio) declares that the forward power to the antenna is superb, but a bad earth or poorly fitted ATU can make you sound like Donald Duck with a sore throat. Only after one or two distant stations have reported that they are receiving you loud and clear should you declare yourself satisfied and part with the cash.

Emergency HF antenna

If you lose the mast, you will almost certainly lose both your HF and VHF antennas. You should have a spare VHF antenna but if that

RADIO FREQUENCY INTERFERENCE (RFI)

RFI is when other onboard electrical or electronic equipment interferes with radio reception or transmission. The ideal solution is to turn off all other electrical equipment when using the radio but this is rarely feasible. Tracking down RFI is a slow, tedious task. The most common sources of RFI are:

- Alternators
- Electrical motors
- Fluorescent lights
- Rotating propeller shafts
- Televisions
- Radars
- Inverters
- Electronic logs and instrumentation

There may also be interference from the guardrails, rigging, other antennas and the ship's wiring. The following hints may help you find sources of RFI:

- Try using a small portable transistor radio to track down the source of the RFI. The louder the interference the closer you are to its source.
- If the RFI is traced to an electrical motor (a very common cause) clean the motor's commutator and brushes. If the interference persists, connect 05–1.0 micro-farad capacitors across each of the power leads and the ground (earth).
- If there is a humming from the radio when the engine is running, see if it changes tone as you change engine speed. If so, the alternator is probably to blame. If the hum does not change pitch or if it is present when the engine is not running then suspect an inverter. Some inverters are very noisy (electronically) because they do not produce a true sine wave.
- Computers can generate a lot of electronic noise, which is fed back to the radio via the demodulator, and completely ruin reception of weatherfaxes. One solution is to fit ferrite chokes.
- When you find a source of RFI, temporarily fit a 1 micro-farad capacitor between the suspect item of equipment and ground. If the RFI disappears fit the capacitor permanently.
- Keep radar scanners as far away as possible from radio antennas.

EMERGENCY ANTENNA

If you have broken the mast, lost your VHF aerial and have no spare then a usable half-wave dipole antenna can be made from the remnants of your coaxial cable. If you are considering buying spare cable then it will most probably have an impedance of either 50 or 75 ohms. Check in your radio's instruction manual. Strip about 20in (500mm) of the outer sheath to expose the braid.

Carefully feed the inner core through the braid where it leaves the outer sheath. Trim both the inner core and the braid so that they are exactly 17.5in (445mm) long. Lay out the inner core and the braid so that they form one straight line and tape to a sail batten. Plug the other end of the cable into your radio and hang the antenna as high as possible so that the batten hangs vertically and you have a VHF half-wave dipole antenna. It has no gain but it should give reasonable performance. More elaborate versions can be made using small-diameter copper tubing, but this model has the great advantage that it can be made with the materials most likely to be at hand.

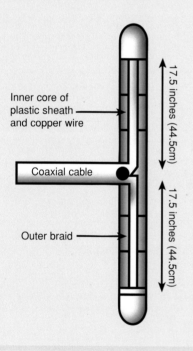

Inner core of plastic sheath and copper wire

17.5 inches (44.5cm)

Coaxial cable

17.5 inches (44.5cm)

Outer braid

cannot be found then it is fairly easy to make a simple dipole VHF antenna using any length of coaxial cable that you can salvage.

SSB transceivers often use a stay as an antenna and if the mast comes down so does your HF antenna. It is possible to make HF antennas but they tend to be fiddly and work only on one frequency. The best solution is to carry a 7–9m (23–30ft) whip HF antenna and plug that into your tuner. Provided you have the power this allows you to use the radio as normal.

Marine versus ham radio

HF radios are normally sold either as ham sets or dedicated marine radios. Both receive on all frequencies but each will only transmit on the frequencies the authorities allocate for either marine or ham use. If you wish to transmit on both marine and ham frequencies you should have two transceivers, but the expense of two sets is avoided by modifying a radio to broadcast over all HF frequencies. This is a task for an expert.

Ham radio is not an alternative to a marine HF transceiver. It opens up the ham chat nets and lets you speak directly to other yachts with ham radios, but it will not handle GMDSS traffic or transmit on any marine frequency. Ham sets tend to have more bells and whistles than the equivalent marine set and can be more demanding to operate, as you will have to remember which sideband you are using, whether you are operating in simplex or duplex mode, and perhaps you will need to manually tune the ATU. On the plus side, not all ships and probably no yachts keep a full time watch on HF frequencies. They only switch on when it's time to join a net. On ham bands thousands of amateurs are straining their ears to pick up that elusive weak, long range (DX) signal. If you are in trouble and relying on the radio (rather than an EPIRB) to bring help there is an argument that you stand a better chance of being heard on the ham bands.

OPERATORS' LICENCES

An operator's licence is necessary to transmit on any HF frequency. In the UK this is a Long Range Radio Operator's Certificate. It can be endorsed for satellite communications. An amateur licence is necessary to transmit on the ham frequencies. This can either be a full or restricted Class A licence. It is obtained by attending a night school course, and taking a test administered by the City and Guilds Institute. A pass entitles you to apply for a Class B licence and this is converted to a Class A licence by taking a separate morse test administered by the Radio Society of Great Britain. Different countries have their own, broadly similar, arrangements.

HAMBAND FREQUENCIES

Band	Comments
10 metre (28MHz)	Best during high sunspot periods.
15 metre (21MHz)	Good for long distance.
20 metre (14MHz)	This is the closest to an all-time, all-place band but it is still subject to atmospheric variation. Lots of short wave broadcast interference.
40 metre (7MHz)	Range of 400–1200 miles in morning and early afternoon.
	Range of several thousand miles in late afternoon, evening, night.
80 metre (3.7MHz)	Range of 350 miles in daylight.
	Range of 1000 miles during night time in summer.
	Range of several thousand miles in winter night time.

RADIO COMPARISON

Type	Power	Range	Comments
Marine VHF	1 or 25 watts	Line of sight. Varies with set. Antenna height up to 30 miles	The workhorse of the sea. Every yacht has at least one
Marine SSB	150 watts	1000+ miles	Ship-to-ship and some shore stations. Can handle email and weatherfaxes
Short-wave Receiver		Worldwide	Can listen to Marine and ham SSB broadcasts and receive weather faxes and Navtex.
Ham (amateur radio)	50–150 watts	Worldwide on HF bands. Two-metre band allowed. Corresponds to marine VHF	Licence needed to operate. No music or profit making
Citizens band	4 watts	Under 150 miles	Different countries have different, non-compatible standards

Prefixes

The prefixes kilo or mega allow the same frequency to be described in different ways. The frequency 4065kHz is 4065000 hertz and can also be written 4.065MHz. One hertz (Hz) is one cycle per second; 1000Hz is also 1 kilohertz (kHz); 1000kHz is also 1 megahertz (MHz) or one million hertz 1000MHz is also 1 gigahertz (GHz) or one thousand million hertz.

Cellphones

In the Eastern Caribbean it is possible to rent a 'Boatphone' which like any cellphone allows you to make and receive telephone calls when you are within range of a cellphone mast. If you already have a cellphone and your provider has an agreement with a local network then you should be able to make calls as usual, but check out your provider's roaming charges first. If you intend to remain in one anchorage for some time consider hiring a cellphone from a local company, or sign up with a local supplier and fit their SIM card or use landlines.

Landlines

Normally, local and international calls are dialled directly. It is usual to pre-pay for calls by purchasing a phone card from one of the many outlets. In some countries, Venezeula for example, international calls can be made only from designated call boxes but these are plentiful and easily identified. On a few of the remoter islands, calls are made by going to the local telecommunications office and waiting your turn.

ADDRESSING MAIL

Spend a little time and effort training your correspondents to address mail properly; simple is best.

Rule 1 Avoid titles and honorifics. Captain John Smith PhD, MA, BSc looks impressive but plain John Smith is better. In Spanish speaking countries, it is common to use both your father's name and mother's maiden name. The middle name is used to file mail. If you have only one Christian name then this is no problem but if you are John Frank Smith drop Frank or be prepared to look under Frank as well as Smith when collecting your mail.

Rule 2 The boat name should be written after your name.

Rule 3 Complete the address.

Rule 4 After the address add the words 'To Await Arrival.'

Rule 5 The sender should write their name and address on the back.

Mail

Traditionally, surface and airmail correspondence awaits your arrival *poste-restante* (general delivery in US islands) at a post office, marina, yacht-club or bar that you have selected and advertised as a mail-drop amongst family and friends.

Post offices are in the mail handling business and take a pride in their job. The drawback is dealing with yet another bureaucracy. You need your passport and will almost certainly be directed to two or three different offices before anyone will admit having heard of general delivery, but if your mail is there then they will find it.

It makes the informal approach of bars, yacht clubs and marinas attractive but the friendly bar of a couple of seasons ago may go out of business between the time you select it as a mailing address and your mail arriving, or may now be an up-market, black tie restaurant that cares neither for boaters or their mail.

Club and bar mail facilities range from custom made A–Z mail boxes to a communal cardboard box. Everyone, including you, sorts through every piece of mail just in case it has been misfiled and by the time you have finished going through the mail – it has been.

Depending on your location, both surface and airmail can take three to four weeks to arrive. Allow for this when handing out mail-drop addresses. Most places hold onto to mail for several weeks but if it is not collected then it is unlikely to be returned to sender.

You may feel happier entrusting mail, especially packages, to companies such as UPS, DHL or Federal Express. Before choosing a company make sure that they have a local office where you can speak to a human being. Obtain a tracking number as soon as possible and check on the company's policy on bringing goods through Customs. Do they see to everything or must you be there to ensure its smooth passage?

Faxes

Facilities for sending and receiving faxes from phone shops or yacht clubs are good. There is usually a small charge for receiving a fax.

Boat cards

Boat cards and stamps are not strictly a means of communication but a quick and easy way of passing your vessel's name and your address to your new friends. Occasionally a boat stamp finds favour with the authorities.

Email

It is rare for a yacht not to have an email address. You do not need an internet service provider (ISP) or even a computer but you do need to sign up with an email service such as Hotmail, Yahoo, Google or AOL. You do this by going an internet café, typing www.hotmail.com (or www.yahoo.com or www.aol.com). Take your pick and look for the box which invites you to sign up to their email service. Click on it and follow the instructions. Apart from paying the internet café, this service is free.

The cost of using internet cafés can be reduced by typing your email onboard, saving it to memory stick and using the shoreside facilities only to receive and send mail. Incoming mail can be saved to memory stick and read at your leisure later.

A variation on the internet café is Pocketmail where mail is typed on a small machine similar to a pocket organiser. This has an earphone and a microphone that is placed against a telephone handset. Mail is sent to and received from an Internet Service Provider (ISP) in the USA. In the USA a freephone number is used but elsewhere normal rates to the USA apply. Widely used within the Caribbean, it is a useful system which frees you from the internet café.

Email afloat

It is possible to send and receive emails aboard your boat. It means either installing a satellite communications device that includes email as one of its facilities or adding bits and pieces to your HF transceiver. This may be generic equipment or modules dedicated to one particular service. Whether satellite or HF, email afloat is really a radio telex service with an email gateway. Not all have the ability to handle attachments and some limit the style of text you can use. Given the number of internet cafés it is probably a luxury in the Caribbean unless you intend spending long periods far from civilization.

CUTTING THE COSTS OF EMAILS AFLOAT

The costs of sending and receiving emails onboard can be reduced by compressing them using a service like ONSPEED or MailASail. ONSPEED compresses both incoming and outgoing mail but before it does so it must establish a connection and doing this can add up to 5–10 per cent of the cost. MailASail scans your email account(s) and then forwards your mail using an email address (eg mgkelly@mailasail.com). As part of its compression system it removes formatting from emails and their attachments and images from pdf files. There is no connection charge but outgoing emails are not compressed.

E-MAIL AFLOAT

The following list is not exhaustive and likely to date as new systems come on line.

Satellite communications

Magellan GSC 100

In 1998 Magellan introduced the GSC 100, a GPS unit which uses the Orbcomm network to send and receive alpha-numeric messages, or 'GlobalGrams' of up to 2000 characters via standard e-mail interfaces.

There are bolt-ons. The ORBWeather service, for example, delivers weather reports covering the current day, the following day and the following evening for your position.

After paying an activation fee, there is a monthly charge and once the monthly allowance of sent and received messages is reached, there is a charge per character (sent or received).

Inmarsat

Inmarsat has been around for about 30 years and offers a wide range of communication packages aimed mostly at the commercial market.

Inmarsat Mini C is a smaller yacht-friendly version of Inmarsat-C which supports two-way store-and-forward communication via lightweight, low-cost and low-power terminals. Depending on model, Inmarsat Mini C supports the same communication functions as Inmarsat C.

Introduced in 1993, Inmarsat M is a briefcase-sized world-wide satphone offering two-way voice telephony, distress alerting, fax and data services at lower data rates. The Mini M is a notebook sized version offering a reduced coverage but still capable of two-way voice telephony, alerting, fax and data services.

Iridium

Iridium uses 66 low orbit earth satellites to provide a worldwide telephony service. Using what looks like a chunky cellphone, you can always reach who you want to call, no matter where you are. Having bought your Iridium phone, you sign up with a provider and there is a charge for incoming and outgoing calls.

HF systems

Those with HF transceivers can, with some additional equipment, make arrangements with a provider to send and receive email over the airwaves.

This is similar to the packet radio of ham radio operators and there is a charge, sometimes per character, for each message sent and received. The service is closer to radio teletype than email proper. It is cheaper than satellite systems but marine SSB can, legally, only be used from a boat. Ham radio systems require a ham radio licence.

For radio hams the Sailmail Association is a 'not for profit' association offering a worldwide email service to its members via its own worldwide network of SSB-Pactor radio stations or through a satellite service such as Iridium, Globestar or Inmarsat. Other than membership fees there is no charge for using Sailmail's network of SSB Pactor stations.

HF signals

An HF signal has two components, groundwave and skywave. The groundwave hugs the sea and has a maximum range of about 200 miles. Given a good signal, the groundwave does not vary with the time of day.

The skywave works by bouncing signals off an ionised layer of gas surrounding the Earth called the ionosphere. Different frequencies are reflected at different angles. The smaller the angle of reflection the shorter the range of the signal so it is important to match the frequency used to the distance you intend to transmit. As a rule of thumb, lower frequencies are reflected over a smaller angle than higher frequencies. The distance between you and where the signal is reflected back to Earth is the skip distance, and beyond the groundwave signal nothing will be heard in this dead zone.

If you opt for email afloat, check the cost of the service before signing up. This can include annual fees, monthly fees, activation fees and a charge per character or per minute. The average email is reckoned to be about 1000 characters. Confirm the true, as opposed to advertised, coverage of the system and its availability, especially at busy times. Otherwise you may find yourself in an area where coverage is poor, or you will wait forever to log on.

chapter 8 Safety on board

Bluewater cruising comes with risks. If you cannot accept them then stay ashore. Managing risk is a bit like lion taming. A risk is only dangerous when it is out of control. Safety comes from correctly identifying risks and putting together a package of measures to manage them. Think carefully about what you include in this package. Real safety is an attitude of mind, an onboard culture created by the skipper and intelligently implemented by all onboard. If your safety strategy relies on technology or mindless obedience to rigid rules then at some point it will fail.

Disasters are never the result of a single hazard. They come from a mass assault by a horde of small, insignificant risks. Individually they are trivial and easily controlled. En masse they are difficult to prioritise and overwhelm the resources that you have to handle them.

Man overboard

Losing someone over the side is one of the most serious emergencies that you can face. If it happens when you are running under spinnaker or twin jibs it may take half an hour before you can turn round and begin the search. In large ocean swells you may only see the person overboard when both the boat and the casualty are on the top of a swell. They stand a better chance of seeing the boat, but spotting a head amongst breaking swells is very difficult in daylight and probably impossible at night. If everyone carries a waterproof flashlight then if they go into the water, they can shine it at the boat to draw attention to themselves. This tactic stands a far better chance of

Body heat is lost 25 times faster in water than in air at the same temperature. The HELP (Heat Escape Lessening Position) can reduce heat loss by up to 50 per cent.

success than people on the boat shining torches on the water to locate the casualty. There is also a choice of radio-locating devices that will lead you to someone in the water. They could be a worthwhile investment.

If everyone wears a harness and clips on, then if they go overboard they remain attached to the boat. If they are clipped into a jackstay running the length of the boat they will receive a severe bruising as they are swept astern. As long as the boat remains underway, they will be unable to pull themselves to the boat. The first action needed by those left aboard is to stop the boat and bring the casualty alongside.

If they are conscious and mobile then put a ladder over the side. If they are unconscious, or unable to help themselves, try to parbuckle them aboard, winch them out on a spare halyard, or detach the mainsheet and use that as a purchase to bring them aboard. If you have a proprietary man overboard system, then deploy it.

Single-handers face particular problems if they part company with their boat. Some tow a long knotted line astern, but unless they have some means of disengaging the self-steering, and bringing the boat into the wind, it would be very difficult, perhaps impossible, to pull themselves towards the boat.

Single-handers must be obsessive about *always* wearing a harness and clipping on. Jackstays should be split into short sections so that a man overboard cannot slide astern. They may not have the upper body strength to haul themselves aboard and should not assume fear

Prusik knot

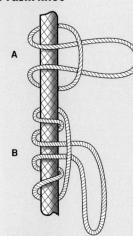

The Prusik Knot was developed by Dr Carl Prusik in 1931 for attaching slings (loops of line) to rope so that they slide up or down when loose but lock and hold under a sideways load. Alternatives are the Penberthy Knot and the Hadden Knot.

A A loop of line is led round the rope.
B The line is led round the rope a second time and the loops brought together and tightened up.

How to use Prusik knots
1 Use two Prusik knots one above the other.
2 Attach top Prusik knot to a sit harness.
3 Attach lower Prusik knot to a stirrup.
4 Push sit harness knot as high as it will go and take weight on sit harness.
5 Bring stirrup knot as close as possible to sit harness knot.
6 Take weight on stirrup knot and push waist harness knot as high as possible.
7 Repeat sequence. It's slow but sure.

A single Prusik knot on a spare halyard and fixed to your harness makes a great safety device if you are being hauled up the mast. Push it up as you go. If the main line fails then as you fall the Prusik knot will tighten and hold you.

Triple bowline

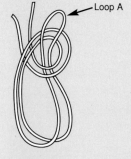

Loop A

Do not worry if you do not have a sit harness onboard. Traditionally sit harnesses were made from a triple bowline and most climbing sit harnesses follow the same principles.

1 Begin by tying a bowline on the bight.

2 Take loop around the back of the bight and down through the hole. Adjust round thighs and waist until it is a snug fit.

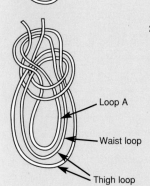

Loop A

Waist loop

Thigh loop

will provide the necessary strength. They should fit short rope ladders or rope loops around the boat that they can pull down and use to climb aboard.

Anchor points for harnesses

Anchor points for harnesses should be spaced so that you clip in before opening the hatch, and by using two safety lines, never unclip until you are back in the cabin and the hatch is shut. This is a counsel of perfection. If the crew complain of infringing their human rights, sling an item of bio-degradable rubbish over the side, count to five and ask them how long they would take to sail back and pick it up. In the Trades, with boomed-out headsails, the correct answer is 'forever'.

Climbing the mast

After the perils of falling overboard, climbing the mast at sea comes next in the catalogue of risks. Installing extra halyards and spare navigation lights during the pre-cruise refit cuts down on the need for mast-climbing at sea. Replacing halyards or burnt out bulbs can wait until you are at anchor. Climbing the mast at sea is very tiring and in a small boat, a combination of extra weight at the top of the mast and swell could lay the boat onto its beam ends.

Traditionally, mast-climbing involves sitting in a bosun's chair and being winched up the mast. It requires four people, one in the chair, one winching, one tailing the winch and one looking after the safety line. Unless the boat has very large winches, cranking someone up the mast is hard work. If the bosun's chair swings away from the mast it, and its occupant, return rather faster and more painfully than they left. Even worse, a bosun's chair can invert and drop its contents overboard.

A bosun's chair makes working at the top of the mast difficult as you are always working with your hands above shoulder height. In a proper harness and foot sling you can stand up to work, see what you are doing, and reach it easily.

Mountaineering systems are far safer. These have evolved into rope access techniques which allow workmen to work on high structures without scaffolding. The methods involved are fail safe, operated by the person climbing the mast, and make it impossible to swing out more than a couple of feet from the mast. It means wearing a climbing harness and using ascendeurs. Climbing harnesses are far superior to bosun's chairs. They are more comfortable and you can hang upside down in a climbing harness and not fall out. Using ascendeurs (sometimes called cloggers or jumars) there is no need for someone to tail a

Using a home-made harness and climber's ascendeurs (detail, left). The risk of swinging away from the mast is much reduced because the halyard is fixed at the top and bottom of the mast.

winch. Ascendeurs come in pairs; one is attached to the harness at waist level and the other to a loop of rope that acts as a stirrup. They go on separate halyards for safety and you push them up alternately for a slow, stately and safe ascent. A short safety line goes from the harness to a third halyard and is fastened with a Prusik knot that slides up as you go, and if all else fails, this will catch you before you hit the deck.

The kit required is available in most mountaineering outlets. In the UK there are firms which train and certify people in rope access techniques who might be willing to teach you how to use this kit.

Abandoning ship

The rule is, only leave the ship when you have to step off the top of the mast into the liferaft. A yacht is definitely the best life raft you can have but if it becomes certain that the boat is lost then the only course of action is an orderly mid-ocean departure, which brings everyone safely ashore. It is important that you develop an abandon ship drill and rehearse it with your crew so that everybody knows what must be done and who does what. After the decision to abandon ship is made there is no time to think about how this is done. Every minute, every second, should be spent executing a carefully thought out, well rehearsed plan in which everyone knows what they have to do and does it.

Floating crash bag

Snaplink to secure to liferaft

Splice

Strobe

Fender

Fender inside crash bag to provide buoyancy in case crash bag becomes separated from lifejacket

Waterproof kitbag. This is VERY securely attached to lifejacket

Lifejacket is inflated once crash bag is out of the cabin

LIFEJACKET

LIFEJACKET

Spare snaplink

The crash box

The crash box needs to contain all you need to stay alive. It must be robust enough to withstand the inevitable abuse, hold its contents securely, be waterproof, buoyant, easily recognisable by night or day and have a foolproof and secure method of attachment to the liferaft. Large, plastic, high-visibility orange flare boxes are good especially if they are liberally covered in photo-luminescent tape that glows in the dark. This makes them easy to find in the forepeak or a locker at night, but also attach a small, waterproof, battery-operated strobe to make sure that if you abandon ship at night then the odds on losing sight of the crash box, if it goes adrift, are much reduced.

Every crash box should have a line spliced to its handle with a snaplink at its free end. Everything you plan to take into the liferaft should have the same arrangement of line and snaplink. Clipping the snap-links to the liferaft's grab line reduces the possibility of anything going adrift even in a capsize.

Hard plastic boxes protect their contents but some people prefer a soft 'crash bag' as it is easier to stow in odd-shaped lockers until it is needed. The comments about the importance of visibility, security and flotation still apply with the rider that the contents must be individually protected against damage. To improve visibility and flotation it might help to lash the crash bag into a lifejacket equipped with its own strobe light.

In the secondary crash box (or grab bag), the one you would take with you if you are taken off by another vessel or open when you reach land, pack the ship's papers, passports, some cash, credit cards, a notebook and pencil.

Emergency rations

The priorities for survival are shelter, water and food. The canopy of a liferaft provides shelter but you should also carry a heavy-duty exposure suit for everyone on board. Solar stills to distil fresh water from sea water are hard to find and small, hand-operated water makers are very expensive, so you may have to carry your water with you and hope to supplement it from passing rain showers.

Alain Bombard claimed that it is possible to drink up to half a pint of seawater a day provided you started immediately that you entered the liferaft and before you became dehydrated. This is an extreme view. He survived, but few will have his confidence in this practice. As a supplement to the canned water in the crashbox carry plastic water containers in the cockpit. Leave some air in each to make sure that they will float. Two five-gallon jugs represent about 20 days of water for one person.

Carry as many cans of food as you can squeeze into the crash box. Try to avoid products high in thirst-inducing salt (it is surprising how high salt comes on the list of the ingredients on many cans) and give preference to food high in fluids. Canned fruit is good. Also include sugary snacks as quick energy and morale boosters. If time allows then the ready-to-use food (about a week's worth of food at normal consumption stored in a plastic box) can be taken into the life raft.

Attracting attention

You must bring your predicament to the attention of other vessels. As well as a 406MHz EPIRB, carry flares, signal mirrors and strobes, but there are too many tales of flares burning unseen to put much faith in them as the principal means of attracting notice. At sea, commercial traffic has only one man on the bridge and relies more on radar than eyeball for maintaining a lookout. The odds on them spotting a liferaft without first being alerted by an EPIRB report are low. Ships, even far from land, tend to keep a watch on Channel 16 and are far more likely to respond to a radio call than a flare. Once you have their attention you can use flares, smoke and strobes to indicate your position. Pack a handheld VHF radio with a spare battery into the crash box; one of your regular chores is to make sure that both batteries are fully charged.

When help comes

It may be several days before help arrives and is most likely to come from a vessel taking part in the AMVER (Automated Mutual Vessel Rescue) scheme which tracks vessels taking part so that the nearest can be diverted to give assistance in an emergency. When it does arrive their priority is to save life. If you have stayed with your boat you may find that it cannot be saved. Few commercial vessels have the equipment or expertise to lift a yacht safely out of the water at sea. Asking for help means the situation is so serious that you should be willing to trade your boat, its equipment and most of its contents for the safety of you and your crew.

If there is no immediate danger of foundering, then this becomes what politicians call a hard choice. A Swiss yacht was becalmed with its engine broken beyond onboard repair north of St Martin. Hurricane Lenny, a Category 4 monster, was expected to pass over them, either that day, or perhaps the day after. In any event, they did not expect to sail out of Lenny's path.

The crew put out a Mayday and were taken off and the yacht was abandoned. Lenny reached St Martin, stopped and turned south. It would never have reached them and the abandoned yacht was eventually found by fishermen and towed, more or less undamaged, into Great Inagau in the Bahamas.

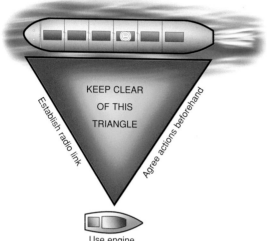

KEEP CLEAR
OF THIS
TRIANGLE

Establish radio link

Agree actions beforehand

Use engine

Going alongside at sea

Asking a passing ship for a few gallons of fuel or water may seem to be the solution to an unexpected shortage, but be careful. Going alongside a larger vessel at sea can fatally damage your boat. To avoid being sucked against the larger vessel, stay outside the equilateral triangle (see left) whose sides are equal to the length of the larger vessel. If you must go alongside to collect supplies or deliver an injured crew member then consider using the dinghy. Without a yardstick to give scale, distances off are hard to judge. Ships are often bigger and further away than they look. If you do not have a radar set then ask them for the distance off.

If help does not come

Before EPIRBs located a casualty's position for rescuers, how did seafarers fend for themselves? Studying reports of sinkings in World War Two, Alain Bombard, a French doctor, was struck by the fact that many crews successfully abandoned ship but died soon afterwards even though they were uninjured and were in tropical waters where hypothermia was not a factor. Bombard concluded that they died because they did not expect to live. He came to believe that survival at sea for long periods with limited resources was possible and cited the example of Second Steward Poon Lim of the SS Ben Lomond which was torpedoed and sank on 23 November 1942; Lim was rescued alive 133 days later.

Bombard argued that it was possible to survive at sea even if you had no food or water. In 1952 he proved his theory by successfully sailing a 15-foot inflatable called *l'Heritique* from France to Barbados, including a 65-day non-stop passage from Las Palmas to Barbados. Apart from one light meal from a passing ship he ate and drank only what he got from the sea. His extraordinary example must have helped folk like the Baileys (118 days adrift), and the Robertsons (84 days adrift).

GMDSS, particularly the 406MHz EPIRB, makes it unlikely that these incidents will be repeated, but what if the EPIRB fails? Impossible? What would happen if a lightning strike blew out every seacock and sank the boat? Lightning kills electrics, including EPIRBs. Even a near miss will make an EPIRB very sick and Murphy's Law of the Sea has a paragraph on this and other circumstances, as yet unknown, where EPIRBs will fail.

If your liferaft can double as a lifeboat then after five or six days spent close to where you abandoned ship, and if the EPIRB has not brought any result, it might be better to continue on your way. To enable you to navigate the lifeboat across the ocean, add to the primary crash box a handheld GPS programmed with a selection of likely waypoints, a compass, and a small laminated chart of the Atlantic Ocean showing the principal shipping lanes, and more spare batteries.

Lifeboat versus liferaft

Liferafts are compact, easy to stow, and quick to launch, but once you are inside you are a passive victim of the winds and currents. In accounts like those of the Baileys and the Robertsons, it is apparent that had they been able to sail in a direction of their choosing rather than drifting at the mercy of the currents and winds, their ordeal would have ended much earlier.

Today, EPRIBs promise help within a few days, and waiting for it to arrive is by far the best option. If you do not carry an EPRIB or prefer a belt and braces approach just in case technology fails, you may wish to explore the lifeboat option.

Very few yachts have the space to carry a lifeboat even if it does double-duty as a tender. Also a lifeboat takes longer to launch and is more vulnerable than a liferaft in heavy weather but in reasonable conditions it could make 40 or 50 miles a day. Locating a lifeboat that fits onto a yacht is a challenge. There is the Tinker Tramp, an inflatable dinghy which can be rigged for sailing or given an inflatable hood to become a liferaft. Even though air bottles can be fitted to inflate it quickly, in an emergency it would still take longer to launch than a liferaft. Deflated and rolled up it is bulkier than both a conventional inflatable dinghy and a liferaft. A big plus is that, unlike a conventional liferaft, it is possible to check its condition frequently, practise using it in its various modes and have confidence that if it is needed it will work. They are not cheap and the argument that they cost little more than the combined cost of a rubber dinghy and a liferaft falls down because most people already have a perfectly good inflatable dinghy.

A Tinker Tramp may not be ideal but the market is not brimming with choice. Its Bermudan rig gives a surprisingly good performance but perhaps not the best for its role as a lifeboat, where most travelling will be downwind and down current, and performance is less important. Perhaps a simple, easily-rigged standing lug on a hard dinghy would be better.

LIFERAFT

Your liferaft should be purpose-made and self-inflating with a valid inspection certificate from the manufacturer or approved servicing agent. It must large enough to accommodate all those aboard. It should be one of the following:

1 A SOLAS model

2 An ORC model in compliance with ISAF Offshore Special Regulations Appendix A, Part I, provided that the liferaft was manufactured before 01/2003

3 An ISAF model in compliance with ISAF Offshore Special Regulations Appendix A, Part II

4 An ISO Standard 9650 Type 1, Group A with service Pack 1

It should be possible to launch the raft within 30 seconds. This means it must be stowed on deck with a quick release system. If you lash it down to make sure it stays aboard in heavy weather, then tape a sharp knife to its lashings.

With its detachable hood, gas bottle and drogue, the Tinker Tramp can double up as a liferaft and a dinghy.

Dinghy liferaft

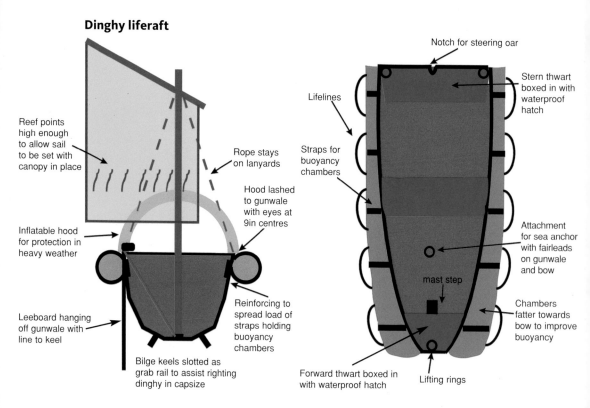

Reef points high enough to allow sail to be set with canopy in place

Rope stays on lanyards

Inflatable hood for protection in heavy weather

Hood lashed to gunwale with eyes at 9in centres

Leeboard hanging off gunwale with line to keel

Reinforcing to spread load of straps holding buoyancy chambers

Bilge keels slotted as grab rail to assist righting dinghy in capsize

Notch for steering oar

Lifelines

Straps for buoyancy chambers

Stern thwart boxed in with waterproof hatch

Attachment for sea anchor with fairleads on gunwale and bow

mast step

Chambers fatter towards bow to improve buoyancy

Forward thwart boxed in with waterproof hatch

Lifting rings

A perfect sailing day in the Caribbean – but there is always the chance of a sudden squall approaching, so be prepared.

SAFETY EQUIPMENT

The following safety equipment should be onboard:

- Buckets (at least two) fitted with lanyards with a capacity of at least 2 gallons (9 litres). A bucket is the most efficient pump a frightened sailor can have

- Drogue or sea anchor. This reduces the risk of capsize in heavy breaking seas. A drogue deploys over the stern; a sea anchor, over the bow

- Emergency grab bag

- Emergency tiller or secondary steering device

- Fire blanket kept near the galley

- Fire extinguishers: at least two

- First aid kit and manual

- Flares stowed in a watertight container with at least:
  6 red parachute flares
  4 white hand held flares
  4 red hand held flares
  2 orange smoke

- Hacksaw and spare blades

- Bolt croppers are essential for cutting rod rigging. To be effective, bolt croppers must be very large (and therefore heavy and awkward to use) or have hydraulic powered cutters

- High powered light – usually called a steamer scarer

- Jackstays along port and starboard side decks

- Lifebuoys(two) both within reach of the helmsman with the yacht's name painted on them and fitted with marine grade retro-reflective material

  Both should have a drogue, with a self-igniting light, and whistle; a danbuoy should have a pole with a flag.
  At least one should have permanent (eg foam) buoyancy Inflatable lifebuoys should be tested in accordance with the manufacturer's instructions

  One lifebuoy can be replaced by a proprietary MOB system

- Harnesses. There must be a harness and lifejacket or a lifejacket/combined harness for each crewmember. These must be adjusted to fit the crewmember before leaving port. Every lifejacket must have:
  A crotch strap
  The yacht's name
  Retro-reflective tape
  Spray hood
  Light
  Whistle

Harness only This must have a crotch strap and a safety line not more than 2m (6ft) long with a snaplink at each end.

Combined lifejacket and harness This must have a safety line not more than 2m (6ft) long with a snaplink at each end and a crotch strap

- Lifelines aka guardrails securely fitted around the entire deck

- Liferaft

- A recognised secondary method of navigation eg sextant should GPS signal be lost

- One manual bilge pump operated from on deck with companionways and hatches shut and a second manual bilge pump below decks. Consider fitting the engine raw water intake with a diverter so that the engine can be used to pump the bilge

- Radar reflector permanently mounted, or capable of being hoisted to a position at least 5m (15ft) above deck. Octahedral reflectors must have a minimum diagonal measurement of 18in (457mm). Other reflectors must have a radar cross-section of at least 10sqm (12 sq yds)

- Handheld marine VHF transceiver. Keep battery fully charged. Plus an Emergency Position Indicating Radio Beacon (EPIRB) transmitting on 406MHz or an Inmarsat type 'E' EPIRB

- Softwood plugs. These should be securely attached adjacent to each fitting to enable any through-hull fitting to be closed off

- Throwing line 15m-25m (50ft-75ft) length, readily accessible to cockpit

- Washboards capable of being fastened shut and secured with lanyards to prevent accidental loss

- Water resistant torch with spare bulb and batteries for each crew member

NB Heavy items of equipment (anchors, batteries, spare gas bottles and stoves) should be firmly secured so that they stay in position in the event of a knock-down or capsize.

chapter 9 Caribbean living

Victualling

On a long passage, meals give rhythm to the day and provide an opportunity for the crew to socialise. It is usual to carry rations for the estimated time on passage plus 50 per cent. In practice you often carry much more for it pays to stock up where food is cheap.

Find out what everyone likes to eat and prepare half a dozen different standard daily menus that more or less please everyone's palate. This makes buying food easy, tracking consumption simple and rotates the choice of meals just enough to avoid boredom. Plan on giving everyone breakfast, a snack lunch and dinner plus a choice of snacks and goodies. Aim to cook proper meals, not all-in-one stews eaten out of doggie bowls.

Food and water

Many boats have freezers and depend on frozen food. Without a freezer, after a couple of weeks fresh food is any fish silly enough to be caught and so you will mostly be eating canned and dried food. Provided they are stowed in a dry locker it is not necessary to remove the labels from cans or dip them in varnish to protect them from rust.

Fresh fruit and vegetables kept in nets suspended from the deckhead keep remarkably well. Hard fruits and vegetables like apples, potatoes and onions survive for weeks, soft fruits and vegetables not so long. The contents of the nets must be checked daily and any beginning to deteriorate must either be eaten or thrown overboard.

Bringing food on board is an opportunity for unwelcome stowaways. Eggs from creepy crawlies such as cockroaches can be hidden in vegetables and cardboard boxes. Once these beasts have settled in it is extremely difficult to eliminate them from the dark corners and cracks they call home. Prevention is the only sure answer. Rinse all fruit and vegetables in a solution of fresh water and chlorine bleach shore-side and never allow cardboard boxes on board.

Even yachts with freezers carry considerable amounts of dried and canned food.

Dried food

Dried peas and beans (there is a huge variety of dried beans) need soaking overnight before cooking. They are best cooked in a pressure cooker and go well with rice, or fish or both. Along with lentils, onions, tomatoes (canned or fresh) and rice, they can form the basis of a decent meal besides being good sources of protein, carbohydrates, fibre and vitamin B.

Some people extol the virtues of soya that is formed to resemble ground meat or stew-sized chunks. If this is to your taste then it is a useful addition to the larder. Dried vegetables, rice, flour and pasta, even if bought in sealed polythene packets, can harbour weevils. Keep packets separate. Use Ziploc bags and put those inside Tupperware-type boxes that, besides discouraging insect life, also protects against damp. When a packet is opened, empty it into a container – glass jars with rubber sealed lids are good – and carefully check it for nasties. Dried vegetables, rice and pasta should be rinsed before use. Sieving flour or sugar is supposed to be one way of removing weevils.

Variety is provided by spices. Curry powder is the obvious standby but depending on your palate, and expertise, the use of different spices can make the same ingredients taste like

▲ *The best and freshest fruit and vegetables are found in market halls and street markets, not in supermarkets. Search out the markets that all the locals use.*

◀ *You can usually rely on finding a plentiful supply of fresh fish on sale in Caribbean harbours.*

OVEN FREE BREAD SUBSTITUTES

On passage it is easy to become obsessed with the need for fresh bread especially if you do not have an oven.

Pan bread

This is a soda bread but cooked in a frying pan instead of being baked. It has the great advantage of being quick to make and economical in gas.

- Four heaped tablespoons of flour
- 1 heaped teaspoon of baking powder
- Salt to taste
- Water

Mix everything together to make a soft dough and roll it out until it is about half an inch thick. Heat a little oil in a heavy frying pan and fry the dough for about ten minutes with a lid on the frying pan. It should rise a bit and set on the bottom. Turn it over, fry for another five minutes and eat. It does not keep well.

For variety try using half wholemeal flour or substitute oats or bran for some of the flour or add grated onion or cheese, or use sugar instead of salt, throw in some dried fruit and call it cake.

Potato scones

These go well with fried eggs and tomatoes, canned or fresh.

- Potatoes (dried potato will do)
- Flour
- Salt to taste
- A small knob of margarine

The ratio of flour to potato is about 1oz (25gm) of flour for every 4oz (100gm) of potato. Mash or sieve the potatoes. Add the salt and margarine. Knead in the flour. Roll out and cut into rounds with a cup. Fry in a hot heavy frying pan for two to three minutes. Turn over and fry for another two to three minutes. If any are left over they can be fried with bacon and eggs for tomorrow's breakfast.

Dropped scones

- 2 eggs
- 8oz (225gm) plain flour
- 1oz (25gm) butter or margarine
- 1 teaspoon baking powder
- Sugar to taste, probably about 1oz (25gm)
- Half a pint of milk

Put the flour in a bowl and then break in the eggs and mix well. Mix in the sugar. Add the milk and beat to a creamy batter. Melt the butter (or margarine) in a pan, add to the batter and mix in. Heat a frying pan wiped with oil. Add a dollop of batter. When the bottom begins to brown, turn over. Eat with butter, jam, honey or as it comes.

Pancakes

- 4oz (100gm) plain flour
- 2 eggs
- About 1/2 pint (10fl oz) milk mixed with about 1/3 pint (7fl oz) water
- A little butter

Mix the flour and eggs. Slowly add the milk/water mix and whisk into a smooth batter. Heat a frying pan. When it is really hot melt the butter. Pour in a small ladle full of batter and swirl around so that it covers the bottom of the pan. When it starts to bubble flip it over. Wait a few seconds and take it out. Repeat until the mixture is used up.

Chinese or Italian cooking. It is amazing how many ways corned beef can be disguised.

Canned food

Canned food can be expensive in the Caribbean so stock up in the Canaries. If, in any port, you come across cheap supplies that keep, then buy as much as you can afford and have space to stow. Good examples are rum in Venezuela and wine in the Canaries.

It is supposed to be good practice to remove all labels from cans, and identify their contents in paint or felt tip pen before coating them in varnish. The intention is to protect them from rust. Few take this precaution; instead, stow cans in large plastic tubs which keeps them dry. If cans get soaked in sea water, rinse in fresh water and leave to dry. Ring-pull cans are vulnerable if they are soaked.

Salting, drying and bottling food

For those who have the skills and inclination, it is possible to salt, dry or bottle shop-bought fresh food to make it last longer.

Water supplies

Theoretically it is possible to survive on half a gallon (2 litres) of water a day. Presumably this is the more generous imperial rather than US gallon. Provided this water is reserved for drinking, cooking and cleaning your teeth, then half a gallon a day is just about adequate, but it is approaching the limit for staying healthy. If you include the liquid in canned vegetables, fruit and soft drinks, it adds around another couple of pints but it is still close to the limit.

A gallon of water (4.5 litres) per person per day is a more sensible ration and if you can manage more then so much the better. Boats with large water tanks and/or water makers can be more generous but it may be prudent to switch off pressurised water systems and ration fresh water by pumping up by hand.

Boats without watermakers should carry their water supplies in several separate containers so that losing one container does not mean losing all your fresh water.

You may worry about hygiene but the meat and fish are fresh.

All these fruit and vegetables have been rinsed ashore in a weak solution of chlorine bleach and brought aboard in a plastic bucket.

Stowage

Divide your stowage into:

1 **Ready-to-use** for items needed every day. This stowage should be easily accessible and include the next few days' food as well as a few tools, the ready-to-use medical box and the crash bag.
2 **Regular stowage** for items accessed no more than once a week which includes fuel and water filters, next week's food, the main medical box, serious tool kits and the supplies to replenish the ready-to-use stowage.
3 **Deep stowage** for items you do not expect to have to use or not use very often. It is the least accessible stowage; reaching items in deep stowage normally involves dismantling much of the boat.

It is usual to number the lockers and prepare an inventory which lists everything in each one. This works well provided everyone can remember your numbering system. You could paint the numbers on each locker or try photographing each locker and including the pictures in the inventory book. List the locker's contents opposite each picture.

Waste disposal

Waste disposal is a problem throughout the Caribbean. Each island has arrangements (usually a skip placed near dinghy landings) for collecting waste from yachts. When visiting uninhabited islands or remote islands where no such facilities exist, then either burn, bury or take your rubbish with you. There are few sadder sights than an empty shoreline littered with the detritus of civilisation. When carrying out maintenance it can be difficult to dispose of oil, batteries, paints and thinners but this must be done safely. Sailing through several miles of drifting garbage in the Windward Passage or finding an otherwise idyllic anchorage blighted by a festering landfill underlines the problems the islands face in dealing with litter and makes purists of us all.

BOAT BOYS

South and west of the Canaries, boat boys are everywhere and like any service industry, range from the good, through the cunning, to the criminal. In some places, trade associations weed out less desirable elements; the best offering accreditation to those who complete government-sponsored training programmes and successful graduates normally wear a suitably labelled T-shirt as proof of their status.

Types of boat boy

There are two types of boat boy. There are those offering a specific service such as supplying fuel or water or laundry or a water taxi. They have fixed prices and come alongside when called up via the local cruiser net. Then there is the general-purpose boat boy claiming to have anything you might want – mostly home-made souvenirs, fruit and vegetables. His prices are based on how much he reckons you are willing to pay.

Dealing with boat boys

General-purpose boat boys hunt for trade and come alongside, sometimes miles offshore, in all sorts of craft. Some paddle out on old surfboards, or wrecks of dinghies. If their boat has an engine it is a matter of pride for them to travel flat out and stop only after ramming your topsides. Refusing the services of one is taken as permission for every other boat boy to pester you. Rig a wall of fenders before the first comes alongside. Ask his name and tell him that right now you don't need anything but when you do he is your guy. For the price of some fruit bought later the rest should leave you alone.

Dinghy watch schemes

When you go ashore in the dinghy it is likely someone will offer to keep an eye on it for you. All dinghy watch schemes have a hint of blackmail. Unspoken but hovering on the edge of your mind is the worry that if you don't take up this offer then you will return to a missing or shredded dinghy and a commiserating boat boy claiming that if only he had been there it would never have happened. So to be on the safe side, you smile and pay up. Frequently the dinghy guardians are young children, and by giving kids a few dollars for doing nothing they may 'earn' more in a day than their parents. This cannot be good.

Beggars

Beggars are found only in towns, and contrary to what you may expect, do not pester. One or two might bother you but not for long if you ignore them and keep walking. That is one answer, but to them anyone who can spend a year or more sailing around in a big glossy boat is, obviously a millionaire and can spare a dime. If you feel they have a point carry a few small denomination notes in the local currency and hand them out until your daily charity budget has gone. Warnings that giving money to beggars means a close-bosomed friend pestering you for life are not true but if they occupy a regular pitch it is hard to walk by when you have given once.

Dinghies

Life at anchor means running a shuttle service between the boat and the shore, and the dinghy does service as both ferry and bulk carrier. Sometimes there is a dinghy dock; here a dinghy anchor thrown over the stern as a kedge prevents damage by holding the dinghy off the dock while ashore. More often you will be faced with a beach landing through surf with the threat of capsize. Having to then drag the dinghy up the beach adds interest and exercise. If an involuntary inversion looks likely, then take papers, cameras, cash and valuables ashore in a waterproof bag.

A small outboard engine takes the strain out of rowing. Otherwise it is important to choose a dinghy that rows well into a head wind. Except for short distances, soft bottomed inflatables are tiring to row. A small RIB is a good workhorse but performs best with an outboard. Hard dinghies are the most versatile but are heavy and difficult to stow. Inflating and deflating dinghies is a chore, so they spend a lot of their time in the water gathering weed. They do not take kindly to scraping tools, and cleaning their hulls before weed builds up is a necessary regular task. Patches and adhesive should be carried for small repairs. If you are competent at this type of work then a spare valve or two might be useful.

MAIN PICTURE *Dinghies and outboards are an easy target for thieves so at night make sure it is up on deck or very securely chained to the boat.*

LEFT *Dinghies spend much of the time in the water and grow weed just like any other boat. If you catch it when it is short, it will scrape off with an old phone card.*

BELOW *The dinghy can have a dual purpose – as a bath as well as a ferry boat.*

At night, dinghies do not always show lights but carrying a torch is prudent. If you wish to find your own yacht easily, a good anchor light will help to guide you home. If you are worried about draining your batteries, it is simple to rig a light-sensitive switch that will switch the anchor light on as darkness falls.

Towing the dinghy

The only way to discover how your dinghy tows is to take it to sea behind you. It is an education to watch it surf down a wave as though it is about to vault over the stern and then, when collision seems inevitable, skid to a stop and wait for the tow line to jerk it into motion like a recalcitrant mule. Mile after mile of this action strains the dinghy fittings beyond their design limits. Sometimes they fill with water and act as a drogue. Bailing a dinghy at sea is never easy and can be dangerous. Anyone doing this should wear a lifejacket and be attached to the mother ship. Sometimes in strong winds, inflatables take to the air and always crash land upside down. It is a good idea to take everything out of the dinghy before setting off.

There are supporters of long tows and short tows; of single and multiple attachment points for the tow line on the dinghy and at the stern of your yacht. Most systems work some of the time in some conditions. As a precaution against fouling the prop, try fitting along the tow line the sort of floats used to mark swimming pool lanes. Towing a dinghy is never straightforward and the only certainty about your choice of dinghy and how to tow it is that your views when you start out will not be the same when you return home.

Caribbean refit

After a few months at sea your thoughts will inevitably turn towards a refit. There may have been a time when anywhere away from the American or European coasts, boat services and chandlery were few and far between but this is no longer true. Like anywhere else, the choice will be best, and the range of services greatest in the principal yachting centres, but it is a fast-changing scene. Ask around before starting work.

There is no set refit time in your cruise programme. Oil changes and replacing fuel and water filters are dealt with during the day-to-day checks. Sometimes you will stumble across great facilities for lifting out and yield to the temptation to scrub the bottom and apply a new coat of antifouling. Occasionally you

A broken mast is a major problem. A new mast, complete with rigging and bottle screws will have to be brought to the boat, which may take some weeks in remoter locations. New sails will also be needed. It is a good idea to write down your sail measurements.

may need to find someone who can replace worn stitching on a sail or carry out some major work on the engine.

Dealing with contractors

If you employ a specialist then before work begins make sure that both you and he are agreed on the work to be carried out. Check:

- What is included in the price
- What standard of workmanship is required
- When the work is to start and finish
- How much it will cost
- Are materials extra?
- If the price includes materials how do you ensure that they will be of the quality you specify and not some cheaper alternative?

On small jobs it is sensible to pay in full only when the work is completed to your satisfaction. On larger jobs, such as having your boat painted, stage payments are fair but a substantial percentage of the total bill should be retained until you are satisfied with the work. If afterwards you have any complaint, you may discover that the contractor has already started another job and without the leverage cash brings, scope for redress is limited.

Shipping-in parts and other goods

If you cannot find what you need locally, then shop online through your usual home port suppliers. Shipping is simplest, safest and cheapest by arranging for a joining crew member to bring your purchases out, although they may have difficulty explaining why their hand luggage includes a diesel engine or 60lb anchor.

If you rely on your supplier as shipping agent, insist that they fax or email you the tracking number. Without this, any enquiries you may make will run into a brick wall, especially if they pass the task of delivering your goods onto a third party. Shipping companies ought to know that packaging should be boldly marked 'ship's stores in transit'. This is a mantra which might just see your goods safely through customs without paying local taxes or import duty. Even so it does not promise freedom from form filling, and extracting your goods from Customs can become a drawn-out saga involving fruitless trips to distant airports.

It is much easier if you choose to take delivery in a duty-free zone such as St Martin. Customs may insist that you employ an approved agent to clear goods in. In some countries procedures are so complex there is no choice but to use an agent. Sometimes the shipping company sees goods through customs as part of their service, otherwise you find your own agent. Some have a fixed charge, a few have a minimum charge and others base their fee on a percentage of the value of the imported goods.

If the local chandler does not have what you want in stock they might offer to obtain it for you. The key phrase they use is 'We can get that for you in a couple of days.' It sounds heaven: prompt delivery, no shipping charges, and no hassle (to you) with Customs. There is an understandable tendency to readily agree before engaging your brain; so before taking up their offer, check that you are talking about the same item and that you are paying no more than the catalogue price. Do not be surprised if they add shipping charges and do not be upset if 'a couple of days' becomes several weeks. Chandlers may wait until their order book fills a shipping container before your gear begins its journey to you or they may import everything in a weekly or monthly container. If your item has not made this month's container it will arrive next month or, perhaps, the month after that. It is not a good idea to pay in advance.

Lost in transit

Sometimes when you collect your goods, you will find that they have been opened and items are missing. The chances of recovering them are low to zero. Your package has passed through too many hands for the finger to point at any individual. Even if you identify the culprit there is very little possibility of finding the missing items. The only sure way of making good the loss is to insure the goods while they are in transit. Sign only for what you receive and not for what is on the invoice, and have this confirmed in writing by the shipper, Customs officer and anyone else involved. Report all losses to the police but do not expect too much. It will, however, help your insurance claim.

On an extended cruise your boat will need on-shore maintenance work and repairs.

RIGHT *This steel-hulled yacht developed a leak that threatened to sink the boat. It was lifted out using a crane meant for containers and stood against the harbour wall. An ex-shipyard welder was found on another yacht who carried out the necessary repairs.*

chapter 10 Staying healthy

A number of books and magazine articles suggest that you are about to visit the Islands of Doctor Moreau or that your appendix is primed to burst in mid-ocean, but if you start out fit and take a few common sense precautions, you will probably stay healthy.

Immunisations

Some immunisations take time to become effective, so about two months before departure, everyone must discuss the voyage with their doctor and seek advice about how the trip may affect their health, together with any particular precautions they should take. This is especially important if they have a pre-existing medical condition.

Reciprocal health agreements

Nationals of the European Economic Area (the EEA comprises the members of the EU plus Iceland, Liechtenstein and Norway) can obtain free or reduced cost health care inside the EEA. The UK has reciprocal health care agreements with Anguilla, Barbados, British Virgin Islands, Monserrat, and the Turks and Caicos Islands.

TEN USEFUL HEALTH TIPS

1 Speak to your doctor before you sail and heed his or her advice.
2 If you are on medication before you leave then ask your doctor for written details and take spare prescriptions with you.
3 Always wear sunscreen, sunglasses and sunhats.
4 Avoid dehydration by drinking plenty of (bottled) water.
5 Never go barefoot ashore.
6 Never handle animals.
7 Take sensible precautions to avoid mosquito bites.
8 Never share hypodermic needles.
9 Always practise safe sex.
10 If you receive medical treatment make sure you have full, written details ... preferably in English.

Sources of advice on health

Specialist advice on particular risks can be obtained from organisations such as MATSA (UK) or Centers for Disease Control (USA). Both have websites. Other UK based helplines are found at the Hospital for Tropical Diseases (0839 337733) and the Malaria Healthline (0891 600350). These are both premium rate telephone numbers. If you choose to obtain medical advice via the internet, pick reputable sites that give information written or checked by named, qualified professionals. Visit more than one site and be cautious of accepting information provided by commercially sponsored sites; if in any doubt check out your findings with your doctor.

Health risks on board

Health risks differ depending on whether you are at sea or ashore. At sea falling ill is always a worry but with the possible exceptions of toothache or food poisoning either from careless preparation or eating that last morsel of dodgy ham, bugs are scarce at sea. The greatest health risks are from traumatic injuries like strains, slips, falls, scalds and cuts. Warning people to be careful is good advice but difficult to follow because these injuries come from momentary inattention, thoughtlessness or plain bad luck. The best way to prevent accidents is to make the errors that cause them self-correcting. This takes you back to crew training, ethos and individual responsibility.

Sea sickness

Persistent sea sickness causes dehydration. Most deaths from diarrhoea are from dehydration. Oral Rehydration Therapy (ORT) replaces fluids and salts lost. If fluid intake is increased as soon as diarrhoea starts, it is reckoned that around 90 per cent of acute diarrhoea cases can be treated successfully at home or on board.

Oral Rehydration Salts

Oral Rehydration Salts (ORS) approved by the World Health Organisation, and UNICEF contain:

- 3.5g sodium chloride
- 1.5g potassium chloride
- 2.9g trisodium citrate
- 20g anhydrous glucose

This comes as a powder in a standard packet whose contents are dissolved in one litre of water. Packets that use bicarbonate of soda (2.5g) instead of trisodium citrate are acceptable but cannot be stored for long.

Sugar-salt solution (SSS) is a home-made ORS containing 3g (half a level standard 5ml teaspoon) of salt, and 18g (4 teaspoons) of sugar all dissolved in one litre of water.

As a guide, the amount of ORS or SSS given should be:

- A child under two years old should be given about 50–100ml (¼–½ cup) of rehydration fluid after each loose stool.
- Older children will require 100–200ml (½–1 cup) after each loose stool.
- Children over ten years old and adults can drink as much as they want.

Other good drinks include yoghurt drinks, water in which a cereal (such as rice) has been cooked, unsweetened tea, green coconut water and unsweetened, fresh fruit juice. Avoid fizzy drinks or drinks containing stimulants such as caffeine.

Drinking ORS is not a cure. It prevents dehydration. It does not stop the sea sickness or diarrhoea and if the sea sickness or diarrhoea persists seek medical advice.

Shoreside health risks

Injuries from road traffic accidents and violent muggings almost certainly head the list of shoreside health risks.

The tropics do provide a number of exotic dangers to your health carried by insects, in food and water or from person to person. However, most folk take sensible precautions and stay healthy. The most important of these precautions are to:

- always treat drinking and cooking water;
- keep the galley clean;
- be careful about what you eat, particularly fish and meat.

TROPICAL HEALTH RISKS

In the tropics you may come across some unfamiliar illnesses. The following list covers the more common. It makes scary reading. The best way of avoiding these dangers is to be aware of their existence and so minimize possible contact or at least reduce the danger to an acceptable level. Not all risks are equal. The mosquito probably tops the list. If its bite does not give you dengue fever, malaria or yellow fever you can still have an allergic reaction that ruins your day.

Aids

HIV and AIDS (SIDA in Spanish speaking countries) is found throughout the Caribbean. In some countries the incidence of infection is very high.

Avoid casual, unprotected sexual contact. Be aware of the risk of infection from treating wounds and giving first aid. Hospitals, medical centres, doctors and dentists are all aware of the transmission risk from re-using hypodermic needles, but if an injection becomes necessary, you may wish the reassurance and using your own needle. Supplies of sealed needles and syringes can be obtained from MATSA in the UK and Travel Medicine in the USA.

Allergic reaction

Even if mosquitoes are not carrying malaria or dengue fever it is still possible to suffer an allergic reaction to insect bites. This may be so severe as to require anti-histamine injections.

Take your pills regularly. Fit all hatches and ventilators with screens, wear sensible clothing, burn mosquito coils and candles and use personal sprays.

Cholera/diarrhoea

Cholera is found in South America and threatens to spread to the Caribbean. Infection comes from drinking water or eating food that contains cholera bacteria. Cholera begins with sudden diarrhoea and occasional vomiting. It can look like, and is often mistaken for, diarrhoea or dysentery, which are caused by parasites or food poisoning. The distinction is more academic than real. Left untreated both can kill.

Be scrupulously clean in the storage, preparation and serving of food. Keep flies and insects from food. Watch where and what you eat. All food should be thoroughly cooked. If fruits are eaten raw then stick to those that are peeled first. Fish and shellfish (eg oysters, shrimp, conch which appears as *lambie* on menus, and lobster) can be especially risky.

Anyone suffering from diarrhoea must drink lots of fluids. Oral Rehydration Salts (GESOL) are available in health centres and some drug stores. Medical attention should be sought as quickly as possible.

Ciguatera

This is a nerve toxin that gives humans a potentially fatal illness. The cause is free-swimming, single-celled dinoflagellates called *gambierdiscus toxicus* which attach themselves to coral-dwelling algae eaten by reef grazing fish. These, in turn, are eaten by larger fish. The cigatoxin accumulates without harming the fish. About 400 species of fish can be infected.

Over 150 different symptoms of cigatoxin poisoning have been described. The most common include nausea, stomach cramps, vomiting, diarrhoea, numbness around the mouth, breathing difficulties and joint pains. Symptoms usually appear within three to ten hours of eating infected fish. Susceptibility varies but those who have suffered once are more likely to suffer again and more severely at lower levels of exposure.

It is impossible to identify infected fish. The surest way of reducing the risk is to avoid eating reef fish and larger (and therefore older) fish where poison has had an opportunity of accumulating. Fish caught off soundings are generally regarded as being safe.

Dengue fever

Dengue fever comes from infected *Aedea aegypti* mosquitoes which are active during the day. The incubation period is normally between three to five days but can be as long as fifteen days. It is an acute, usually non-fatal disease, characterized by sudden high fevers, severe headaches, backache and pains in other parts of the body especially muscles and joints. (It is sometimes called breakbone fever.) On the third or fourth day there may be a rash on different parts of the body. Recovery from dengue fever may take several months to over a year, during which time the patient may suffer from depression, lassitude and general fatigue.

In addition to the precautions against malaria, check all water containers, bottles, plastic cups and tubs. They can be a breeding ground for mosquitoes. Wash and scrub them thoroughly to destroy any *Aedes aegypti* eggs which may be clinging to their sides, but be aware that the eggs can resist drying out for up to eight months. Keep water containers securely covered and provide all refuse containers with close-fitting covers.

Drinking water

Not all drinking water is safe. In some areas fresh water supplies can contain a parasite which gives rise to an infection called schistosmiasis. Fresh water swimming pools and even some inshore waters are not necessarily safe.

Filter and treat all water going into the ship's tanks with either proprietary water purification tablets or chlorine bleach or iodine at a rate of one teaspoon of bleach to 40 gal (182 litres) of water and/or boil on a rolling boil for five minutes before using it. Store water in sealed, clean containers. Ashore, preference should be given to drinking bottled or canned carbonated (fizzy) water and be careful about adding ice to your rum and coke. Do not swim in fresh water pools.

Hepatitis

There is 'infectious hepatitis' which is transmitted by infected food and drink and 'serum hepatitis' which is passed on by infected blood. Hepatitis brings a loss of appetite, fever and headaches. The whites of the eyes turn yellowish and the liver becomes tender.

General precautions include washing all fruit and vegetables and boiling or treating all water. There are vaccines which offer some protection and they should be obtained before sailing and kept up to date during the cruise.

Hookworm

This is caused by a parasitic worm whose larva bore their way into a victim's feet, and from there, travel to the gut and feed on blood. The resulting disease is called ancylostomiasis and is potentially fatal. Although many folk go barefoot with no ill effects, the simplest and best preventative measure is always wear shoes when ashore.

Malaria

Malaria develops from the bite of the female *Anopheles* mosquito which are active evening and night. They feed mostly at night so the risk of infection is greatest between dusk and dawn. Malaria has a 14 day incubation period and the symptoms are fever, headache, sweats, chills and general weakness.

Begin taking anti-malarial pills before entering a malarial area and continue taking them for a couple of weeks after leaving the area. If possible, between dusk and dawn, avoid areas where there are mosquitoes. Reduce exposed skin to a minimum by wearing long trousers and long-sleeved shirts: white or light colours are better than dark colours which seem to attract mosquitoes.

Fit mosquito screens to all hatches and vents. Sleep under mosquito nets tucked well under the mattress. Treat all nets with Deet. Use insect repellents on exposed skin. Those containing the chemical 'deet' appear to work better than other types of repellent such as citronella or tea-tree oil which are reckoned to be about 50% as effective as 'deet' preparations. Spray cabins nightly with a preparation containing pyrethrum or other insecticide or burn coils containing pyrethrum

Rabies

Take the risk of rabies seriously. Avoid dogs, monkeys, bats and other biting animals. If bitten, wash the wound with alcohol or iodine (iodine is supposed to be better) and seek immediate medical attention.

Snakes

The Caribbean has its fair share of snakes. It is unusual for someone to be bitten by a snake and since not all snakes are venomous it is rare for anyone to be bitten by a venomous snake. Even then not all is lost. It is hard work for a snake to produce venom and they like to keep it for something they will eat. Humans are not on their menu so they may just give you a dry bite to scare you away or just use a touch of venom to let you know they mean business. This is very reassuring unless you are the exception when the usual advice includes killing and keeping the snake to assist identification since administering the wrong anti-venom can be fatal.

If travelling where snakes may be found, then dress sensibly, wear high ankle boots, not flip-flops and watch where you are putting your hands and feet. Be sure that the branch that you are about to grab is not already occupied. Look out for warm, sunlit areas where snakes like to sunbathe. Folklore says that snakes are more scared of you than you are of them but this should not be put to the test.

Venomous marine animals

For those who enjoy snorkelling or diving, some marine inhabitants such as cone-shells, stoney and elkhorn corals, touch-me-not sponge and jellyfish can give nasty cuts and stings. Marine venom is nearly always more potent than that of land animals.

The golden rule is, do not touch. If treatment becomes necessary, the aim should be to reduce the possibility of infection and to minimise the stinging and swelling. Traditionally this is done by applying vinegar or lime juice followed by applications of antibiotic creams.

Yellow fever

The World Health Organisation (WHO) considers yellow fever to be endemic in Columbia and Ecuador and several Caribbean islands. It is a viral illness carried by female *Aedes aegypti* mosquito and has an incubation period of three to five days.

Mild cases may escape with fever and headache but symptoms in severe cases can include fever, chills, bleeding into the skin, nausea, constipation, jaundice, delirium, coma and death.

There is a safe and highly effective yellow fever vaccine, which gives immunity within a week of being administered and lasts for at least ten years. It should not be given to children under six months, anyone sensitive to eggs, those with suppressed immune systems (eg suffering from AIDS) or pregnant women. Vaccination should be done before leaving and the certificate kept with the ship's papers. Some countries will insist on seeing it. Prevention is far better than cure for there is no specific treatment for yellow fever. Paracetamol and oral rehydration salts can help control dehydration and fever.

HYPOTHERMIA

Symptoms	Stages
Shivering	Shivering
Numbness	Apathy
Weakness	Loss of consciousness
Impaired vision	Slowing heart beat and breathing
Confusion	Death
Impaired judgement	
Dizziness	

If you go snorkelling or diving, look but do not touch, for some underwater inhabitants might object. If you wish to wander along jungle paths wear sensible shoes and clothing and watch out for the occasional sunbathing snake.

Medical facilities in major Caribbean ports range from adequate to good but even the best medical centres possibly lack specialised resources and equipment. In more remote areas, medical provision is likely to be a visiting nurse or a doctor holding a weekly or monthly clinic. Far off the beaten track, the position is exactly the same as if on passage: you are on your own until you reach civilisation.

First aid

At least one person, and preferably everyone, should hold a recognised, current first aid certificate and it is advisable for one crew member to attend the more advanced Ship's Captain's Medical Course. But unless there is a qualified doctor on board, therapy is unlikely to go much beyond treating casualties for shock, immobilising injuries, avoiding or reducing infection and controlling pain. The best place for the sick, including the seasick and wounded, is their bunk. So the time spent before you sail making sure that the cabin is warm and dry, the bunks are comfortable, and the boat is rigged for short-handed sailing (you are now a crew member short) pays off.

The medical box

You need two medical boxes. The principal box contains all the pills, potions, ointments and tools for serious treatment. It should include a good stock of broad spectrum antibiotics (check if any of your crew are allergic to penicillin) and strong pain killers so that infections can be contained and pain controlled until proper medical assistance is reached. With luck it will remain unused. The box ought to be waterproof to keep out bugs as well as moisture and it should be stowed in the coolest, darkest, driest locker aboard. Some medicines need storing in a fridge. If you do not have one then ask your doctor for an equivalent drug which will survive the temperatures you are likely to experience. It is possible that some of the contents will reach their 'use by' date during the voyage and these should be discarded and replaced. Carry repeat prescriptions.

The second medical box is the ready-to-use box. It should contain plenty of sticking plasters, butterfly stitches, antiseptic creams, painkillers, seasickness remedies and dental kit. It should be waterproof and its contents replenished at each port of call.

Speak to your doctor about the exact contents of both medical boxes. He or she will advise you about what you need and if prescription drugs are required, supply the prescription for the initial supply and any replacements needed en route.

Before you sail make sure everyone has had a medical check, stocked up on their chosen anti-malarial pills and had their jabs for hepatitis and yellow fever. If they have a chronic medical condition, especially one requiring regular treatment or which limits their mobility, their doctor must agree that they are fit to sail. It is also very wise for everyone to visit their dentist.

THE MEDICAL BOX CONTENTS

The medical box should contain:

- Analgesics
- Antibiotics
- Antimalarial pills
- Antiseptic solutions and creams
- Remedies for allergic reactions
- Remedies for eye and ear disorders
- Remedies for gastro-intestinal disorders
- Remedies for seasickness
- Remedies for skin problems and allergies

Many treatments will be either by controlled drugs, available only on prescription, or obtainable only from a chemist (pharmacy). Many are sold under both their generic name and proprietary brand names. Senna, for example is a stimulant laxative found in Ex-lax, Senlax, Senokot and Californian Syrup of Figs.

It is important that you are absolutely certain of:

- The illness that each medicine can treat
- The correct dosage to be given and if it differs for children and adults or pregnant women
- The side effects
- How it is administered
- How it interacts with other drugs
- How it should be stored
- Its shelf life. Most will come marked with its batch number and expiry date but this may be missing on some dispensed items
- Who are included in the risk groups? The young? Old? Pregnant women?

These details for each medicine should be written down and kept on laminated sheets in the medicine box. The surest way of getting it right is to discuss it with your doctor. He can provide a list of recommended medicines and prescriptions where necessary. Do not forget to ask him for a letter which will act as certification that you are carrying these drugs for medical purposes. This is to satisfy curious Customs officers, and as some medicines may become out-of-date during your cruise, ask for repeat prescriptions so that you can obtain replacements for controlled drugs and those available only on prescription.

Equipment and dressings

If you are not already carrying the following items in your first aid box consider adding them before you sail.

Adhesive plasters

Brook airway

Clinical thermometer

Crepe bandages (10cm) and (5cm)

Gauze swabs

Inflatable splints

Jelonet

Mediswabs

Needle packs

Sphygmomanometer (for blood pressure)

Steristrips

Stethoscope

Rolls of sticking plaster, including butterfly stitches

Sticking plasters of various sizes

Surgical scissors

Toothfil dental kit

Wound dressings

Zinc oxide tape

Apart from the main medicine box and the ready-to-use medical box, make up another and keep it in the crash bag just in case you have to abandon ship.

Sailing green

1 Dispose of all litter ashore at recognized facilities.
2 Use the least toxic product that will do the job. Use bio-degradable products wherever possible. Look for 'bio-degradable' and 'phosphate free' on the label. Do not assume that bio-degradable means safe. Some bio-degradable products are dangerous to the users if improperly applied.
3 Wipe spills up. Do not wash them overboard.
4 Share leftover supplies with other cruisers or dispose of them safely.
5 Keep your engine well tuned.
6 Check fuel lines regularly. When filling tanks always use a funnel and have a spill kit handy.
7 Minimize the use of engine cleaners.
8 Use non-toxic bilge cleaners.

ENVIRONMENTALLY FRIENDLY ALTERNATIVES

Chemical	Alternative
Bleach	Borax or hydrogen peroxide
GRP stain remover or shower cleaner	Baking soda
Copper cleaner	Lemon or lime juice and salt
Locker top cleaners	Vinegar and water
Interior wood cleaner	Olive or almond oil
Chrome cleaner	Apple cider and vinegar mixture
Window cleaner	Vinegar and lemon juice mixture

part three **weather watching and caribbean sailing**

chapter 11 **Atlantic weather**

On a typical Atlantic circuit the incidence of gales is theoretically below one per cent, so good odds on good weather. Much of the weather you will encounter is day after day of pleasant winds and warm seas. But it is a certainty that at some point you will meet a gale, or a series of squalls so close together it is difficult to tell the difference between them.

Heavy weather makes even the simplest task a challenge. After the first day, your mind is screaming for a time-out but the battering of the gale is relentless. As days go by during very heavy weather, your stress increases and you are the weakest link.

Now the effort put into creating an easy-to-use galley and comfy bunks pays off. Those off-watch can eat well and curl up warm and dry. Easy sail-handling steadies the boat without causing exhausting deckwork. Pramhoods, doghouses and dodgers keep those in the cockpit dry and protected from wind.

Handling heavy weather

Ocean waves are big but they are also long, typically lasting for six to eight seconds. They may be 20 or 30 feet high but their long wavelength makes it seem more like plodding up a hillside than climbing a cliff face.

There are three principal strategies for handling heavy weather:

1   If the wind is blowing in the direction you wish to go, then run downwind. Unless you are approaching your destination you are unlikely to run out of searoom. The trick is keeping your speed down so there is no possibility of jumping off the crest of a wave. In strong winds you will be surprised how little sail it takes before you start surfing. Even under bare poles it may be necessary to stream a warp or even a small drogue to slow the boat and hold her steady.

2   If the wind is unfavourable then the traditional response is to heave-to. This is done by putting the helm down, backing the jib and balancing jib and mainsail so that the boat takes up a steady position with its bows at an angle of about 45° to wind and seas. As the wind perks up you may find yourself constantly reducing sail until you are under bare poles and lying a-hull broadside to the waves. This is extremely uncomfortable but unlikely to be dangerous.

3   Lastly, even in unfavourable winds you can sail upwind in wind strengths that would be impossible in the short, sharp waves of coastal waters. The boat is remarkably stable and

life aboard reasonably comfortable. The technique involves pointing the bows somewhere between 45–60° off the wind and setting the windvane; with a scrap of jib or even no sail at all you will make between 1–2 knots. This gives enough steerageway to hold the boat steady but compared to the oncoming waves you are stationary. The boat rises and falls over the waves like a cork. The only drawback is rogue waves coming across the predominant wavefront that pick you up, knock you down and shake you by the scruff of the neck before running away.

It would be wrong to over-emphasise bad weather or to display a stiff upper lip nonchalance. Everyone meets it and no-one enjoys it but passages on the Atlantic circuit are made at times to avoid bad weather. When it does arrive it seems to last forever but it makes up a very small proportion of your total sea time.

Thunderstorms

Warm, moist air close to ground level rises and as it does so it cools and the water vapour it contains becomes water droplets forming clouds. If the clouds are warmer than the surrounding air they continue to rise and form the characteristic anvil of a thunderstorm.

The steeper the temperature gradient between the cloud and the surrounding air, the more vigorous the thunderstorm will be. If there are sizeable differences in wind speed and direction within the cloud then a cyclonic circulation can develop. At certain times of year this could be the beginning of a hurricane.

The formation of thunderstorms is associated with land and sea breezes, cold fronts and tropical waves. They are common in tropical waters, especially during the rainy season, and though their rain brings opportunities to fill water tanks, items like biminis, awnings, pramhoods and dodgers may be vulnerable and flog in winds that reach 20–40 knots.

Squall line

A squall line is a non-frontal line of thunderstorms bringing rain and strong winds and can occur anywhere at any time. Their approach is normally marked by rain streaking the sky black and a narrow white line where the rain bounces off the sea. There is no doubt when the gust front hits, but there is usually time to prepare.

Downbursts

A downburst is a thunderstorm at its nastiest. Their sudden, unexpected appearance is believed responsible for overwhelming and sinking small craft and it is reckoned that the loss of the *Pride of Baltimore* near Puerto Rico in 1986 was due to a downburst. Eyewitnesses reported that the ship was blown over onto its beam ends and sank in less than two minutes.

Downbursts form when warm water under a thunderhead cloud (cumulonimbus) creates an updraft that displaces cold air as it rises. The

Downbursts

Thunderstorm

Rain induced downdraft

Updraft

Evaporation and cooling accelerates downburst

Winds can exceed 100 knots

3 miles

cold air drops, accelerating as it goes until it hits the sea and explodes. Winds can reach over 100 knots in an area around three miles in diameter. Once the downburst is over then the winds decrease to that of a normal, ferocious squall and spread out over a much wider area.

The good news is that they are over in less than ten minutes although a single thunderstorm may produce a sequence of downbursts lasting over an hour; the bad news is that it is not possible to tell if a squall line, or an isolated cumulonimbus, contains downbursts.

Electrical storms

Electrical storms are found anywhere. In the Caribbean they tend to follow the mountains fringing the mainland shores rather than the offshore islands. You can expect to meet at least one electrical storm. Whether at anchor or on passage it is a frightening experience. Your mast is the highest feature for miles around and there is no way to escape from sitting under it.

Lightning occurs when part of the atmosphere (air, ground or sea) develops a high negative charge and another part creates a high positive charge. When the difference between the two is sufficient, a thunderbolt carries an electrical charge from one to another to equalise the electrical potential. Lightning heats the surrounding air to around 30,000°C (54,000°F) and accompanying thunder is caused by the explosive expansion of super heated air. Every five seconds between seeing the lightning flash and hearing the sound of thunder places the storm is one mile further away.

If your boat is struck by lighting, check all seacocks and skin fittings as these could be blown out. Only check for other damage when you are sure the hull is watertight. It is likely all electronic devices are fried. A near miss can condemn them to a slow death. Stow a hand-held radio, compass, GPS, cheap watch, torch and lots of spare batteries in a metal box. An army surplus ammunition box is a good choice as it is also water resistant. The box acts as a Faraday cage and protects its contents from a lighting strike, making sure that you have the essentials for navigation and communication.

Land and sea breezes

In the Caribbean, the North East Trades are affected by topography and other weather features such as tropical depressions, and land and sea breezes.

During the day the land heats up quicker than the sea and becomes a low pressure area relative to the sea. Warm air rising from the land expands and cools. This increases the relative humidity and clouds form. The rising or upward branch of air associated with land and sea breezes can often be detected by the presence of clouds.

At altitude, the rising air moves horizontally and the clouds in this air mass indicate the upper wind direction as it moves out to sea. Over the sea the air cools and drops down to sea level where it moves towards the land. Air blowing from the sea towards the land is called a sea breeze. This cycle of air movement is called a Hadley Cell after George Hadley who first discovered the principle in 1735 and used it, on a far greater scale, to explain the existence of the Trade winds.

During the night the sea cools more slowly than land. The warm sea is now a low pressure area relative to the cooler land. The Hadley Cell is reversed and the surface winds now blow from the land towards the sea. This is called a land breeze. Topography affects how far sea breezes can travel inland but land breezes can travel up to 25–30 nautical miles offshore.

Small, low lying islands such as those in the Bahamas lack the land mass that allows land and sea breezes to form, but in the mountainous islands of the Greater Antilles or along the coasts of Venezuela and Central America they are so strong that they can negate the Trade winds.

Sources of weather forecasts

Whenever possible try to find local forecasts produced by local forecasters. National meteorological offices understandably concentrate on their local waters and as the forecast moves further offshore a broader brush gives a general, rather than a detailed picture. The British Meteorological Office treats Biscay as a single sea area. It is a much more important region to the French Météo-France and they split it into 4 sea areas for greater detail. When you come to cross Biscay it may pay to check www.meteoconsult.fr for the latest forecast.

Ashore and afloat a SSB receiver brings regular access to a range of weather forecasts throughout the day. Weather routeing for yachts is not concerned with today's or even tomorrow's weather. For good or ill you cannot outrun the weather. The trick is to look three or four days ahead and then adjust your course to miss any nasty weather that *may* lie ahead.

The Atlantic weather forecaster

For some years Herb Hilgenberg, call sign VAX498, has been providing yachtsmen in the Caribbean and Atlantic with individual weather forecasts and weather routeing advice. It is a superb service.

He broadcasts each day on 12.359MHz. Vessels begin to check in at 1930 UTC giving their name and position. At 2000 UTC Herb lists those vessels he has heard check-in and, in turn (by sea area, not first come first served), he asks each boat to give their present weather conditions.

OTHER SOURCES OF WEATHER FORECASTS

Newspapers	Most newspapers include weather forecasts in understandable pictorial form.
Commercial radio stations	Local radio stations in coastal areas often include weather forecasts for leisure sailors. There are private radio stations like Herb (see text box opposite) for the North Atlantic who broadcast forecasts tailored for yachtsmen. You learn about these stations from the grapevine in your sailing area. Unless you speak the local language fluently or they broadcast in English, learn the local terms for gale warnings, wind speeds and direction and listen very carefully.
TV	All television stations broadcast regular weather forecasts. They are mostly concerned with weather over land but are better than nothing. Services such as Teletext broadcast shipping forecasts.
Internet	The internet is full of weather sites. Use a search engine like Google and type in 'weather forecast' and take your pick. The internet allows you to compare forecasts from different national weather agencies. If you are planning a Biscay crossing, you can compare the UK Met Office forecast with Météo-France. National weather agencies tend to be at their best around their coasts. The UK Met Office treats Biscay as a single sea area while Météo-France divides it into four.
Navtex	The international Navtex broadcasts are in English. The national Navtex broadcasts are in the local language.
Wefax	To receive a weatherfax you need either a dedicated Wefax receiver or a SSB receiver, demodulator, laptop and weatherfax programme such as JVFax. JVFax is a shareware programme and can be downloaded from the internet. You also need the frequencies and times of the weatherfax broadcasts for your area. Weatherfaxes can be received onshore or at sea.
Local Coastguard	Most Coastguard services broadcast inshore weather forecasts and issue strong wind warnings. Abroad, these are usually in the local language.
Harbour authorities	Port authorities and marinas often display the local forecast.

USCG forecast areas

1 Gulf of Mexico
2 South of Nova Scotia
3 George's Bank
4 South of New England
5 Hudson Canyon to Baltimore Canyon
6 Baltimore Canyon to Hatteras Canyon
7 Hatteras Canyon to Blake Ridge
8 Savannah to St Augustine
9 St Augustine to Jupiter Inlet
10 Jupiter Inlet to Key Largo
11 Key Largo to Dry Tortugas
12 Cape Sable to Tarpon Springs
13 Tarpon Springs to Apalachicola
14 Apalachicola to Pensacola
15 Pensacola to Gulfport
15a Gulfport to Mississippi
16 Mississippi to Intracoastal City
16a Intracoastal City to Port Arthur
17 Port Arthur to Port O'Connor
18 Port O'Connor to Brownsville
29 Puerto Rico to US Virgin Islands

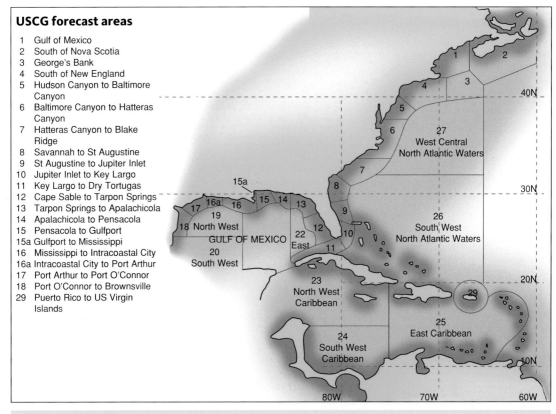

RADIO WEATHER FORECASTS FOR ATLANTIC AND CARIBBEAN

Time GMT	Station	Frequency	Remarks
0440	USCG Offshore	4426 / 6501 / 8764	
0415	David 'Mistine'	4003	Followed by TX on 8104 at approx 0445
0530	USCG High Seas	4426 / 6501 / 8764	
0800	UK Marine Net	14303	
1000	USCG Offshore	4426 / 6501 / 8764	
1130	Radio France International	15300 / 21645	
1130	USCG High Seas	8764 / 13089 / 6501	
1300	USCG from Florida	4363 / 13092 / 22738	
1330	Trans-Atlantic Net	21400	
1600	USCG Offshore	6501 /8764 / 13089	
1730	USCG High Seas	8764 /13089 / 17314	
1800	UK Marine Net	14303	Weather at approx 1830
2000	Herb 'Southbound 2'	12359 / 8294	
2200	USCG Offshore	6501 /8764 / 13089	
2300	USCG from Florida	4363 / 13092 / 17242 / 22738	
2330	USCG High Seas	6501 /8764 / 13089	

WEATHER WEB SITES

The internet is full of sites dealing with weather and weather forecasts and everyone has their own favourites. These are just a few but some have links to other sites. They are not in any particular order or ranking.

Web address	Comments
www.marineweather.com	Good synoptic charts and weather buoy data
www.qeocities.com/thewavepage	Good selection of forecasts for various Met Offices
www.amiwx.com	Good selection of forecasts for various Met Offices. Good satellite pictures
www.ndbc.noaa.gov	Worldwide weather buoys
www.qreatweather.co.uk	Has a huge number of useful links
www.franksingleton.clara. net	A great site for sailing weather information
www.onlineweather.com	Useful range of stations giving winds and temperatures
www. bbc.co.uk/weather	Useful range of stations with a five-day forecast
www. nws.noaa.gov	US government site with excellent links for worldwide weather forecasts
www.theyr.net	World wide three-day synoptic charts showing temperature and winds
www.meteo.fr	Under *nos previsions* look for *par activite*, click on *mer*, click on *côte* and then on appropriate area for forecast.
http://weather.noaa.gov/weather	A useful site with worldwide weather and useful links. Select a country, then a location for current weather and the forecast for the last 24 hours
www.windfinder.com	Good for worldwide winds
www.windguru.com	A surfers' site with information on wind and seas at worldwide locations
www.wetterzentrale.de	In German but has a good range of links

WEATHERFAX STATIONS

There are over 21 weatherfax stations around the world, each with its own frequencies and schedules. They include:

Halifax (CFH), Canada	Moscow	Offenbach (DDH), Germany	US Coastguard (NMF) Boston
4271 (4269.1) kHz	4318 (4316.1) kHz	3855 (3853.1) kHz	4235 (4233.1) kHz*
6496.4 (6494.5) kHz	5108 (5106.1) kHz	7880 (7878.1) kHz	6340.5 (6338.6) kHz
10536 (10534.1) kHz	7670 (7668.1) kHz	13882.5 (13880.6) kHz	9110 kHz (9108.1) kHz
13510 (13508.1) kHz	10611 (10609.1) kHz		12750 (12748.1) kHz
	13886 (13884.1) kHz		

* The figures in brackets beside the frequencies are a reminder to deduct 1.9kHz when tuning in for weatherfaxes.

French forecast areas

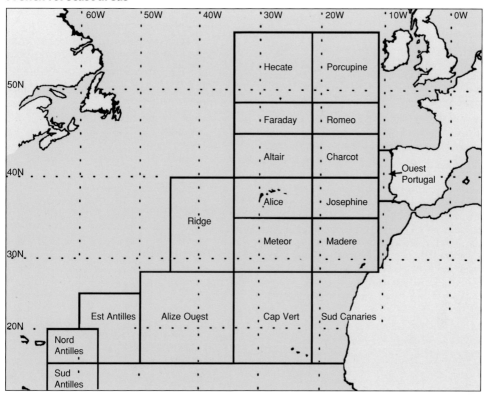

The schedule and frequencies for the Fleet Weather and Oceanographic Centre at Northwood (GYA), England are:

NORTHWOOD (GYA) Frequencies
2618.5 (2616.6) kHz
4610 (4608.1) kHz
8040 (8038.1) kHz
11086.5 (11084.6) kHz
18261 (18259.1) kHz

Broadcast type	Times in UTC/GMT
Surface analysis	0300, 0400, 0500, 0900, 1100, 1200, 1500, 1800, 2100, 2300
Surface prognosis T24	0524, 0800, 1000, 1300, 1736, 2200
Wind	0812, 2112
Fronts centres	0848, 0912, 1124, 1136, 1400, 1600, 1700, 2000, 2012, 2024, 2036
Gale summary	0348, 0600, 0700, 1148, 1548, 1900
Sea swell	0924, 1912

GRIB FILES

Using a binary format to minimize file size, GRIB (Gridded Information in Binary) files are used to transfer data between national meteorological services. They allow forecasts for several days ahead to be sent as an email attachment of only a few kb rather than the 50–80 kb required for a synoptic chart. Turning the GRIB data into a chart showing the wind and wave forecasts for your chosen sea area is done using a GRIB viewer offline.

Because they transmit data, not pictures, GRIB files are cheaper to receive over your cellphone, or satellite phone when out of cellphone range. This makes them either an alternative or supplement to weatherfaxes.

The free SailDocs (info@saildocs.com) system provides a free GRIB viewer called Viewfax that can be used with most other services. For a copy of Viewfax go to http://www.siriuscyber.net/ sailmail/amdisk1.exe floppy disk link. This is a 1.1mb download that creates a folder called Airmail. Run this program. Then download the Viewfax viewer from http://www.siriuscyber.net/wxfax/ 'Fax companion' page. Look for Grib/Fax Viewer and its 'Click here to download Viewfax' button. GRIB files can also be viewed with MaxSea and Raytech charting programs. A MaxSea viewer can be obtained at no charge from the GMN site or MaxSea site.

Free services include Saildocs,GMN, and MailASail. Météo-France Navimail, Movingweather and ProGRIB charge. You could also try PassageWeather (www.passageweather.com).

Herb then gives each vessel their forecast for the next couple of days. It may take some time to reach your sea area.

To receive a personalised forecast from Herb all you need to do is to log in at 1930 hours UTC but once you have done so you are expected to maintain daily contact until you have completed your passage. If you can, email him before you set out with details of your trip. His email address is hehilgen@aol.com.

Winds

Although winter gales and the hurricane season determine your timings, the Westerlies, the north-east Trades and the Horse Latitudes are the winds that govern an Atlantic Circuit and dominate your route planning.

The Hadley cell

Warm air at the Equator rises, causing a low pressure area to form roughly 5° north and south of the Equator. This is the Doldrums. When the air reaches an altitude where it is at the same temperature and density as the surrounding air it heads north (in the northern hemisphere), cooling as it goes until it sinks back to Earth creating a high-pressure area on the surface around 30° latitude. As it sinks, the air becomes warmer and holds more moisture, giving clear skies and little rainfall. When it reaches the surface, air from the high-pressure area travels south to the equatorial low-pressure area. This movement of air produces a closed cell called a Hadley cell after George Hadley who was the first to recognise it in 1735.

The Coriolis effect

Due to the Coriolis effect, winds in the Northern hemisphere are deflected to the right, and so the winds blowing towards the Equator from the high-pressure area at 30°N do not blow from north to south but from north-east to south-west. This had been known for centuries, but the explanation had to wait until 1835 when Gaspard Gustave de Coriolis discovered that the Earth's daily rotation deflects all free-moving objects to the right in the northern hemisphere and to the left in the southern hemisphere. Since the equatorial Hadley cell is very stable, these winds are persistent and steady in their direction. They are the north-east Trades.

The Westerlies

There is a second Hadley cell between 30° and 60° north and here the Coriolis effect means that the surface winds blow from the south-west to the north-east and are called the Westerlies. In the northern hemisphere, weather generated by the seasonal heating and cooling of the continents (Africa, the Americas and Europe) disturbs the Westerlies so that their regularity cannot match that of the north-east Trades. It is salutary to remember that in the southern hemisphere, where these winds are not so affected by land masses, they are, with good reason, called the Roaring Forties. The Horse Latitudes lie between the Westerlies and the north-east Trades.

Tropical revolving storms

As the tropics approach so does the threat of tropical revolving storms (TRS). The received wisdom is that a fall in the barometer of 5 points below the seasonal average comes with a gold-plated promise of a full-grown, genuine tropical revolving storm. It is unusual for these to be part of the Christmas festivities, but they may turn up when least expected. Detailed records began some 150 years ago and show a sequence of good and bad years linking their activity to the following conditions:

El Niño Every few years the waters off Peru and Ecuador became warmer around Christmas time. Local fishermen called this the Christ Child. We call it the warm phase of the El Niño-Southern Oscillation (ENSO). Like a pendulum every three to seven years conditions swing between El Niño (warmer water), normal conditions, and La Niña (colder water). Although El Niño has been traced back to1525, it was the 1960s before meteorologists recognised that El Niño pumped heat into the troposphere and affected weather worldwide. La Niña encourages hurricane formation in the Atlantic and El Niño discourages it.

The Atlantic Conveyor Belt High sea surface temperatures and high salinity in the North Atlantic is called the Atlantic Conveyor Belt and it was strong during the 1930s to the late 1960s which was also a time of high hurricane activity. The belt was weak between 1900–1925 and 1970–1994 when hurricane activity was less intense.

Stratospheric equatorial winds Easterly stratospheric equatorial winds are reckoned to discourage the formation of hurricanes.

The entire Caribbean falls within the hurricane zone but they are rare south of Grenada and are generally confined to the months between June to November, with activity peaking in September and October. In the northern hemisphere, the official hurricane season is from 1 June to 30 November each year. Worldwide there are about 85 tropical storms a year and 45 of these will grow into hurricanes or typhoons. Oral accounts of tropical revolving storms in the Caribbean go back to the 16th century. These tales concentrate on extreme storms whose severity made them part of the local folklore. Detailed records go back just over 100 years. Between 1886 and 2000 there were 997 tropical storms, an average of nine each year; about six become hurricanes and two intense or severe hurricanes.

In the last thirty years the number of category four and five hurricanes has almost doubled and since the mid-1990s, activity has picked up. Some experts believe that the early part of this century will bring more hurricanes and more of these will be of the most severe class. Some of this increased activity may be linked to global warming.

Late season hurricanes

It is unwise to suppose that as the end of the hurricane season approaches, the likelihood of a hurricane diminishes or that hurricanes always obey the rules. Towards the end of November in 1999, a tropical wave popped up off the Colombian coast and was soon classified as a tropical depression. Almost instantly it became a tropical storm and was named

Lenny. In hours Lenny grew to a category four hurricane. For days it ambled east, although every forecaster promised that it was about to turn north. Eventually it heeded the forecasters' pleas but then it stopped at St Martin, where it spent a couple of days touring the island before heading south and finally disappearing in the Atlantic.

Lenny's winds and storm surge trashed homes on the beach on Bonaire and did damage in the Lesser Antilles as far south as Grenada, which is generally considered safe from hurricanes. Just before Lenny occurred, many boats had left Trinidad, Venezuela and the ABC Islands for the winter season in the Virgins. Sarifundy's bar in Spanish Water, Curaçao, pinned up a list of yachts lost or damaged, including one that never arrived. It was heartbreaking reading.

The power of hurricanes

It is difficult to meaningfully express a hurricane's power. Satellite pictures show that they are not the neat arrangement of winds and isobars popular in illustrations but a whirling mass of ferocious winds, thunderstorms and torrential rain. In a single day even a modest hurricane will produce as much energy as most European countries use in a year. There can be 914mm (36in) of rain in 24 hours. In 1928 one hurricane dropped two and a half billion gallons of water on Puerto Rico. In Deshaies on Guadeloupe, cement mooring blocks lying in 40 feet of water were thrown onto the beach. In 1970, one hurricane killed 300,000 people in Bangladesh. Barometric pressure in the hurricane's eye can be less than 914mb (27in of mercury). Any right-thinking yachtsman will consider meeting a force 10 storm a very serious proposition. The wind force (not speed) in a hurricane is 12 to 16 times as great.

How hurricanes form

Hurricanes usually begin life when thunderstorms along the African coast drift out to sea. If the sea temperature is 27°C (80°F) then warm moist ocean air rises. As it does so it cools, the water vapour condensing to form storm clouds.

The cooling also releases latent heat which warms the air above. This rises, sucking in more warm, moist ocean air that, in turn, rises, cools, condenses and releases yet more latent heat. As this cycle repeats itself, more heat is transferred from the ocean to the upper atmosphere and, helped by the coriolis effect, strong, higher altitude winds create the typical swirling wind pattern of every hurricane. At the same time, converging sea level winds push more warm moist air skywards, reinforcing the spiral wind pattern and speeding up the wind.

There are four stages in the birth of a typical hurricane:

1 **Easterly wave** This is a shallow low pressure trough sometime called a 'tropical wave' or 'tropical disturbance'. A new tropical wave forms in the Atlantic every four or five days and between 80 and 100 reach the Caribbean. They travel west at about ten knots bringing overcast skies and showers and the possibility of thunderstorms and strong squalls. In the hurricane season every tropical wave should be treated with respect; about 5–15 per cent develop into a hurricane.

2 **Tropical depression** If an easterly wave develops a closed circulation it appears on synoptic charts with one or more closed isobars and becomes a tropical depression with forecast winds of force 7 or less.

3 **Tropical storm** In suitable conditions a tropical depression can grow into a tropical storm with winds between force 8–11.

4 **Hurricane** When sustained wind speeds reach 64 knots (force 12) a tropical storm is classed as a hurricane.

TOP *Locals claimed that these boats were blown ashore during a hurricane.*

CENTRE *Any wind that can blow this tree down will blow your boat over.*

BOTTOM *If you get caught out by a hurricane near a lee shore – this could be the result.*

NAMING HURRICANES

In the 1930s an Australian forecaster, using the names of unpopular politicians, began naming hurricanes. Between 1950 and 1952 the phonetic alphabet was used to name Caribbean hurricanes. From 1953 they were given the saint days of islands, later they were christened with female names and nowadays hurricanes are given male and female names in alternate years. The names given to particularly severe hurricanes are 'retired' and not used again.

A tropical wave can develop into a hurricane in a matter of hours if:

- The surface sea temperature is at least 26.7°C (80°F) to a depth of at least 50m (150ft).
- Upper and lower winds are similar. If the surface winds are light and the stratospheric winds are strong then wind shear destroys a hurricane before it is born.
- There is an existing front or low pressure system or some other mechanism to initiate cyclonic surface winds.

Hurricanes live for between three to fifteen days. They move from east to west at speeds of 9–13 knots. Most make a landfall somewhere between Martinique and St Martin. At some point they turn north towards the American seaboard and as they do they increase speed to between 15–20 knots. There are many exceptions to this generalised picture and when a hurricane is in the neighbourhood it is safest to adopt an attitude of positive pessimism and plan for the worst.

The structure of hurricanes

A deep depression in temperate latitudes has a central pressure of around 960mb and a diameter of 1200 miles. Tropical revolving storms have a similar or lower central pressure but a diameter of only 40 –500 miles, sometimes less.

In temperate depressions, winds increase steadily from about 15 knots on the periphery to gale force at the centre. In a hurricane they reach gale force about 125 miles from the centre and then increase rapidly with lines of thunderstorms, torrential rain, hail, lightning, tornadoes, and downbursts radiating from the eye wall at the centre.

When the eye wall is reached, the winds fall to about 15 knots. Once the eye has passed then the winds and thunderstorms will just as suddenly return at full strength.

Hurricane warning signs

The warning signs of an approaching tropical revolving storm include:

- In the open sea, swell pushed ahead of the storm.
- Cirrus clouds in bands point towards the storm centre followed later by alto-stratus, then broken cumulus and scud carrying rain squalls.
- If after being corrected for latitude, temperature and diurnal variation, the barometer is 3mb below the average then a tropical revolving storm is likely: 5mb below the mean and this is a promise. In the tropics the greatest changes in barometric pressure come from diurnal variation. At 10 o'clock in the morning and evening the barometer will rise a point or two and at four o'clock morning and afternoon it will drop a couple of points. A slowly falling barometer with the diurnal variation still evident means the storm centre is 120–400 miles away. If the diurnal variation is masked by the falling barometer then the storm centre is within 120 miles.
- Any change in wind speed or direction should be regarded with suspicion.

Avoiding tropical revolving storms

The most certain way of avoiding a tropical revolving storm is to remain in the Canaries until at least the end of November or beginning of December, and once in the Caribbean, either head for Europe before the start of the hurricane season or spend it cruising the Trinidad and Venezuelan coasts.

CALCULATING HURRICANE ODDS

There are three ways of calculating the odds of a hurricane hitting a particular location. Remember, odds are not a promise of certainty; they are something you bet on.

The hurricane year – month by month

You can check when a hurricane is most likely by counting the total number of hurricanes in each month over as long a period as possible. This graph is based on tropical storms by month from 1886 to 1998.

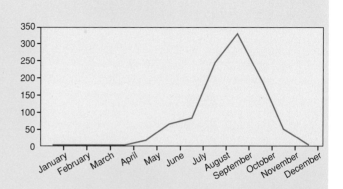

Average interval between hurricane strikes in different locations

If you are in Antigua and it has been seven years since its last hurricane then it is due for another.

Location	Time in years between hurricanes	Most likely time of year
Antigua	4/6	August–October
Bahamas	3/5	July–October
Barbados	9/12	July–October
Belize	8/10	June–September
Dominican Republic	7/9	August–October
Jamaica	4/6	July–October
Martinique	6/8	August–September
Puerto Rico	6/8	August–October
Trinidad	35/40	June, August, October
Virgin Islands	4/6	August–October

Areas most at risk

Check which months that specific areas are most at risk and take care to avoid them at such times.

Area	Month most at risk
Eastern Gulf of Mexico and NW Caribbean	May
The area given above expands east	June
The area now includes Bahamas and Eastern Lesser Antilles	July
Water temperatures of 25.6°C found from Central America to Cape Verde Islands	August
Peak month and all Caribbean is at risk	September
West and South Caribbean	October
South West Caribbean	November

Hurricane tactics

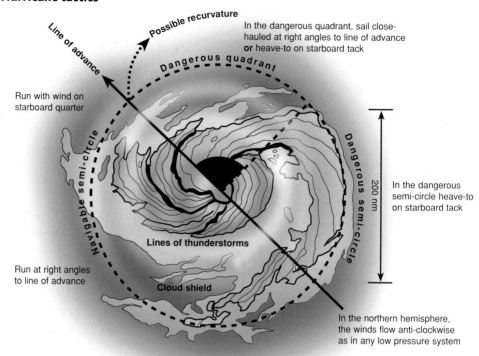

Possible recurvature

Line of advance

In the dangerous quadrant, sail close-hauled at right angles to line of advance **or** heave-to on starboard tack

Dangerous quadrant

Run with wind on starboard quarter

Navigable semi-circle

Dangerous semi-circle

200 nm

In the dangerous semi-circle heave-to on starboard tack

Lines of thunderstorms

Run at right angles to line of advance

Cloud shield

In the northern hemisphere, the winds flow anti-clockwise as in any low pressure system

Caught out in a tropical revolving storm

At sea the safest way of dealing with a tropical revolving storm is to declare a 200 mile exclusion zone around its centre. If you are in harbour and a hurricane is forecast to hit then leaving harbour is unwise. You may believe you are sailing away from the hurricane but a sudden change in its course could bring you head-to-head, placing you and your crew in extreme danger.

Observing your exclusion zone should bring nothing worse than a force 6. If it looks likely you will approach closer than 200 miles to the hurricane, you have two options. The first is to put out a Mayday call immediately. Hopefully, this will be heard and a vessel diverted to take off you and your crew. This option must be taken early to allow time for a vessel to reach you before the weather becomes too bad to make abandoning ship dangerous.

The second option is to ride it out. This is the choice of last resort and not to be undertaken if any other course of action is available. Your first task is to put as much searoom between you and the storm as possible. Hopefully, this will take you clear of any danger.

If you cannot win enough searoom to avoid the storm, try to place your vessel in the navigable semi-circle where the winds are least. If a hurricane is travelling due west at 10 knots then to the north of its centre its speed of advance is added to the windspeed and a 70-knot wind feels like 80 knots; to the south of its centre it is subtracted with the apparent wind therefore giving 60 knots. As wind force increases as the square of the windspeed, this 20-knot difference could be important. Even so, for a small yacht the difference between navigable and dangerous semi-circles is relative. In both there are violent and strong winds and extraordinarily dangerous seas. Once the wind is backing then you are in the navigable semi-circle and the traditional advice is to run with the wind on your starboard quarter, altering course as the wind continues to back. If there is insufficient room to run then it may be necessary to choose between the lesser of two evils and enter the dangerous semi-circle to avoid the eye.

In the dangerous semi-circle, the traditional advice is to heave-to on the starboard tack, altering course as the wind veers. If the wind remains constant or backs it is likely that you are in the direct path of the eye or possibly in the navigable semi-circle and, as before, you should run with the wind on the starboard quarter. There is some evidence that the use of parachute sea-anchors is helpful in extreme conditions, particularly if you do not have the searoom to run before the weather.

Encountering and surviving a hurricane at sea will take careful and consummate seamanship leavened by a heavy dose of good fortune. It will require estimating the relative position of the storm, using information gleaned both from weather forecasts and by frequent and meticulous observations of the wind direction under extraordinarily difficult conditions, in order to reach safer waters as soon as possible.

HEAVY WEATHER CHECKLIST

- Bring your navigation up to date.
- Decide on your heavy weather strategy eg divert to a harbour of refuge, or if that is not possible, heave-to; if these actions are not an option then decide when to run before the weather, or lay to a sea anchor.
- Calculate the wind strengths and sea states and decide when you will change your heavy weather strategy and note this down in the log.
- If you intend to stream warps, then make sure that they are to hand in a convenient locker together with anti-chafe materials. The same applies to sea anchors and drogues.
- Check stowage arrangements. Stowage that is fine in normal weather can result in flying objects that could hurt you.
- Dig out your warm clothing, oilskins, seaboots, harness and lifejacket and put them on.
- Check that the grab bag is to hand and fully packed with all you need.
- Check that the liferaft is secure.
- Check that all halyards and lines are secure.
- Check that every item of deck equipment is secure. This includes dinghies, lifebuoys, danbuoys and their lights.
- If you drop the mainsail and tie it to the boom, then plan to do this before working on deck becomes dangerous. Makes sure the sail is secure. Use additional sail ties to stop the sail from blowing free.

- If you plan to use either a trysail and/or storm jib then these must be rigged early rather than late.
- If you have hank-on headsails, then do not tie unwanted headsails to the guardrail. Bring them below or stow them in a cockpit locker.
- Pump the bilges.
- Top up the fuel tanks; you might wish to run the engine and filling tanks in heavy weather is a nightmare.
- Turn off all seacocks that are not immediately required.
- Top up your ready-to-use food supplies.
- Feed the crew before the bad weather arrives.
- Prepare food and drink. Put hot drinks and soups in flasks before the heavy weather hits. A hot meal such as an all-in-one stew, prepared in a pressure cooker which is allowed to cool without the pressure being taken off is effectively canned and will keep for several days. In prolonged heavy weather, this ready-cooked stew can be brought out and heated up with the minimum of effort to provide a good, nourishing meal. In extremis it can be eaten cold. Have lots of nibbles and easy to prepare hot drinks to hand; variety is important. There are times when everyone wants savoury nibbles, at others only sweets. Unless you are absolutely sure of how your and your crew's taste buds perform carry a wide selection.
- Monitor weather forecasts and the barometer.
- Make a final check to see that all above and below decks is in order.

WEATHER FORECAST TERMS

On passage, daily weather forecasting is a mixture of single observations (reading the barometer and looking out of the hatch) plus interpreting a mixture of voice forecasts and weather faxes. Knowing exactly what terms mean that are used in forecasts will help.

Advisory In the USA advisories are issued in respect of poor weather conditions that are occurring, or imminent, or likely but not so severe that they meet the criteria for issuing a warning.

Coastal forecast In the USA this covers the area between the coast and up to 60 miles offshore.

Cold front The leading edge of a relatively colder air mass. In the northern hemisphere, winds ahead of the front are southwest and shift northwest as the front goes through.

Complex gale or storm A low-pressure system with more than one centre and each centre generating gale-force winds.

Developing gale or storm An extra-tropical low where winds of 34 –47 knots (48 knots or greater in a developing storm) are expected on surface analysis charts within 36 hours: in the 48 hour forecast within 72 hours and in the 96 hour forecast within 120 hours.

Downburst A severe, localised downdraft from a thunderstorm.

Extratropical low L A low-pressure system in middle and higher latitudes.

El Nino A warming of equatorial waters in the Pacific, which occurs every three to seven years.

Fair No precipitation, no extremes in temperature, winds or visibility and less than 4/10th cloud cover.

Frontogenesis The birth of a front, frequently found when an air mass moves out of the US mainland into the Atlantic.

Frontolysis The death or dissipation of a front.

Gale warning Sustained winds of 34 to 47 knots expected.

High pressure An area of higher pressure with clockwise circulation in the northern hemisphere.

Hurricane watch This means that the storm will make a landfall inside 24 hours. If your anchorage is in a hurricane watch area, gale force winds and an unpleasant time are certain with the possibility of worst to come.

Hurricane warning Sustained winds of over 64 knots expected.

ITCZ Inter-Tropical Convergence Zone: the area near the Equator where the northeast and southeast trades meet, creating a band of clouds and thunderstorms.

Jet breeze A narrow band of strong winds high in the atmosphere that often affects the direction taken by fronts and low pressure systems.

Land breeze A wind blowing from the land towards the sea, also called an offshore breeze.

La Nina A cooling of the Equatorial waters in the Pacific *see* El niño.

Likely A 60-70% of forecast weather conditions actually occurring.

Low pressure An area of low pressure with anticlockwise circulation in the northern hemisphere.

New Used when a new low is expected to form within a specific time. The time will be given.

Occluded front The union of two fronts formed when the warm front catches up with the cold front; generally leads to frontolysis

Offshore forecast In the USA this covers from 60 to 250 miles off the coast.

Onshore breeze A wind blowing from the sea towards the land, also called a sea breeze.

Overcast Over 90% cloud cover.

Partly cloudy 30-70% cloud cover

Rapidly intensifying A low where the surface pressure is expected to fall rapidly by at least 24mb in 24 hours.

Ridge Elongated area of relatively high pressure usually associated with anticyclonic winds.

Scattered clouds 10 to 50% cloud cover.

Small craft advisory This warning is issued when winds between 18-33 knots are expected. A small craft is a vessel under 65 feet.

Special marine warning In the USA, this warning is when sustained winds of over 35 knots but lasting less than two hours are expected. Normally associated with thunderstorms, squall lines and cold fronts.

Squall line A non-frontal band of thunderstorms.

Storm warning Sustained winds of over 48 knots expected.

Sustained winds The average windspeed over one minute.

Stationary A front that has not moved from its last position.

Trough Appears as 'trof' on weather faxes: an area of relatively low pressure associated with cyclonic winds.

Warm front The leading edge of a relatively warm air mass. In the northern hemisphere winds are from the southeast and behind the front they are southwest.

Windchill The level of cooling felt from a combination of wind and air temperature. For those interested, the formula for calculating wind chill is:

WC = 0.0817 x ((3.71 x) + (5.81 -)) x (T − 91.4) + 91.4

Where V = wind speed in mph and T = temperature in Fahrenheit.

ABBREVIATIONS

The following abbreviations are found on weather charts

COMB	Combined
DCRS	Decrease
DSIPT	Dissipate
DVLPG	Developing
FRMG	Forming
INCRS	Increase
INTSFY	Intensify
INLD	Inland
MOVG	Moving
Q-STNRY	Quasi-stationary
RPDLY	Rapidly
STNRY	Stationary
WKNG	Weakening

Heaving to

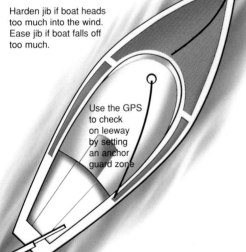

1 Back the jib. This is easy if you tack and do not release the jib sheet.
2 Ease mainsail.
3 Put the helm down. You will need to experiment to find the best balance of jib, main and helm.

Harden jib if boat heads too much into the wind. Ease jib if boat falls off too much.

Wind and Seas

Use the GPS to check on leeway by setting an anchor guard zone

Heaving to is useful for:
1 Weathering a squall
2 Putting in a reef
3 Making a quick repair
4 Waiting for the tide.

The Pardy sea anchor

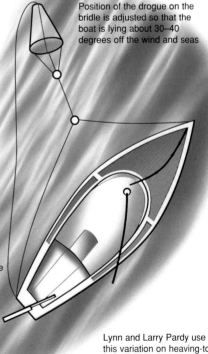

Position of the drogue on the bridle is adjusted so that the boat is lying about 30–40 degrees off the wind and seas

Wind and Seas

Watch for chafe where lines leave the boat

Lynn and Larry Pardy use this variation on heaving-to and reckon that it gives a more comfortable ride

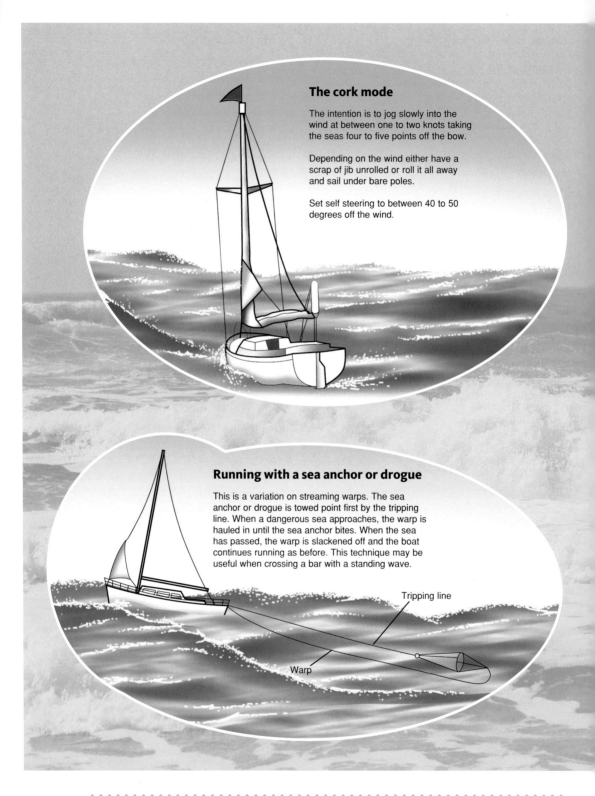

The cork mode

The intention is to jog slowly into the wind at between one to two knots taking the seas four to five points off the bow.

Depending on the wind either have a scrap of jib unrolled or roll it all away and sail under bare poles.

Set self steering to between 40 to 50 degrees off the wind.

Running with a sea anchor or drogue

This is a variation on streaming warps. The sea anchor or drogue is towed point first by the tripping line. When a dangerous sea approaches, the warp is hauled in until the sea anchor bites. When the sea has passed, the warp is slackened off and the boat continues running as before. This technique may be useful when crossing a bar with a standing wave.

Tripping line

Warp

Lying to a sea anchor

The sea anchor should be at least one wavelength, preferably two wavelengths ahead of the boat. This requires a VERY long warp.

Buoy (optional)

Warp

Tripping line

chapter 12 Caribbean sailing

Sailing amongst coral is a bit like wandering blindfold through an ever changing maze where the slightest error brings disaster. Coral atolls, reefs and cays are low lying, often only a few metres above sea level and rarely visible at ranges over ten miles. Many are unlit and beacons or lighthouses are 60-80 feet high. This is about the same height as a palm tree. Never assume that the first tall feature you see is the beacon you expected, or that your GPS and chart agree. Since your chart was last updated the coral could have moved to pastures new.

If your boat is not to become a permanent feature on a reef, then once in the Caribbean landfalls must be made with great care and never at night, in heavy weather or poor visibility. The chart may show lights to guide you through holes in the reefs that surround so many anchorages. It would be unwise to assume these are working and you may be committed before you discover that they are not. You should stand off at a safe distance and monitor your drift by setting the anchor watch function on the GPS to a suitable range and wait for conditions to improve. Reefs can extend some distance from land and it is not good practice to use radar as a substitute for eyeballs. Do not rely on the echosounder to give warning of a reef's approach, for depths can change from over 1000 metres to nothing in less than half a mile, which is no more than five or six minutes sailing.

Chart datums and accuracy

When sailing in coral, an error of a few feet can put you aground. You must be confident that you are navigating within the limitations of your chosen system. These limitations may not be immediately obvious.

The Earth is not a perfect sphere. Geographers call it a geoid meaning 'Earth-shaped', which is no help when deciding the whereabouts of the centre of the Earth. Agreement on this is important for it is the starting point for measuring latitude and longitude. Different centres give different positions for the same co-ordinates. Historically, different hydrographic offices picked a centre that suited their purposes best. The disparities were (and are) never huge and until the arrival of satellite position-fixing systems they were usually within the realm of normal navigational error.

Celestial navigation brought earlier mariners to their landfall and then they relied on sightings, for although their marine charts were not as accurate as today's they were pretty good at land surveys. This means that although the chart showed the island in the wrong place its size and shape and the relationship of one island feature to another is correct. Old leadline surveys can still figure in modern charts and this can lead to a disagreement between your plotted GPS position and your actual position on the ground. The error is likely to be in cables or less. If you require a greater degree of accuracy then positions obtained by plotting cross-bearings on suitable, correctly identified, charted features will almost certainly give a better answer.

The first attempt to produce a world-wide standard for latitude and longitude came with the World Geodetic System in 1960. This became known as WGS 60 and was followed by WGS 66, WGS 72 and WGS 84. There is also the North American Datum 83, which is considered the equivalent of WGS 84, but you may find some charts using the older NAD 27 and until fairly recently some Admiralty charts used a datum called OSGB 36. GPS systems offer a selection of datums. Make sure that you are using the correct one for your chart.

Reef navigation

The higher you are, the easier it is to see a way through the coral. It helps if you have some means of quickly scrambling up and down the mast. If you have mast steps make sure they are usable with the mainsail raised and underway. Home made ratlines can be either of rope or lengths of wood lashed across the lower shrouds at suitable intervals. Both work, although rope ratlines cut your feet and wooden ratlines can chafe headsails when you are hard on the wind.

When approaching a reef from seaward it will first appear light green with a brown or dark fringe that quickly changes to blue as deeper water is reached. If there is a big swell running, you might see a line of white where the breakers meet the reef, but do not count on it. The light green colour is the shallow sandy area inside the reef. As you come closer, this area may be pock-marked by brown coral heads, and areas less than 10 metres deep are a greenish blue. The brown fringe is the reef and the blue the deep water outside.

When sailing in reef areas it is important to keep your plot up-to-date, to correctly identify every feature in sight and to stay orientated. This is easier said than done for the landscape is pretty much the same whichever way you face. Use the compass, wind and the sun to confirm that you are pointing in the right direction. Do not approach beacons or marks too closely for they may be on the reef, some distance from deep water, and never cut corners, however tempting. Reef navigation is nautical map reading with a constant, pernickety attention to detail. The chart lives in the cockpit where the helmsman can see it.

Approaching a reef

Do not make your approach into the sun. A sparkling sea makes a pretty picture but it is impossible to see the bottom, and safe reef navigation relies on being able to see underwater hazards. Polarised sunglasses will help. If you must approach into sun, try sailing, under motor if necessary, in a series of tacks which take you across the sun, but best of all is to approach with the sun aft the beam with the bottom clearly visible. Arranging this can determine your timetable for the day.

As you approach the reef, a pair of eyes in the ratlines will help you to make out the path through the reef for some distance ahead. Failing that, send a lookout into the bows; single-handers have to make do with jumping up and down on the cockpit coamings.

Entrances to a reef

Not all gaps or cuts through the reef are obvious. Choose the widest channel available and remember that if there is a heavy sea there may not be enough water in the troughs of waves. When the tide is running it will be strongest in the cut, and wind-over-tide can throw up horrible sea conditions. A slow

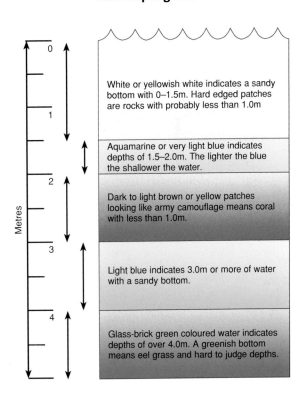

Reef depth guide

White or yellowish white indicates a sandy bottom with 0–1.5m. Hard edged patches are rocks with probably less than 1.0m

Aquamarine or very light blue indicates depths of 1.5–2.0m. The lighter the blue the shallower the water.

Dark to light brown or yellow patches looking like army camouflage means coral with less than 1.0m.

Light blue indicates 3.0m or more of water with a sandy bottom.

Glass-brick green coloured water indicates depths of over 4.0m. A greenish bottom means eel grass and hard to judge depths.

approach, and a reconnaissance carried out by sailing across the entrance a few times, will help you to decide if conditions are suitable. It is usually possible to approach close to the reef for a decent view. Entering with a following sea can be tricky so keep the stern straight to the seas or you may broach. If in doubt, stay out and look for a well-marked, navigable channel; most reefs have at least one.

Navigation inside the reef

Once inside the reef, have a crewmember in the ratlines for they can guide you through coral heads and unexplained patches of dark water. Cloud shadows can be mistaken for coral and sometimes the only way to be sure is to stop the boat and see if the 'coral' head moves.

The few navigation marks inside the reef: withies or plastic bottles or the occasional mooring buoy, are usually ambiguous and can be used only with local knowledge. Although the colour of the bottom is a useful guide to depth, the water can be so clear that judging depth by eye is difficult. Cutting over a coral head may put you aground or the echo-sounder may show 20 metres. Either way it may look exactly the same.

Anchoring in coral

Never anchor on coral because this will destroy entire ecosystems. It is usually fairly easy to find a suitable anchorage on an area of sand or mud bottom if you take the time to look. In popular areas such as the US Virgins and parts of the Bahamas, moorings have been laid to keep yachts off the coral. If there are no moorings, try to find an area where you can swing through 360° without fouling a coral head. If this is not possible then lay out a stern anchor so you do not swing.

If an anchor becomes trapped under a coral head use the dinghy to lay a second anchor in clear water, buoy the trapped anchor and then dive to free it. If you are anchoring near coral, you must use chain because of the risk of chafe. Make sure you anchor before dark and, for safety, dive on the anchor to check it before retiring for the night. (See also the following chapter.)

Marinas provide the convenience of life ashore while creating the illusion of being afloat. They make folk lazy. In home waters as night falls the sails come down, engines fire up and bows rise out of the water as everyone makes for the nearest pontoon. Anchoring is for picnics or waiting for the tide. By the time you reach the Caribbean anchoring tends to be the norm. Anchorages are floating communities where you meet old friends and catch up on the latest gossip.

Yachts are left unattended when crews go ashore to shop, play tourist or party. Come bedtime, folk take to their bunks until breakfast. Anchor watches are unknown. The confidence to do this comes partly from lying to a steady wind but mostly from lots of chain and a bower anchor at least one size above that recommended for your yacht.

Many yachts carry a second, equally large anchor of a different type ready to be let go. Second anchors often live on the pushpit, as stern anchors are useful to reduce swing in busy anchorages, or if you are lying to the swell in a cross wind, an anchor laid at an angle to the stern is used to haul the yacht round until its bows are pointing into the seas.

Choice of anchor and rode

Everyone has their own firmly-held opinion on the best type of anchor and has the figures to prove it. Experience has shown that the best anchor is a tractor engine, encapsulated in concrete and buried deep. Failing that, big is beautiful and it helps to have at least two different anchors to meet differing conditions and a third 'thank God' anchor just in case.

The weakest link

An anchor system is only as safe as its weakest link. If you choose an oversized anchor then its chain, shackles, swivels, bitts, anchor roller and winch must be sized to match and the work to make this possible is best done during the refit before you sail.

Whether you use chain, chain and warp, or all warp depends on you. Boats appear to sheer less with all chain but yachts on warp do not snatch quite as much. Those using all chain often have a snubbing line tied to their anchor chain. Warp is lighter to haul in than chain but it does not self stow and it is liable to chafe where it lies along the bottom or wraps round a coral head. Perhaps these are arguments in favour of a mixture of chain and warp. Warp is also likely to chafe where it enters the boat but this is easily prevented by using long lengths of thick plastic hose.

Entering an anchorage

There are those sailors who have the confidence to roar into a busy anchorage, throw the anchor over the side, leap into the dinghy and be ashore before the anchor has reached the bottom. For everyone else it is a fraught time. If you have a shallow-draft yacht you can usually anchor inshore of the mob. Otherwise picking the right spot is not easy. There is the fear of fouling someone's anchor or dropping back onto another yacht. It is best to creep in slowly, find a vacant parking place and check that its emptiness is not because it hides a sandbank, wreck or reef.

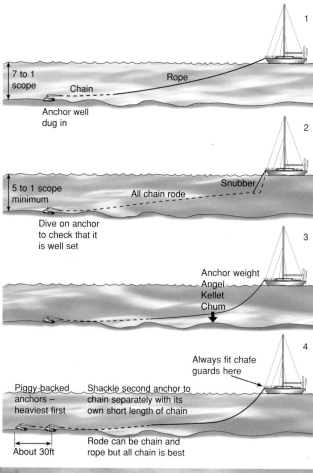

1

7 to 1 scope

Rope

Chain

Anchor well dug in

2

5 to 1 scope minimum

All chain rode

Snubber

Dive on anchor to check that it is well set

3

Anchor weight
Angel
Kellet
Chum

4

Always fit chafe guards here

Piggy-backed anchors – heaviest first

Shackle second anchor to chain separately with its own short length of chain

About 30ft

Rode can be chain and rope but all chain is best

In most anchorages the water is so clear, and the underwater environment so colourful, that diving to check the anchor is a pleasure.

If there is life on nearby yachts casually enquire about the holding and where their anchors lie. Evaluating their replies needs careful judgement, for some yachts seeking peace and solitude tell fibs. When you are happy that all is well go close to the stern of the yacht that will end up immediately ahead of you, lower the anchor and drop back into your chosen spot. When you stop, the engine can be run astern for a couple of moments to make sure the anchor is dug in. In remote areas without shore-lights, check how you are lying during the night by laying a lighted dan buoy nearby to give a reference point. Stay out of prohibited zones. You will be asked to move.

When some boats enter a crowded anchorage they initially lay out a long anchor rode, go hard astern to dig the anchor in, then they wind in much of the rode so they are lying to a short scope, occupying as little space as possible. This works as long as the wind holds steady. If it changes, the boat swings round, the anchor unhooks from the bottom and the short scope prevents it re-bedding. Suddenly you have an anchorage full of boats travelling backwards, collecting anchors and chains as they go. It is a well intentioned but misplaced anchoring technique.

Checking the holding

Most anchoring takes place in depths of between five and ten metres. If you desire peace of mind, and space permits, then forget the rule that says three times the depth for chain and five times for warp and let it all hang out. You bought it to use when anchoring, not as ballast, so why not use it?

Once you reach warmer waters, it is no hardship to dive, visually check how the anchor is set and, if necessary, pick it up and move it around until you are happy. A snorkel, mask and fins are enough for this task.

In commercial harbours, the bottom is often foul and the water quality discourages diving to check the anchor. It is a good idea to always use a tripping line.

The use of a 'kellet', 'chum' or 'angel' to improve the catenary and holding power of an anchor is well-known but few boats carry one just in case. If needed, one can be easily made up from a short length of chain and almost any small weight such as dive weights or grapnel type anchor. Another option is to double up and piggy-back two anchors.

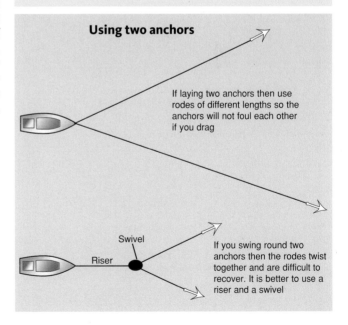

Using two anchors

If laying two anchors then use rodes of different lengths so the anchors will not foul each other if you drag

Swivel

Riser

If you swing round two anchors then the rodes twist together and are difficult to recover. It is better to use a riser and a swivel

Popular anchorages are always busy. Finding a safe spot to anchor is always a challenge and often the bottom has been so ploughed up by anchors that the holding is poor.

Carlisle Bay, Barbados.

There are quiet anchorages. This one is in a bay off an uninhabited island in the Les Saintes group.

Ports of entry

On arriving in a new country, your first port of call must be a recognised port of entry in order to clear in. Similarly, when you come to depart, your last port must also be a recognised port of entry to clear out.

Most islands have one port of entry, or perhaps two. Even though these may not always be convenient for yachts it is not wise to tuck into a quiet yacht anchorage and take the local maxi-taxi (a private bus service using minibuses) to Customs and Immigration. It is rare for yachts to be boarded on arrival but you will make officialdom's day if you are economical with the truth when they ask, 'Where is your boat?'

Paperwork can take up to half a day to complete. Some countries, such as Venezuela, insist that you clear in and out of that country's internal districts or regions as well as internationally.

The paperwork

When you clear in or out have a folder which contains:

1 Ship's papers
2 Passports for all on board
3 A crew list: a blank crew list form may be provided free, or for a small charge, or you may be expected to provide your own
4 Papers from clearing out of the last country visited or your copies of clearing in forms when clearing out
5 Immunisation certificates for everyone on board
6 A pen

Even if officials insist that you use their forms (they might charge for providing them) it still helps to have filled out one of your own crew lists, for then you have all necessary information relating to the crew on one sheet of paper and you can complete the official forms without fumbling through a stack of passports. A boat stamp is not strictly necessary but occasionally its use persuades officials that you are taking their procedures seriously.

Often the forms of the different agencies are very similar and much may be inapplicable to pleasure craft but leaving blank spaces sends you to the back of the queue. Smile, admit ignorance, and ask for help. Officials have their preferred stock answers to the questions on the forms, but unless you own up to ignorance, they assume you know the right form of words even if they are in Spanish. See Appendix: Boat Details and Crew List.

Clearing in and out

Without exception officials are smartly dressed and courteous. They work hard to explain what is needed, often without a common language to ease understanding. Even so, moaning about bureaucracy is a popular pastime amongst the cruising community but some streetwise savvy helps you glide through the bureaucratic jungle. Always dress smartly. Or rather, do not turn up unshaven, unclean, barefoot and wearing nothing but a torn T-shirt and tattered

During October and November the marina in Las Palmas fills up and the anchorage outside becomes overcrowded. Putting out a kedge anchor so that you lie to the seas rather than the wind reduces your swing and makes life more comfortable.

Porto Santo has the principal and perhaps the only beach in the Maderias. Yachts can anchor off, just outside the harbour, but in onshore winds they must move inside for protection.

A classic Caribbean view – from the beach at Carlisle Bay, Barbados.

shorts. Officials are not impressed by down-market dress codes. It is not a good idea to argue with officials but there is a fine line between being obsequious and easy-going; insisting on a policy of mutual respect from all parties develops the best relationships.

Smile a lot and be prepared to take it easy. Although the procedures everywhere are similar, each country has its own system and locally some officers may have their unique and variable interpretation of the rules. Without fail you will have to report to Customs and Immigration. In addition, the port authority, port health authority, Ministry of Transport, Ministry of Agriculture, Ministry of Interior, and police may wish to become involved. There are usually charges for cruising permits, a levy on each crew member, and light and harbour dues to pay, usually in a separate office. Some countries also ask you to pay a departure tax when you clear out. It is not normally necessary to clear in with Customs in free ports like Saba, Saint Martin, Sint Eustatius or Sint Maarten but you must visit Immigration and the harbour authorities.

On weekdays, officialdom's working hours are normally 9.00am–4.00pm. Outside these hours or at weekends there are overtime charges. When clearing out in the morning and you are asked, 'When are you sailing?' then even if you plan to sail late afternoon or even the following morning the truthful answer is 'As soon as possible.' Any other reply may see you being told to go away and return nearer your sailing time. Normally you should have 24 hours to sail after you clear out but do not count on it.

Length of stay

Every country places a limit as to how long visitors may stay. Immigration officers always ask, 'How long do you wish to stay?' Take the maximum on offer. Extending a stay involves more form filling and additional fees. If you wish to stay beyond the maximum permitted time then it will probably be necessary to briefly leave the country and start all over again.

Cruising permits

Most countries issue cruising permits. In Spanish-speaking countries, a *despacho* will be issued and on it you will be asked to name all the ports you intend to visit. List everywhere you might or might not visit. There is no penalty for not going to a named port but stopping at a port not on your list may require filling in more forms and paying for another *despacho*. At each port the authorities will stamp your *despacho*, though some may insist on issuing their own and expect the appropriate payment.

Passports

Make sure that your passport is up-to-date. Most countries require it to be valid for three months beyond your intended length of stay. Passports will normally be stamped 'specifically excluding working in paid employment' or some similar form of words. Some countries expect you to carry your passport at all times.

Visas

You may need a visa. These may be obtainable on arrival or need to be arranged beforehand. Check this out in good time through your country's foreign office or State Department website. Visas can take several weeks to arrange.

Pets

Yachts with pets aboard must keep the animals on board until clearance has been given, usually by the Chief Veterinary Officer, and under no circumstances take your pet ashore before this is given.

Agents

In some countries, Venezuela for example, there are formidable difficulties in doing your own paperwork and it is usual to employ an agent to deal with all official matters relating to the boat and its crew, including clearing in and out. Charges for this service are reasonable.

Searches

A few countries search all visiting vessels as a matter of routine. At sea you may be stopped by the local Guarda Costa, Coast Guard, local

Lack of a common language is no barrier to communication, provided that everyone is willing to try. This Cuban Customs officer is using the ship's phrase book to ask questions – not about the boat or crew but about the family in the photographs on a bulkhead.

defence force, police or navy. They will wish to see the ship's papers and the crew's passports. They may or may not search your yacht. Within two or three hundred miles of the USA waters, US Coast Guard ships or aircraft may ask for details of you, your crew and the boat.

chapter 15 Security

The risk of crime is no greater in the Caribbean than anywhere else. Your home town probably has areas where you wouldn't venture alone at night, but an unfamiliar environment, strange customs and language difficulties can create an unwarranted fear of crime which could ruin your cruise.

Having said that, security is low on the yachting priority list compared to the attention given to gear failures, storms and strandings. Yet it is the most likely cause of grief to you, your purse and your vessel. So, pay your crime prevention dues before you sail or pay them with interest later.

No one knows the true scale of boat crime. It is a worldwide phenomenon but no law enforcement agency has an overall picture. Only a fraction of all crime (surveys of land-based crime suggest it could be as low as 20 per cent) is ever reported to the authorities. Since many bluewater cruisers are uninsured, hold only third party cover or are faced with huge deductibles, few claims ever reach the usually well-informed insurance companies. A modest guess gives boat crime a multi-million dollar price tag. Ashore this would encourage vote-winning government initiatives. Afloat, individual yachtsmen are cast adrift to do their best.

Piracy

Being boarded whilst underway is bad news whether your unwanted guests are 'professional' pirates or opportunist fishermen. They have a faster, more manoeuvrable vessel than yours, outnumber you and are probably armed. Nowadays such attacks are rare but tales still circulate of assaults, rapes and killings and yachts, like the *Marie Celeste*, found adrift without their crew. Some may once have had a grain of truth. Areas where this type of attack is likely change but are generally well known and the best defence is to give them a wide berth.

For the latest information, or to check out past years, the International Chamber of Commerce's International Maritime Bureau (IMB) has online world maps showing where incidents of piracy, actual or attempted, have taken place. Clicking on the symbol of an incident brings up further details. The maps can be found on the IMB's website at www.icc-ccs.org.uk/extra/display.php.

Theft

Nowadays pirates prefer the easy life and wait for you to come to them rather than go to the effort of hunting you out. Their lairs of choice are popular anchorages with an abundance of victims and they prefer working when you are either ashore or asleep. With luck you remain unaware of your unwelcome visitors until they have left.

They like high-value items with a ready resale market. Outboards and dinghies head the list. Wire strops and padlocks are no obstacle. The best answer is an old, unattractive dinghy and rusty, worthless looking outboard motor. Failing that keep the dinghy on deck at night or at least pull it up on a halyard so that it is out of the water. Any attempt to steal it should lead to a banging and clattering that brings you out on deck. Thieves do not like drawing attention to their activities. Anything left lying on deck can disappear and for smaller, less valuable items the real loss is not in what is taken but in finding suitable replacements far from home.

Police in tourist areas tend to be friendly but it is a good idea to ask before pointing a camera in their direction.

Mark equipment with the name of your boat. Try to make these markings obvious and difficult to remove. If it is stolen then the damage done removing the markings reduces its resale value. Knowing this, thieves prefer unmarked property.

Unattended vessels

Unattended vessels are at special risk. During the day neighbouring yachts will probably respond if strangers are seen aboard but this is unlikely at night. When you leave your yacht for more than a day then it should be locked up; the decks cleared of easily removed equipment and the dinghy deflated and stowed below. An anchor light with a sensor to switch it on at night gives the illusion that someone is aboard. If you are leaving your vessel for a week or more while you fly home or visit distant tourist attractions, consider putting it into a marina with good security or hauling out and storing in a secure compound.

TEN WAYS TO BEAT THE THIEF

1 Be aware of the local situation. Check the local radio net (VHF or HF) for latest information on crime hotspots, and before setting out, speak to those who have very recently visited the areas you plan to cruise.

2 Cruise in company. The mutual support of two or three yachts may be sufficient to deter the local opportunist, especially in remote anchorages.

3 Invest in good quality physical and electronic protection. Consider having removable grilles made and fitting them to every hatch at night. This allows ventilation but makes it difficult for thieves to enter the cabins. It might be useful to create a secure area to retreat to if boarded or to keep valuables in. Think about rigging personal attack alarms with trip wires on deck and in the cockpit to give warning of intruders coming aboard. Fit either a complete, zoned alarm system or stand-alone, battery-powered movement detectors and use them when you go ashore and in areas of yacht not normally occupied at night. These can be rigged to sound an alarm and/or switch on lights.

4 Mark all gear with the boat's name.

5 Secure dinghies with chain and padlocks, not line. Lock outboards to dinghy transoms. A few minutes work with a couple of cans of matt green and brown spray paint can make a brand-new outboard look as if it has spent the last year on the seabed.

6 Never leave valuables lying around so that a passing thief can grab them and run. Stow them away out of sight in lockers. This applies above and below decks. Chain your outboard and dinghy to your yacht and raise the dinghy out of the water at night. Always secure your yacht when you leave it, even for five minutes.

7 When you go ashore or visit other yachts, leave the lights on and radio playing to give the impression that there is someone aboard. When you go ashore always leave your dinghy in a secure area.

8 A dog trained to bark whenever strangers approach your yacht is a splendid deterrent. A small yapper is fine but a pitbull or doberman is also a visual deterrent. The downside is dog hairs in the bilges and in some countries there are restrictions on taking animals ashore.

9 In high-risk areas, marinas tend to look like prison camps complete with perimeter lighting, fencing and guard dogs. They are not cheap. Prices tend to be at US or European levels but it could still be the cheaper option.

10 Having weapons aboard needs very careful consideration. If you decide to carry weapons then be sure that:
a) They are legal
b) You are proficient in their use
c) You have thought through the circumstances in which you would use them.

SECURITY – THE 3 DS

These simple guidelines are a mnemonic to help when drawing up your security plan. Remember to keep it simple. Man plans and God smiles. Simple plans are easier to change when something unexpected happens.

Divert potential thieves into some harmless activity. This can be as simple as paying a boatboy to guard your dinghy instead of stealing it – it is cheaper than buying a new dinghy.

Discourage thieves by making your vessel look as though it has nothing worth stealing, or by anchoring close to vessels that are easier or richer targets, or by having obvious security.

Delay the thief reaching your valuables by installing alarms, chains, locks and lights. Ideally, the delay period should exceed the interval between the thief being detected, the alarm being raised and your response. Give some thought about what form your response will take. Confrontation may not be a good idea.

SHORESIDE SAFETY TIPS

1   Always be aware of what is happening around you.

2   Know where you are going and have your route planned.

3   If you become lost, always ask for directions when in busy public places. Be wary of people offering to act as a guide especially if they lead you down dark alleys.

4   If approached by suspicious characters, avoid eye contact or conversation and keep moving.

5   Only use Automatic Teller Machines (ATMs) in busy well-lit areas. Never count your money by the machine.

6   Keep bumbags (fanny packs) out of sight under your shirt. Make sure bags are securely closed. Hold purses or shoulder bags in front of you.

7   Carry an old wallet or purse containing a few dollars, any old store loyalty cards, business cards, photographs (not of you, your boat or your family) and other worthless paraphernalia to make it real. If given the choice of your money or your life then hand it over and disappear before it becomes apparent how little it contains.

8   If you think you are being followed, head for busy areas with bright lights.

9   If stopped and challenged by criminals, give them what they want. It is better to lose money than risk injury or death.

10 Know the local telephone number for the police and other emergency services.

Shorebased crime

Countries value happy tourists. Popular tourist districts are well policed but nowhere is entirely safe; in urban neighbourhoods the more truly 'ethnic' an area then the greater the risk of experiencing crime.

Weaponry

Most countries impound any guns and ammunition on entry and return them on your departure. It is a serious offence not to declare a firearm. As crime is most likely to occur after you have cleared in there seems little point in carrying firearms.

Mace and pepper sprays are close range 'shoot and scoot' weapons. Scooting may be difficult on a yacht. Flares and Very pistols have been used to frighten off intruders but their use in a confined space or close to other yachts is not advisable.

A weapon is not a deterrent. Your first action after producing it would probably be to use it. But, if you fire without warning as soon as you are aware of an intruder, then your victim could be an 'innocent' youngster who has just come on board to welcome you to his island or the local police chief doing his rounds. Force is not the simple answer it may first appear. Its use, successful or not, will involve you rather too closely with unfamiliar legal and penal systems.

part four **the routes**

chapter 16 **Passage planning**

You may think that preparing a formal passage plan is for pedants. Everything you need to know is in your head and your crew know what you are thinking. What more do you need? Believe this and you are guaranteed an adventurous passage ... if you survive.

In 2002, Chapter V, Regulation V/34 of the International Convention for the Safety of Life at Sea (SOLAS V) made it mandatory for all craft, **including leisure craft**, to prepare a passage plan for each voyage. The International Maritime Organisation (IMO) Resolution A.893 (21), *Guidelines For Voyage Planning*, lays down four stages to passage planning:

- Appraisal
- Planning
- Execution
- Monitoring

These together cover 50 different elements on passage planning with the emphasis on routeing.

A good passage plan should enable you, your crew and your boat to make your proposed voyage in a safe, seamanlike and enjoyable manner. This does not happen by happy accident, especially on ocean voyages. If you forget some piece of kit or do your sums wrong, then you live with the consequences and the knowledge that five minutes forethought could have prevented weeks of misery. Plans come with the warning: plan in haste, suffer the consequences at leisure.

Your plan is tailor-made for you, your boat and your crew. It is unique. Adopting, rather than adapting, a plan written by someone else means unquestioningly accepting their judgements, decisions and limitations, whether or not they are appropriate to your circumstances. This means it is only possible to give general advice. There is no magic form of words that, when slavishly followed, guarantees success; there are only guidelines.

Passage plan timetable

Just how far ahead of your departure date planning begins depends on your expertise, the condition of your boat and the experience of your crew. The work for your Atlantic circuit starts months before you set out. Most of that time is spent making the boat ready for sea, and if you need it, going on courses to learn essential skills. Once en route, the planning for a major leg of your voyage probably begins a couple of weeks before your proposed departure date.

There are four phases, each with its own set of tasks which must be complete before you can safely move on. In theory, the workload decreases as the sailing date approaches. In practice it grows in unexpected directions.

Phase one – the months before you sail

Besides taking an overview and beginning the research on your proposed voyage, this phase deals with items like rigging, sails, engines, pumps, radios and watermakers that take time to service, repair or replace. It also includes gathering together all the charts (paper or electronic), pilots, sailing directions, almanacs, tables and other publications you need. A plan is only as good as the information it is based upon. If you do not have a particular chart or publication then beg, borrow or buy what you need.

The timescale of this phase is not always within your control. A useful rule of thumb is that when you start one repair you will unearth at least three other defects demanding attention. You may be relying on others for some or all of this work. Thanks to the internet, sourcing spares, publications and supplies is straightforward but their delivery and clearance through customs less so. Always allow for some delays.

This is also the time to prepare your boat management plan. When at sea normal life goes on. Meals are cooked, pots, pans and dishes washed, shirts laundered, checks carried out and running repairs made. None of this happens by accident. You will need to prepare the following:

Duty roster This is the allocation of areas of responsibility. If you are single-handed then there is no question about who does what. Otherwise think about what are the duties of the following posts and who is best to be the:

- Mate
- Watch officer(s)
- Bosun
- Engineer
- Electrician
- Navigator
- Cook/purser
- First aider

When allocating roles, play to people's strengths. Make them aware of their role in the duty roster early so that they can play an active part in preparing the passage plan, and if necessary send them on training courses. Sharing the work reduces the load on you and makes your crew feel they have a real role in preparing the ship for sea. On most yachts everyone wears at least two hats. Try to make them complimentary.

Chain of command Boats are not democracies. You can, and should, delegate duties but you can never delegate responsibilities. There must be a clearly understood chain of command starting with the skipper and ending with the cabin boy. Mostly the chain of command is invisible but if problems or dramas arise, as skipper you earn your rations by solving them.

Standing orders These lay down where an individual's authority to make decisions runs out and yours begins. Standing orders may be general and apply to everyone. For example, you may wish to be called every time another vessel is sighted or be specific to an area of responsibility, for example the engineer alerting you to excessive fuel consumption.

Watch-keeping Select the watch-keeping system best suited for your boat and crew.

Daily routine This is the programme which lays down who is doing what and when each day.

Phase two – within a few days of departure

This is when you finalise your passage plan research. Research is used in the broadest sense possible. Read the accounts of others who have made similar passages. Bear in mind that their stories may be heavy on adventure, but you will learn how they deal with heavy weather, calms, equipment failure and daily life on board. If you are amongst other boats preparing for the crossing, there will be some that have done it all before. Seek them out and learn from their experiences. Do not forget those who set off earlier. Most boats take part in at least one daily radio net. Listen in and discover what the conditions out there are really like.

As part of this phase start making your final preparations:

- Fill up the gas bottles.
- Service the engine.
- Change oil and fuel filters.
- Check fanbelts and batteries.
- Test EPRIBs and MOB devices.
- Begin stocking up on non-perishable food.

You should aim to carry supplies of food, fuel and water for your expected time en route (ETE) plus 50 per cent. In other words, if you expect the passage to take 20 days then stock up for 30 days at sea.

Phase three – within a couple of days of departure

Your passage plan should be complete. You should start looking for a weather window for your departure and to finalise your departure date. Top up water and fuel tanks and start bringing fresh food on board.

Brief the crew on your passage plan. Although you have discussed it with them as it developed, it is sensible to formally go through your final plan so that everyone is working to the same edition, not some personalised version which they believe you and they had agreed over a cup of coffee.

Once the briefing is over then you can begin going through spills, drills and safety procedures. How far you go with these depends on your crew. If you have sailed thousands of miles together, a simple reminder may be sufficient. At the other extreme it may be necessary to go to sea for a couple of days and practise sail-changing, reefing, tacking, gybing, man overboard, fire-fighting and abandon ship drills. Return to harbour only when the crew claim that they can do these drills in their sleep and you are happy to believe them. Leaving this marlinspike seamanship until you are en route or expecting the crew to teach each other is not an option. Nor does it matter whether everyone aboard is an experienced sailor and knows their sail drills. If they have not sailed together then they are not a team.

Finally begin stowing for sea. This means fixing the galley so that you can cook three meals a day in a seaway, preparing sea berths, stowing kit so that it will not fly around the boat looking for someone to hit, and checking that the contents of the crash bags are complete and up-to-date.

Phase four – departure day

The day begins with checking the latest weather forecast. Is it within the limits you have laid down? Is there any nasty weather that will catch up with you in the first two or three days before you are properly clear of land? If so, are you happy to face this weather before everyone has their sea legs?

If you are happy, then bring the last of the fresh food onboard, carry out your final engine and equipment checks and prepare the first meal at sea. This can be a pre-cooked all-in-one-stew that just needs reheating or a huge batch of sandwiches. Make sure there is a good supply of sweet and savoury snacks to hand.

Check that everyone is on board, stow the dinghy, hand out seasickness remedies to anyone who may need them, remove the sail covers, fire up the instruments and cast off.

Routeing

Overview

1 Charts and pilots SOLAS V requires you to use the appropriate nautical charts and publications when planning your passage. Increasingly, this means electronic charts and the add-ons that come with them. There is nothing wrong with this but it is prudent to ask how you would navigate if you lost all electric power. The answer, of course, is a battery-powered GPS and/or paper charts. If you are using paper charts then list those required and check that they are corrected up to date. If you are using printed pilots, then list them and mark the pages relevant to your voyage.

2 Lights Make a note of the position, characteristic and range of all relevant lights en route. On an ocean passage this information is normally confined to the lights of the departure and arrival ports with perhaps a landfall light like Needham Point on Barbados. If you are coasting or cruising through an island chain you may follow a sequence of lights and it helps to know beforehand where they are and when you should expect to pick them up.

3 Navigation warnings A few minutes spent in the harbourmaster's office checking the latest Notices to Mariners is time well spent.

Port information

There are three types of port: departure ports, arrival ports and ports of refuge. For each of them you need to know:

1 Position This may be nothing more than a port's latitude and longitude but there may be other information that helps you to fix its position. If you are sailing towards an island how far off do you expect to pick it up? Barbados is a low rounded hump you may pick up from 10 or 15 miles away but it has an airport at the south end of the island close to Needham Point. Aircraft taking off and landing can be picked up much further off, especially at night when their landing lights appear like demented satellites. Pico is the highest point in the Azores and lies opposite Horta. It can be seen 60 miles away, possibly further if it has a cap of cloud.

2 Restrictions on entering/leaving/berthing Some ports and anchorages may be dangerous or even impossible to enter or leave in some winds or sea states. They may be tidal. They may be unlit, ruling out a night entry/departure. If you have to clear customs and immigration then know precisely where you are expected to anchor or berth.

3 Lights You must know the position, characteristic and range of all lights, and if sailing down a lit channel, the course, distance and ETE between each light. This is especially

Pico, the highest point in Portugal is immediately opposite Horta harbour. If it is wearing a cloud cap then bad weather is on its way and it is not a good time to leave.

important for arrival ports. After days, perhaps weeks at sea you may be overexcited, completely exhausted or both and more than ready to make mistakes.

4 Communications Know the port VTS channels.

Departure pilotage
This is your route out of the harbour or anchorage to your point of departure where you begin passage-making. Even if you have a chart plotter, pilotage means using Mark 1 eyeball. The plotter confirms what you already know. A point of departure is chosen to be clear of all coastal hazards and points you towards your first waypoint on the passage-making element of your voyage.

Passage-making
Ideally, passage-making is plodding from one waypoint to another en route to your point of arrival but when theory conflicts with reality, change your plan. The most likely clashes come from winds blowing from an unexpected direction or altering course either to miss bad weather or to pick up better weather. Before modifying your plan, take a moment to evaluate the information that is giving you second thoughts. Only make changes if you are satisfied that the new information is reliable.

Arrival pilotage
This is the mirror image of departure pilotage, taking you from the point of arrival to your berth.

Weather and currents
Your choice of route is largely determined by the expected weather and currents between you and your destination. At the planning stage, all you can do is use the information on routeing (pilot) charts and dry-sail each option and find which suits you best. As a rule, this exercise

gives a fair overall picture of what you can expect but when using average winds, seas and currents there can be significant departures from 'the average' along your route and you must change your route accordingly.

Limitations to departure/arrival Wind direction or strength, sea state or visibility may be such that it is imprudent to leave or enter harbour. If the latter applies then the decision to stay out must be made in good time so that you can either divert to a harbour of refuge or heave-to without any risk. In deciding when conditions are unsuitable you must take into account the performance envelope of your boat and the strengths (and weaknesses) of yourself and your crew.

Weather trends From the moment you begin passage planning, compare each daily forecast against the actual weather experienced. This gives you a feel for the pattern behind today's weather and helps you to judge the accuracy of tomorrow's forecast. If for some reason you miss a forecast, you can make a fair attempt at drawing up your own.

Weather forecasting en route Sources of weather forecasts en route are discussed in Chapter 11. Note the time each forecast is broadcast. Put all the times into the same time zone and list them in the sequence they are broadcast during the day. GMT is a good choice and there should be one clock aboard which shows GMT so that there are no complicated sums to work out at the time of the next broadcast.

Single observer forecasts Regularly log the barometric pressure, temperature, wind direction and strength, sea state, cloud cover and type. Ideally this should be done hourly but, short-crewed on a long passage, this is not going to happen. Investing in an electronic weather station which holds details of a readings of a day or more could be a wise investment. Changes in the readings should be in accordance with the forecast weather. If not, then it is possible that your earliest warning of a change in your weather comes not from the forecast but these local changes.

Timings

Your expected time en route (ETE) is the Great Circle distance divided by your average speed made good. At the planning stage, it is tempting to knock a knot or two off your boat's maximum speed, take the answer as your average speed and use it to calculate your ETE. If your boat's maximum speed is seven knots your average speed becomes five or six knots and the 3000 miles from the Canaries to the Caribbean takes 21–25 days. As you are in the Trades and the favourable North Equatorial Current, you may consider knocking a day off. You will be disappointed. Even on a Trade Wind passage there are calms where you spend days chasing zephyrs, gales where you are hove-to, and the North Equatorial Current is not a conveyor belt running to a schedule but a maze of swirls and eddies. Unless you are driving the boat flat out all the time, your average speed will be close to half your boat's maximum speed.

Some passages involve crossing time zones. On an ocean passage ship time is adjusted every few days so that it more closely reflects local time. Traditionally, ship time changes at local noon. It also helps to know when you cross from one time zone to another and whether or not it is adjusted for some daylight-saving scheme.

Know the times of sun and moon rise and set as well as the moon's phase.

Communications

Write down the times and frequencies of:

- Any radio nets you intend to use.
- Stations broadcasting weather forecasts and weather faxes.
- Port working and VTS channels for departure port, arrival port and ports of refuge.
- Coast radio stations.

Pin this list up somewhere near the chart table.

Formalities

If sailing from one country to another then, before leaving, you must clear out with customs, immigration and perhaps the harbour authorities. When that is done, the following documents must be stowed safely in a waterproof container in the crash (grab) bag.

Ship's papers

- Registration documentation.
- Clearance papers.
- Insurance certificate together with details on how to contact your insurance company.
- Evidence that tax has been paid on vessel.
- Ship's radio licence.

Personal documents

- Passports.
- Certificates of competence.
- Radio licence. At least one member of crew should hold a radio operator's licence.
- Medical insurance documentation.
- Cash/credit and debit cards.

Shore contacts

Every boat should have a nominated shore contact whose particulars are logged with the Coastguard. Before departure, pass details of each passage to your shore contact and confirm your arrival with them when you reach your destination.

If you have an SSB transceiver there is always a choice of radio nets whose participants keep track of your progress en route. If you have a satellite phone then keeping your nearest and dearest up to date, even from the middle of the ocean, is straightforward. If you call them on a regular schedule then one or two missed calls warns them that something is amiss. A couple more missed calls and they should alert the authorities. If you do not have a satellite phone and are not taking part in a SSB net then on longer voyages your shore contacts endure several weeks of silence.

Even if you have a satellite phone or plan to participate in an SSB net it is a good idea to tell your shore contact by snail or email of:

- Your destination.
- Your ETD.
- Your ETA.
- Action to be taken by shore contact if you do not contact them within X hour(s) of ETA (*X varies with the passage*).

- Names of everyone onboard with details of their shore contacts and telephone numbers.
- Estimated length of time at sea.
- Description of boat including sail numbers.
- List of safety equipment carried.

In the UK, the Coastguard operates the CG66 Voluntary Safety Identification Scheme. CG66 registration Forms can be obtained on line at https://mcanet.mcga.gov.uk/public/cg66/ or from your local marina or sailing club or any Coastguard Co-ordination Centre or Sector Base, MCA Marine Office or RNLI boathouse. The information requested includes:

- Name of vessel
- Type of vessel
- Size and colour of vessel
- Radio
- Navigation equipment carried
- Lifesaving equipment carried
- Your usual area of operation
- Berth or mooring
- Details of a shore contact.

Send completed forms to your nearest Coastguard Co-ordination Centre. The scheme is free. Many countries run similar schemes.

In UK waters you can advise the Coastguard by VHF of your passage when you leave and of your safe arrival when you reach port. Further afield, the role of Coastguard is carried out by your shore contact.

Even so it is still a good idea to register with the Coastguard. If you do run into trouble and activate your EPIRB then the Coastguard can contact your shore contact and keep them informed.

Finally

A good passage plan is the result of much hard work but you are not chipping it into stone. As Odysseus discovered when man plans, the gods play the game by their rules. Once underway your task as skipper is to monitor the execution of your plan and continuously modify it to more closely reflect reality. Without a plan, every change means that you are inventing and reinventing the wheel from scratch. With a plan you are tweaking the existing model. This promises a better and faster response, keeps the additional workload on yourself and the crew to a minimum and gives your crew the impression that you are in control.

chapter 17 Planning your route

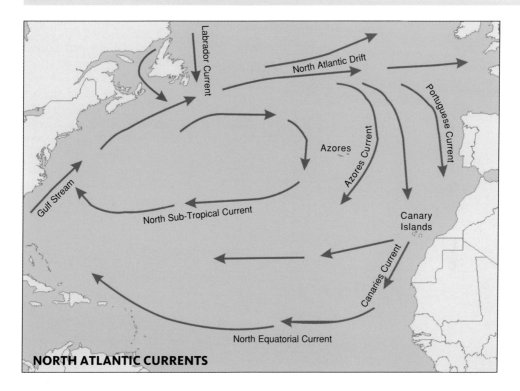

NORTH ATLANTIC CURRENTS

As departure approaches you can expect to experience a few moments of apprehension and doubt. When the idea of an Atlantic crossing first popped into your mind you would have sailed without a second thought but as your sailing date nears your concerns grow stronger. It is a form of nautical stage fright. The trip round the coast to Falmouth is invaluable as a shake-down cruise. For most sailors this is the first longish sail of the season: the first time gear is worked hard and the first chance for you to find your sea legs. Don't forget, you also need to carry out your sea trials.

As the *The Sober Sailor's Sensible Bedside Handbook* puts it, 'A properly planned transatlantic cruise is a series of day sails to make new friends and discover new cruising grounds separated by the occasional and unavoidable longer passage.' On the traditional tradewind route, only three voyages are over 1000 miles. There are a couple of passages consisting of a few hundred miles and the rest is day sailing ... that's right, *day* sailing.

Key ports

If you insist on looking at the circuit as a whole, there is the risk that you will fret over difficulties that may never arise. Long before you sail, the terrors of these illusory fears can build up in your mind. You lose the knack of dealing with the here and now and start worrying about what might happen in a far away, never-to-be future. The most valuable advice for anyone

KEY PORTS

In the planning phase some ports stand out as the starting point for a longer than normal passage. When you break your Atlantic crossing into a number of separate legs you are not committed to making this passage. Instead, at each of these key ports you can choose your next destination from a range of options.

Once west of the Canaries then you are probably committed to reaching the Caribbean but by then you will have made three fairly lengthy passages and are in a far better position to make an informed decision.

Key ports	Options
Falmouth to La Coruña	**1** Falmouth to La Coruña via Brittany **2** Mediterranean via French Canals **3** Azores and to the Caribbean **4** Madeira and to the Canaries **5** West coast circumnavigation of UK **6** Go home
La Coruña to Lisbon	**1** Iberian cruise **2** Falmouth direct **3** Falmouth via Brittany **4** Azores and to the Caribbean **5** Madeira and to the Canaries
Viano do Castelo/ Lagos to Madeira/ Porto Santo	**1** Gibraltar and the Mediterranean **2** Canaries direct **3** Use as cruising base for a season
Madeira to Canaries	**1** North Africa and the Mediterranean **2** Gibraltar and the Mediterranean **3** Azores and home
Canaries to Caribbean	**1** Iberia direct **2** Gibraltar and Mediterranean **3** Azores and home **4** Use as cruising base for a season or more

planning an Atlantic circuit, is take it one port at a time and see how far you can go. Sailing is for pleasure and this cruise should be fun.

It is a good idea to break up the cruise into small, easily-digested legs which will help you and your crew to concentrate your minds on achievable goals. First draw up a list of key ports. A key port is one where you choose between a long committing passage and a range of shorter passages. Falmouth is a good example. You can sail directly across the Bay of Biscay for La Coruña or make for the Mediterranean and the Canaries via the French canals. You can also hug the French coast with a detour through the Channel Islands. Even if the decision is to go home, then the return passage can be a lazy cruise zigzagging up the Channel or sailing up the west coast round Britain.

The passages

I have given each passage a route number and information to help you plan your trip. Co-ordinates are given to place you in the approaches to the start and finish ports.

No port information is given because changes happen so quickly that even the most up-to-date and detailed harbour guide is out-of-date before it is printed.

Weather

The likely weather conditions given are based upon data extracted from pilot charts. These give averages. An average is a mathematical fiction that conceals extremes. If you put your head in an oven and your feet in a fridge then, on average, you are warm. The weather data describes, within reason, the conditions you can expect, but do not be surprised if you encounter something entirely different and must modify your plans and route accordingly.

Passage times

The estimated times en route for each passage are based upon a 35ft (10.6m) heavy displacement sloop and a minimum sailing speed of one knot. Below one knot you must switch the engine on to maintain your average speed. Obviously, smaller yachts take longer

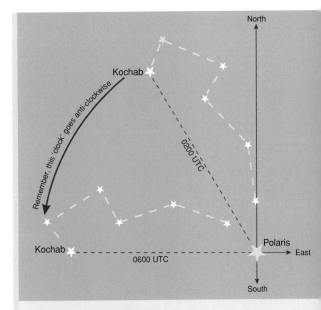

THE POLAR CLOCK

In the northern hemisphere you can pretend that the Pole Star is the centre of a clock face and the Little Dipper (Ursa Minor), or Kochab, is the hand. Imagine one line running north-south through Polaris and another line running east-west. These are the reference points for your clock but they cannot represent 3, 6, 9 or 12 o'clock because Kochab circles Polaris anticlockwise. Find Kochab, note its position relative to Polaris and look at your watch. This is your start time and for every hour, Kochab will move 15 degrees anticlockwise. Looking at your watch may be cheating but it is the easiest way of calibrating this 'clock' and after a couple of nights you can probably manage without your watch.

and larger yachts are quicker but not by as much as you would expect.

Actual daily mileage and average daily mileage are very different. Some days the winds are kind and you romp along. Other days you stand still. Based on almost 150 small boat crossings of the Atlantic from 1886 to the 1960s and regardless of the improvements in design and equipment over this period and whether or not they were sailing east to west or west to east, their average speed for the whole trip worked out at half their maximum hull speed (Maximum hull speed = 1.4 ÷LWL knots). After 1960 racing yachts dominate the readily accessible published data and skew the figures. The record for crossing the Atlantic under sail is less than seven days!

Your average speed also depends on how you choose to sail your boat. A racing boat chases the slightest wind shift, changes sails at the least puff and trims sails all day long. A cruising boat sets the sails up and leaves them alone. This is not idleness. It is relatively easy to get a boat moving at 80 per cent efficiency for 50 per cent effort. Then the law of diminishing returns kicks in and every percentage increase above 80 per cent demands another 10 or 20 per cent effort. Unless there is a good reason to drive the crew hard, there is rarely the manpower or motivation on cruising boats to work so energetically for so little return.

Ocean navigation

Not that long ago, attempting to cross an ocean without being competent at celestial navigation would have been criticised as foolhardy, and while it may not be a black art, there is as much skill in using the tables that accompany the arithmetic of astro-navigation as there is in understanding what you are doing. On small boats, and sometimes not so small boats, pinpoint accuracy is rare and, at best, a fix is only possible two or three times a day: between times, positions are obtained from DR calculations.

Columbus relied exclusively on DR for his first crossing. His first attempt at finding his latitude by celestial navigation was made at anchor off Cuba. He used a Quadrant, and his sums had an error of 20°, which put him close to Cape Cod. His subsequent efforts were no better and to the end Columbus remained a confirmed DR navigator.

He would have loved GPS. It has changed navigation from an art to a branch of computer literacy. No knowledge or understanding is required beyond the ability to press keys and follow the on-screen commands. Nowadays, anyone who can use a cellphone can navigate.

Yacht transport

If long-distance voyaging has no appeal but you still wish to cruise the Caribbean then you can hire a delivery crew who, for a price, will take your boat to the destination of your choice.

Alternatively you can arrange to ship yourself and your boat out. Some carriers like Dockwise Yacht Transport (DYT) have ships designed to carry motor and sailing yachts from Europe to the Caribbean and back. In port they behave like a floating dock to allow the yachts to sail aboard. Water is then pumped out of the vessel's tanks and the yachts are fastened to cradles welded to the deck. Fresh water, electrical and sewage connections are provided to allow the yacht's crew (the limit is one but more might be possible) to live on board. Prices include three meals a day and crossings take about 16 days. The time can be spent refitting your boat. Others carry yachts as deck cargo. The following list of contact addresses is far from exhaustive.

DYT USA
Dockwise Yacht Transport LLC
1535 S.E. 17th St, Suite 200
Ft. Lauderdale, Florida 33316
USA
Tel.: + 1 954 525 8707
Toll Free: 1 866 SHIP DYT (744 7398)
Fax: + 1 954 525 8711
Email: dyt.usa@dockwise-yt.com

DYT Europe
Dockwise Yacht Transport Europe Srl.
Corso Paganini 39/2
16125 GENOVA
Italy
Tel.: + 39 010 2789411
Fax: + 39 06 91594458
Email: dyt.europe@dockwise-yt.com

Sevenstar Yacht Transport b.v.
Radarweg 36
1042 AA Amsterdam
P.O. box 409
1000 AK Amsterdam
The Netherlands
Tel: +31 20 - 4488590
Fax: +31 20 - 4488596
Email: info@sevenstar.nl
Website: www.sevenstar.nl

Sevenstar Yacht Transport b.v. UK Agent
Yacht Shipping Ltd
Bowling Green House
1 Orchard Place
Southampton
SO14 3PX United Kingdom
Tel: +44 238 022 3671
Fax: +44 238 033 0880/1
Email: info@ysl.wainwrightgroup.com
Website: www.yachtshipping.com

Sevenstar Yacht Transport b.v. US Agent
Global Yacht Transport Agencies, Florida
2401 PGA Blvd., Suite 230
Palm Beach Gardens, FL 33410
Tel: +1 5616227997
Fax: +1 5616227211
Email: info@globalyachttransport.com
or
Global Yacht Transport Agencies, Newport RI
Tel: +1 6035688188
Email: Durham@globalyachttransport.com

Sevenstar Yacht Transport b.v. also has representatives in Australia, Finland, Germany, Monaco, New Zealand, Spain and Turkey

chapter 18 Direct routes to the Caribbean

The few who choose to sail direct to the Caribbean from Europe are either in a great hurry or challenging for the record as perhaps the fastest, smallest, oldest or oddest boat to cross. For some reason the Atlantic attracts such attempts.

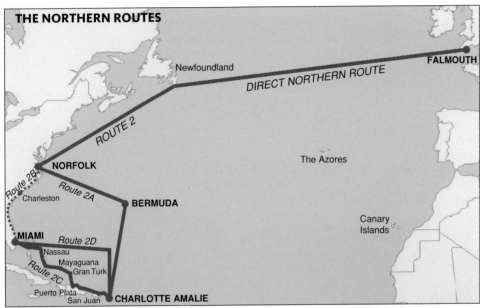

Dusk approaches in the harbour in St John, US Virgin Islands.

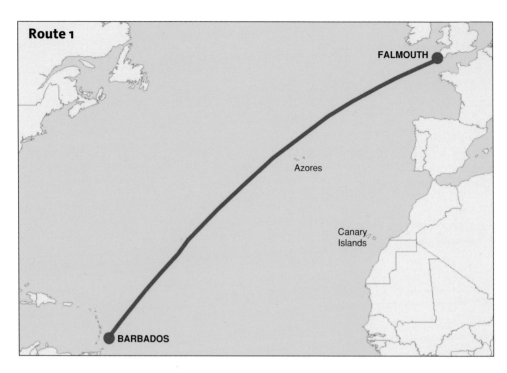

ROUTE 1: The direct Trade Wind Route • Falmouth to Barbados

Route 1 Passage Information	
START: FALMOUTH 50° 1´N 5° 6´W	
Time of year	May/June
Great Circle Distance	3470nm
ETE	24 days
Average SMG	6.2 knots
Average wind direction	250°
Average wind speed	11.8 knots (Bft F4)
Chance of calms	3%
Chance of gales	0.6%
Percentage sailing time beating	0%
Percentage sailing time close reaching	17% (4 days)
Percentage sailing time broad reaching	83% (20 days)
Percentage sailing time running	0%
Average current drift/set	170°/0.5 knots
Average wave height	4.3ft (1.3m)
Average sea temperature	69°F (21°C)
DESTINATION: BARBADOS 12° 55´N 59° 92´W	

This is a variation on the Trade Wind Route passing within sight of the Azores. Choosing the best time for this passage is choosing the lesser of two evils. May or June promises decent weather crossing Biscay, but by the time you are south of the Azores the hurricane season has begun. You may be lucky, maybe not; earlier in the year the odds on meeting poor weather in Biscay rise dramatically. In April the figure for gales is 2.8 per cent and in March 5.9 per cent.

If you choose to sail in November, outside the hurricane season, there is an 8 per cent chance of a gale crossing Biscay. In December it is 11 per cent but there is little chance of encountering a hurricane when you reach the tropics. If you must sail non-stop across the Atlantic then you may wish to consider the northern route.

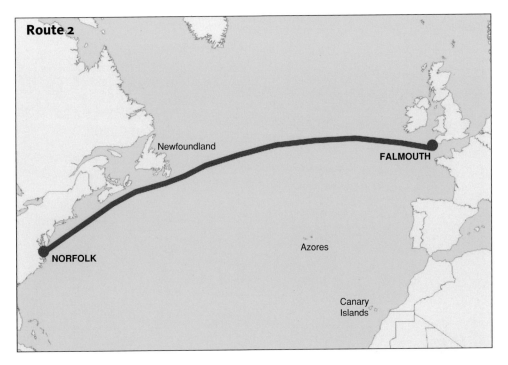

Route 2

Newfoundland

FALMOUTH

NORFOLK

Azores

Canary
Islands

ROUTE 2: The direct Northern Route • Falmouth to Norfolk, Virginia

Pioneered by the early OSTAR racers looking for the shortest route across the Atlantic, the northern route tries to strike a balance between avoiding the Gulf Stream to the south, ice to the north and sticking as closely as possible to the Great Circle Route between Europe and America. It rides the winds blowing round the top of the depressions rushing eastwards across the Atlantic. It is only for the hardiest of sailors and the best prepared boats. Landfall is in ports on the Eastern Seaboard of the USA between New York and Norfolk.

It is the fastest route across the Atlantic, but if you are aiming for the Caribbean it is, in the end, no quicker than the traditional Trade Wind Route. On arriving in the USA, the summer ought to be spent exploring northern waters beyond the hurricane zone. Then, when autumn arrives, you can either make another long ocean passage (Route 2A) to the Caribbean or join the boats following the Intra Coastal Waterway to Miami (Route 2B) and then island hopping to the US Virgin Islands.

Route 2 Passage Information	
START: FALMOUTH 50° 1´ N 5° 6´ W	
Time of year	June
Great Circle Distance	3075nm
ETE	30 days
Average SMG	4.3 knots
Average wind direction	235°
Average wind speed	14 knots (Bft F4)
Chance of calms	3.6%
Chance of gales	1.2%
Percentage sailing time beating	0%
Percentage sailing time close reaching	2% (1 day)
Percentage sailing time broad reaching	40% (12 days)
Percentage sailing time running	58% (17 days)
Average current drift/set	136°/0.5 knots
Average wave height	4.4ft (1.3m)
Average sea temperature	52°F (11°C)
DESTINATION: NORFOLK VIRGINIA 37°N 76° 2´ W	

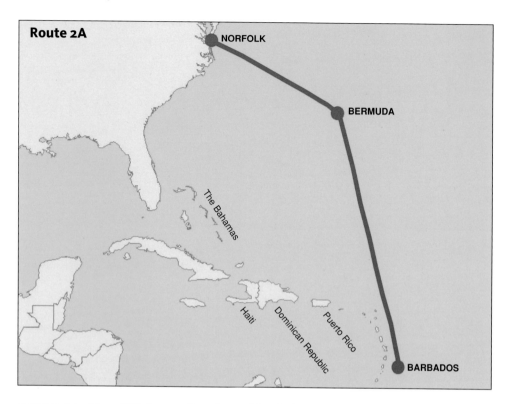

Route 2A

NORFOLK

BERMUDA

The Bahamas

Haiti

Dominican Republic

Puerto Rico

BARBADOS

ROUTE 2A: The Offshore Route • Norfolk to the Caribbean

Route 2A Passage Information	
START: NORFOLK VIRGINIA 37°N 76° 2´W	
Time of year	October/November
Great Circle Distance	1440nm
ETE	20 days
Average SMG	3.7 knots
Average wind direction	083°
Average wind speed	12.8 knots (Bft F4)
Chance of calms	2.3%
Chance of gales	1.4%
Percentage sailing time beating	38% (7.5 days)
Percentage sailing time close reaching	60% (12 days)
Percentage sailing time broad reaching	2% (0.5 days)
Percentage sailing time running	0%
Average current set/drift	302°/0.5 knots
Average wave height	4.7ft (1.4m)
Average sea temperature	78.3°F (25.7°C)
DESTINATION: BARBADOS 13° 01´N 59° 31´W	

This is a demanding sail. If you are not beating then you are close-reaching. Little wonder most yachts take a break in Bermuda (32° 22´N 65° 4´W). The majority make this passage in October when they may choose to join an organised rally such as that organised by the Cruising Rally Association

To avoid contrary currents, yachts must first cross the Gulf Stream. It is customary to time the crossing of the Gulf Stream with the eastward passage of a ridge of high pressure between low pressure systems. Although the Gulf Stream generally follows the line of the coast, loops and whirls branch off so that it is a maze of contrary currents and temperatures. It is advisable to check the US National Weather Service website's satellite pictures of the Gulf Stream in order to plot the best course across.

Once across the Gulf Stream most boats sail directly for Bermuda where they pick up the north-east Trades before making for the Eastern Caribbean.

ROUTE 2B: The Intracoastal Waterway • Norfolk to Miami

The Intracoastal Waterway (ICW) is over 1100 miles of toll free canals and natural inland waterways running the length of the eastern seaboard from Miami to Norfolk, Virginia with links north into Canada and the Great Lakes. It can hardly be described as a direct route to the Caribbean in the sense that it is non-stop. It is more a collection of leisurely day sails with numerous side trips to explore shoreside attractions. It is popular with many American cruisers who, as winter approaches, use it to travel south towards the warmer waters of Florida and the Caribbean.

The idea of linking the natural inland waterways along this coast began in 1643 when a narrow half-mile long canal was dug to link the Annisquam River and Gloucester Harbour in Massachusetts. This is reckoned to be the oldest part of today's ICW. Between 1837 and 1911 the US Congress authorised feasibility studies of different parts of the route and piecemeal work was carried out; but the push to complete a sheltered inshore passage from Florida northwards had to wait until 1919 when, direct from their success at the Panama Canal, the US Army Corps of Engineers began the work to complete the Intracoastal Waterway. It was finally finished in 1936. Starting from Key West in Florida it runs north 1139.5 miles to Norfolk although it is possible to continue to Trenton, New Jersey. Purists claim this is going beyond the ICW.

It has a nominal depth of 12 feet but in places it may be no more than seven to nine feet deep. It is lit so night sailing is possible, but movement is normally confined to daylight hours; for yachts this means 50 to 80 miles a day. Numerous bridges cross it. Fixed bridges with 69 feet vertical clearance have replaced many opening bridges and the remaining bridges mostly open on request, rarely slowing progress. Formerly you warned bridges of your approach with three blasts on the foghorn but nowadays they prefer a call on channel VHF 13

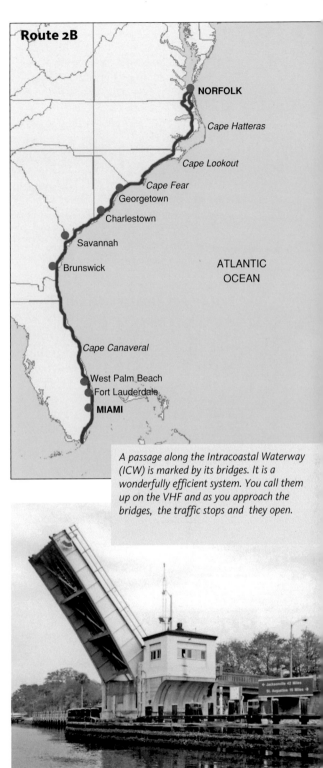

Route 2B

NORFOLK

Cape Hatteras

Cape Lookout

Cape Fear

Georgetown

Charlestown

Savannah

Brunswick

ATLANTIC OCEAN

Cape Canaveral

West Palm Beach

Fort Lauderdale

MIAMI

A passage along the Intracoastal Waterway (ICW) is marked by its bridges. It is a wonderfully efficient system. You call them up on the VHF and as you approach the bridges, the traffic stops and they open.

or 9. Some, like the Bridge of Lions in St Augustine, open to a timetable and if you miss an opening then you are stuck. If you are in a hurry then the twists and turns in Georgia and the Carolinas can halve the distance made good and challenge anyone's sense of direction.

There are marinas beyond number. Details are in Skipper Bob's book on Intracoastal Waterway marinas. Dockage rates vary from 50 cents to $4 a foot plus electricity but members of BoatUS often receive a discount. It is usually possible to anchor (Skipper Bob's ICW Anchorages for details) though for the first time since leaving Europe it is necessary to allow for tidal range. This has more than an element of guess work. The tide enters through the barrier islands and rushes through the ever-branching channels as it pleases. Within the same mile it is possible to have the flood with you and against you.

To Europeans this is 'red-right-returning' buoyage country, and navigation is from one red or green beacon to the next. Fine, except without warning they change to follow the direction of flood tide and the screeching nag of the echo-sounder is explained by missing a change of buoyage and leaving the channel. There is no middle ground. People either like the ICW or hate it. Some prefer to have their boats trucked south to Florida. The savings in time and marina charges en route pays for the cost of transport.

ROUTE 2C: Norfolk to the Caribbean • Miami to Charlotte Amalie, United States Virgin Islands (USVI)

Once in Miami there is a choice of cruising southwards through the Bahamas and the Turks and Caicos to Charlotte Amalie in the USVI. This route is mostly day sailing and would not be undertaken before late November or early December. There is about 1300NM of sailing but there are so many byways to explore that it is impossible to give a timescale. The passages between the Bahamas to the Turks and Caicos and from there to the Dominican Republic are the only ones requiring an overnight sail.

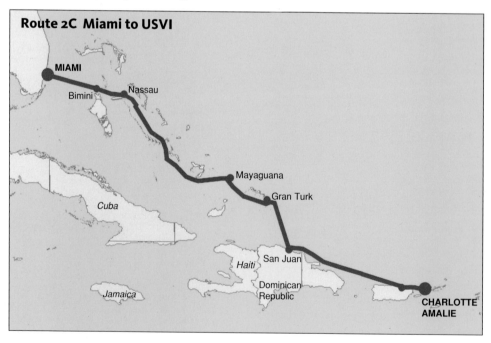

Most boats choose to wait in Florida for a suitable weather window and enter the Bahamas at Grand Bahama or Bimini. Due allowance for the Gulf Stream must be made when laying a course across it. Once in the Bahamas, yachts work their way south towards Mayaguana and then jump across to the Turks and Caicos Islands before heading south to the Dominican Republic and along the north coast of Puerto Rico to the Virgin Islands.

ROUTE 2D: The Offshore Route • Miami to the USVI direct

From Miami it is also possible to sail directly to the Caribbean. The likelihood of adverse winds and currents on this route means beginning with a long board of over 800 miles out into the Atlantic along 25°N, and turning south around 65°W. Hurrying through the more usual route via the Bahamas, the Turks and Caicos and the Greater Antilles would probably take about a week longer but be a more pleasant sail.

Route 2D Passage Information

START: MIAMI 25° 40´N 80° 15´W

Time of year	October/November
Great Circle Distance	1225nm
ETE	14.1 days
Average SMG	3.6 knots
Average wind direction	062°
Average wind speed	13 knots (Bft F4)
Chance of calms	3.0%
Chance of gales	0.7%
Percentage sailing time beating	19% (3 days)
Percentage sailing time close reaching	81% (11.1 days)
Percentage sailing time broad reaching	0%
Percentage sailing time running	0%
Average current set/drift	292°/0.5 knots
Average wave height	4.5ft (1.4m)
Average sea temperature	79.2°F (26.2°C)

DESTINATION: CHARLOTTE AMALIE 18° 22´N 64° 47´W

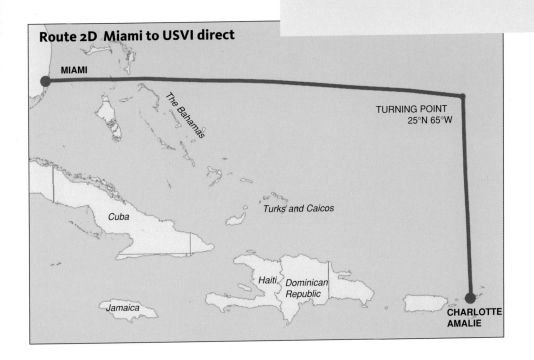

Route 2D Miami to USVI direct

chapter 19 The trade wind route

This is easily the most popular route between Europe and the Caribbean. Contrary to received wisdom it is not a non-stop passage but a series of gentle day sails interrupted by three or four long passages. It takes about six months and is not for those in a hurry.

Route 3 Leg 1 Passage Information	
START: FALMOUTH 50° 1´N 5° 6´W	
Time of year	May/June
Great Circle Distance	415nm
ETE	3.7 days
Average SMG	4.6 knots
Average wind direction	323°
Average wind speed	10.8 knots (Bft F4)
Chance of calms	3.7%
Chance of gales	0.9%
Percentage sailing time beating	0%
Percentage sailing time close reaching	0%
Percentage sailing time broad reaching	80% (3 days)
Percentage sailing time running	20% (0.7 days)
Average current set/drift	210°/0.4 knots
Average wave height	4.5ft (1.4m)
Average sea temperature	58.6°F (14.8°C)
DESTINATION: LA CORUÑA 43° 26´N 8° 28´W	

ROUTE 3: The Trade Wind Route, Leg 1 • Falmouth to La Coruña

The usual time to make this passage is in May or June and it is important to wait for a window of four or five days good weather before setting out. From Start Point, the rhumb line route brings you close to Ushant with its strong tides and busy Traffic Separation Scheme.

Square riggers, fearful that a westerly gale would leave them stuck in Biscay, sailed west from Start Point until the Pole Star was on their backstay and then turned south. It is still

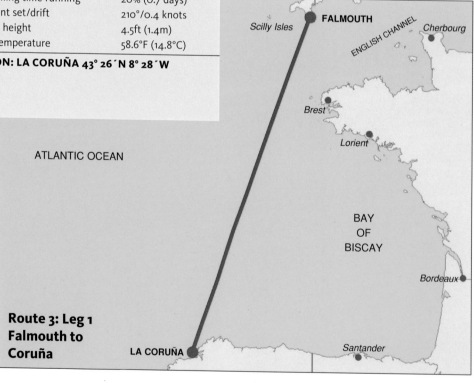

Route 3: Leg 1 Falmouth to Coruña

good advice. It gives a good slant if the wind turns south westerly and sea room to sit out a gale if you are caught out whilst crossing Biscay. Unfortunately sailing west involves some windward work but this can be broken by stops in Penzance or the Scilly Isles. Boats coming down the Irish Sea may wish to consider starting from somewhere on Ireland's south coast such as Dunmore East or Cork.

Biscay's fearsome reputation makes this leg a considerable challenge, not technically, but if you have not sailed off soundings before, it is a great stride into the unknown. The responsibility for yourself and your crew weighs heavily and a thousand 'what if' questions, for which you have no answers, spin round your brain like a demented merry-go-round. The only cure for this is to cast off.

ROUTE 3: The Trade Wind Route, Leg 2 • La Coruña to Lisbon

The 350 mile passage along the Spanish and Portuguese coasts is a wonderful cruise in its own right. Once round Cabo Villano, the north westerly winds, better known as the Portugese Trades, blow steadily. Summer fogs cling to the valleys and from a few miles

offshore, the tops of the hills can be seen peeking above the fog. GPS has removed any uncertainty that poor visibility brings but there is a fairly heavy inshore traffic and a good look-out is essential.

Galacia is a place to linger and explore, not pass by. It is part of Europe's Celtic fringe: a fascinating and largely unspoilt cruising ground, proud of its seafaring traditions and eager to welcome visitors; it is an ideal place to spend the dog days of summer. The coastline is saw-toothed by flooded river valleys called rias, each an easy day-sail from its neighbours. July and August is the fiesta season. Every Spanish city, town, hamlet and crossroads has its own patron saint and every saint's birthday is an excuse for a holiday. This grand celebration is announced days beforehand by fusillades of fireworks that sound like the Spanish army rehearsing for war. On weekdays you can find the nearest fiesta by using the lazy Portuguese Trade winds to propel you towards the sounds of battle. Saturday and Sunday bring fireworks galore, dancing and lots of music. Each fiesta must take months of preparation but even in a city like Vigo there is a sense of great spontaneity, of everyone doing their own thing and having a good time. Progress south slows to a cheerful crawl, fuelled by grilled sardines, churos and red wine.

The Rio Minho, a few miles south of Bayona, marks the border between Spain and Portugal and there is a dramatic change in the

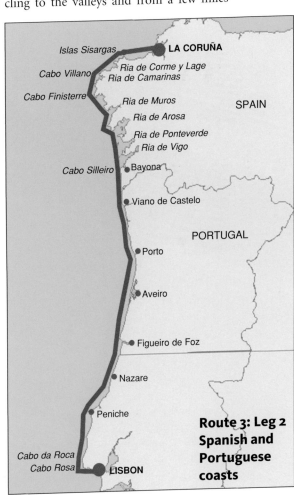

Route 3: Leg 2
Spanish and Portuguese coasts

coastline. The wide mouthed rias with their creeks and inlets are replaced by an undulating cliffy shoreline broken by rivers entering the sea over shallow bars. When heavy onshore weather displaces the Portuguese Trades, this shore is a fearsome place. Entering or leaving harbour is dangerous and sometimes prohibited by the authorities. If at sea you stay out, and if in harbour you retire to the nearest café and thank your lucky stars.

Somewhere between Viano do Castelo in the north of Portugal and Lagos on the Algarve it is time to find another key port and make a final decision whether to continue towards Madeira or make for the Mediterranean. Returning north is not a sensible option unless you are prepared to motor into the teeth of the Portuguese Trades. It has been done but only by those who know no better. The last option is to leave your boat in one of the many marinas and use that as a base for a season or two. The journey home by air or land has not yet become horribly expensive.

ROUTE 3: The Trade Wind Route, Leg 3 • Lisbon to Porto Santo and Madeira

Route 3 Leg 3 Passage Information	
START: LISBON 38° 40´ N 9° 16´ W	
Time of year	September
Great Circle Distance	475nm
ETE	4 days
Average SMG	5.0 knots
Average wind direction	359°
Average wind speed	11.6 knots (Bft F4)
Chance of calms	3.7%
Chance of gales	0.1%
Percentage sailing time beating	0%
Percentage sailing time close reaching	2% (0.8 days)
Percentage sailing time broad reaching	98% (3.2 days)
Percentage sailing time running	0%
Average current set/drift	184°/0.4 knots
Average wave height	4.6ft (1.4m)
Average sea temperature	69.6°F (20.9°C)
DESTINATION: I DE PORTO SANTO 33° 7´ N 16° 15´ W	

Lisbon is a convenient jumping-off point for the long passage to the Maderias. The voyage should be made in late August or early September, before the equinoctial gales begin battering the coast. The Maderias are made up of the islands of Maderia, Porto Santo and the Ilhas Desertas. You can make directly for Maderia but most boats first head for Porto Santo.

Porto Santo

Only 10 miles long and 4 miles wide, Porto Santo is a small target in a big ocean. Boats from the Mediterranean join at Porto Santo after a passage of 575nm from Gibraltar. They experience very similar weather conditions to boats from the mainland and for 90 per cent of the time are on a close reach. From both the Mediterranean and mainland Portugal it is a longer passage than the Biscay crossing but it does not bring as many butterflies. Living aboard for two or three months has honed your passage-making skills and increased your confidence.

The island's only harbour, Porto do Porto Santo, is on the south coast, and yachts sailing from the Mediterranean, Spain, Portugal and Northern Europe all aim for the south-west corner of the island before racing for the finish line at the harbour. It is like Piccadilly Circus and where the Atlantic circuit really begins. From now on every yacht you meet intends to cross the Atlantic, and most are bluewater virgins, pleased to have come so far but uncertain of what lies ahead.

Porto Santo claims to have Maderia's only beach, and burying yourself in its sand to take advantage of its medicinal properties is a popular occupation with day trippers from Maderia.

Route 3: Leg 3 Lisbon/Gibraltar to Ilha de Porto Santo

LISBON

GIBRALTAR

I de Madeira   **I DE PORTO SANTO**

Funchal   Ilhas Desertas

A happy crew arrive at Porto Santo.

In the 15th century, Columbus married the daughter of the governor of Porto Santo and in 1995 his house, the beach and some windmills were the island's only tourist attractions. The rest of the island could star in a spaghetti western. Since then tourism has grown.

Watch out for the Porto Santo effect where mañana is a term of indecent haste. When Joao Goncalves Zarco and Tristao Vaz Teixeira became the first Europeans to land on Porto Santo in 1419 it took them a year to sail 26 miles and 'discover' Madeira.

Madeira

Although Madeira was uninhabited when Zarco eventually arrived, it is reckoned that the Phoenicians reached it first, and an Italian map dated 1351 (nearly 70 years before Zarco 'discovered' the island) shows both Maderia and Porto Santo. If you wish to explore Madeira but believe Funchal's marina will be too busy (visiting yachts raft several boats deep along the wall) and are reluctant to test the poor holding of the anchorage, there is a daily ferry and regular flights from Porto Santo. There is a new marina at Quinto do Lorde, at the eastern end of Maderia. This bay is also one of the very few anchorages on the island but it is some distance away from the bright lights. A day trip from there to Funchal leaves only a couple of hours to explore before catching the return bus. Once it was necessary to visit Madeira to obtain a permit to stop at the Salvage Islands on the way to the Canaries but now that can be arranged from Porto Santo. This, a combination of poor transport links and Funchal's crowded marina encourages some yachts to sail directly to the Canaries from Porto Santo.

It would be a pity to miss Madeira. Lacking a foreshore, Funchal has grown by spreading up the hillside and when you reach the top of the town it is traditional to slide back down in a wicker sledge. 'Slide' and 'sledge' are terms used loosely. The sledge looks like an armchair and its gravity defying slide rarely reaches a brisk walking pace. For the energetic there is levada walking. Levadas are irrigation channels cut into the hillside to bring water from the wet north of the island to the dry south. Slaves began digging them in the 16th century, often hanging over cliffs in baskets to carve out the channel. Now they stretch for over a thousand kilometres and walking the paths alongside is a popular and occasionally spectacular pastime. If you go hiking along the levadas wear boots and take waterproofs and warm clothing.

Apart from Porto Santo, the Madeiras include the Ilhas Desertas and the Ilhas Selvagems. Both are nature reserves and the Desertas are home to monk seals, which are one of the ten most threatened species on the list of animals near extinction.

ROUTE 3: The Trade Wind Route, Leg 4 • Funchal to Las Palmas

It is only three days sail from Madeira to the Canaries. A passage that would have once involved months of planning and been the highlight of a summer cruise is now looked upon as routine. Checklists are ticked, supplies of food, fuel and water topped up and when a suitable weather window appears, off you go.

After leaving Porto Santo or Madeira, if the weather is settled, spend a few days visiting the Ilhas Selvagems (Salvage Islands). This is a scattering of islands and associated, often uncharted, rocks and shoals arranged in two groups about ten miles apart. They lie, more or less, on the route between Madeira and the Canaries, waiting for a visit from the careless navigator, hence their name. They are now a nature reserve and uninhabited apart from a couple of wardens based on Selvagem Grande who will be delighted to see you and show you around their small world.

There are three official anchorages: two on Selvagem Grande and one on Selvagem Pequena that must be used, but they are not particularly good in unsettled weather. There are lights on both Selvagem Grande and Selvagem Pequena, but do not be surprised if either or both are not working.

After the Ilhas Selvagems it is usual to aim for the east end of the Canaries. Graciosa at the east end of the chain is good landfall and from there cruise slowly westwards through the archipelago, arriving on Gran Canaria, Tenerife or La Gomera by late October or early November.

Route 3 Leg 4 Passage Information	
START: FUNCHAL 32° 38´N 16° 59´W	
Time of year	October
Great Circle Distance	290nm
ETE	2.7 days
Average SMG	4.5 knots
Average wind direction	025°
Average wind speed	12 knots (Bft F4)
Chance of calms	3.4%
Chance of gales	0.4%
Percentage sailing time beating	0%
Percentage sailing time close reaching	44% (1 day)
Percentage sailing time broad reaching	39% (1 day)
Percentage sailing time running	17% (0.7 days)
Average current set/drift	231°/0.5 knots
Average wave height	4.7ft (1.4m)
Average sea temperature	71.6°F (22.0°C)
DESTINATION: GRACIOSA 29° 20´N 3° 32´W	

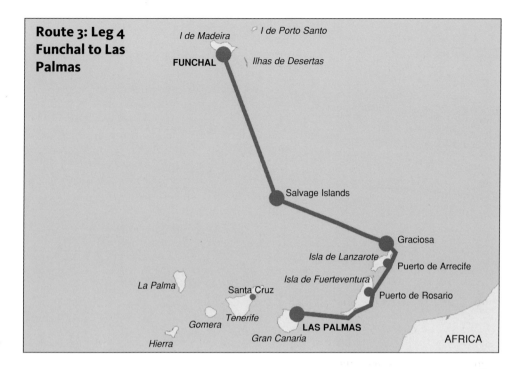

Route 3: Leg 4 Funchal to Las Palmas

I de Madeira

I de Porto Santo

FUNCHAL

Ilhas de Desertas

Salvage Islands

Graciosa

Isla de Lanzarote

Puerto de Arrecife

Isla de Fuerteventura

La Palma

Santa Cruz

Puerto de Rosario

Tenerife

Gomera

LAS PALMAS

Gran Canaria

Hierra

AFRICA

The King of Mauritania was so impressed by the fierce dogs (canis in Latin) found in the islands he called them the Dog Islands, but Pliny was right when he called them the 'Fortunate Isles'. The Arabs set up trading centres and they were followed by the Genoese, French and finally the Spanish whose claim to the islands was finally recognised in 1469.

The nine islands are part of a volcanic ridge and still have active volcanoes with around 20 major eruptions spread throughout the chain since 1341. The original islanders were the fair-skinned, blue-eyed, blond-haired Guanche who were wiped out by subsequent settlers. Little is known about the Guanche and there has been some fanciful speculation on their origins. Recently the remains of step pyramids similar to those found in Mexico, Peru and Mesopotamia were found on Tenerife and they provide food for thought about pre-Columbian links between the new and the old worlds. Did the Guanche gather each November in the Muelle Deportivo on Las Palmas to make ready for their transatlantic voyage?

During the season, Funchal marina is always crowded. Visitors raft up along the harbour wall.

ROUTE 3: The Trade Wind Route, Leg 5A • Las Palmas to Barbados

Route 3 Leg 5A Passage Information	
START: LAS PALMAS 27° 42´N 15° 37´W	
Time of year	November/December
Great Circle Distance	2560nm
ETE	23 days
Average SMG	4.6 knots
Average wind direction	079°
Average wind speed	13.7 knots (Bft F4)
Chance of calms	1.7%
Chance of gales	0.8%
Percentage sailing time beating	0%
Percentage sailing time close reaching	0%
Percentage sailing time broad reaching	57% (13 days)
Percentage sailing time running	43% (10 days)
Average current set/drift	262°/0.6 knots
Average wave height	5.2ft (1.6m)
Average sea temperature	74.7°F (23.8°C)
DESTINATION: BARBADOS 13° 01´N 59° 31´W	

You may have left home believing that each time you reached port, the locals would gather in their thousands to welcome the intrepid, but modest, transatlantic sailor. Nothing is further from the truth. When you arrive in port you will fight to find a berth, not your way through the welcoming crowds. In late autumn, the Muelle Deportivo at Las Palmas on Gran Canaria is crammed with vessels from Europe and the Mediterranean. Berths inside the marina are at a premium and the anchorage outside is crowded. The marinas along the island's south coast are fully booked months in advance.

This is the moment of truth. Sail south from here and the easy way back home is via the Caribbean. The air is heavy with views and news on bluewater passage-making, for amongst its other characteristics, the Muelle Deportivo is a rumour factory where whispers, especially horror stories, are quickly passed from boat to boat. The real surprise is not the number of boats crossing the Atlantic but that any sail at all.

Each year some two hundred boats leave with the ARC at the end of November. Ocean rallies are growing in popularity. The ARC, grand daddy of them all, was started by Jimmy Cornell in 1986 and sails each year from Las Palmas to Rodney Bay in St Lucia. Rallies are big business and very welcome at any port they visit but the number of boats involved can also temporarily stretch port facilities and amenities beyond breaking point. Some boats taking part in rallies believe that when they arrive at an official rally port of call they have first claim on what facilities are available. To them, anyone not in the rally is sailing on the cheap and 'independent' becomes a term of abuse. On the other hand, 'independents' regard themselves as the true guardians of the bluewater cruising traditions. In 1995 there was a club for non-ARC boats, the NARC. Membership was optional and free. It had its own flag, a yellow square defaced by the symbol of your choice, and its only rule was that there were none. The truth is that there is much to be said on both sides and enough sea for everyone.

Avoiding a late season hurricane will keep boats in the Canaries until the end of November or later. To make the most of the Caribbean season, the charter fleet begins leaving in mid-November which is early. ARC boats normally leave on the last weekend of November although some say this is still a little early. Waiting is no hardship. Even for single-handers, an Atlantic circuit is not a solitary pastime. By now you have earned full partying rights as a member of the maritime gipsy tribe.

The last minute refit

The Canaries are a good place to make those last minute modifications and improvements. With well over a thousand miles under the keel, opinions on what works and what doesn't have firmed up and there are a number of good chandlers and marine outlets in Las Palmas.

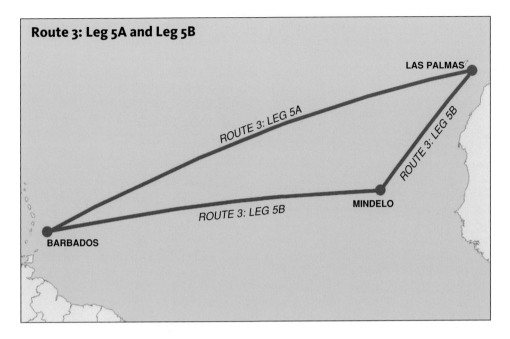

Route 3: Leg 5A and Leg 5B

LAS PALMAS

ROUTE 3: LEG 5A

ROUTE 3: LEG 5B

MINDELO

ROUTE 3: LEG 5B

BARBADOS

If they cannot supply what you need then it is easy and not too expensive to have equipment sent out from Europe or the USA or brought out by a new member of the crew. Lastly, and most importantly, there is access to a huge reservoir of skills. One of the main differences between a bluewater cruise and a summer holiday afloat is that the Bluewater Co-operative Inc supplements commercial shoreside facilities.

The bluewater co-operative

Circumstances encourage every bluewater sailor to be a jack of all trades although only a very few are master of all. The result is that in every anchorage there is a huge, informal pool of skills and on every cruiser is a hoard of hard-to-find odds and ends. Need an electrics specialist, a sailmaker, an engineer, a rigger, or a computer expert? Short of a widget with a left-handed thread? Somewhere amongst the mass of boats is the person with the expertise or item you need and it is possible they are looking for someone with your skills.

Crew changes

The Canaries are also a first-rate place for crew members to take a break and go home or to change over crews. Those with limited sailing time can fly out to join for the crossing to the Caribbean.

Flights

If you can pick up a spare seat on a holiday charter, a flight home can be very cheap. The first rule in keeping airfares down is to fly to and from airports with lots of international flights. If there is a significant number of package holiday flights so much the better. Flights to obscure destinations may be romantic but they cost more. Try to avoid internal connecting flights for they are always expensive. Ask around, somebody is bound to have made the same trip recently. Not every travel agent offers the same range of deals, some offer better value than others. Check out various ticket combinations. Sometimes it is cheaper to buy a return ticket even if only flying one way; avoid expensive high season flights, and, if possible, try to avoid a gap of over two months between flying out and returning. Most airlines consider this reason enough to charge more. Booking early can mean a cheap seat but this may restrict changing flights or dates.

The crossing

Although most boats leave the Canaries for the Lesser Antilles and a few for the Bahamas, it is not mandatory to make directly for the Caribbean. Some yachts head for the Cape Verde Islands, and then sail to the Caribbean. Others make for Brazil, French Guyana, Suriname or Guyana on the mainland of South America before cruising northwards for Trinidad and the Lesser Antilles. As the Caribbean becomes more and more developed, spending some of the season cruising the South American coast will become more attractive.

The greatest danger of the classic route is heading west too early and finding the calms of the Azores High. In winter this lurks west of the Canaries and sailing south-west until you are firmly in the Trades adds miles but proves quicker. The Trades may be found as far north as Madeira, but in the winter they follow the sun south and the space they once occupied is leased to light, variable winds called the Horse Latitudes. In some years these reach hundreds of miles south of the Canaries. In the old days they saw salty, shellbacked skippers throwing horses overboard when passages grew long and water and fodder ran short. Meet these winds and you may begin to believe that it would be quicker on horseback.

Days and nights are spent becalmed or chasing zephyrs with a half-life of minutes. It is rare for an absence of wind to be accompanied by a flat sea. There is always swell enough for the boom to sway, the sails to flap and anything loose to rattle, roll or creak. Nor are calms absolute. Soft breezes momentarily fill the sails and raise hopes high enough for them to be decently dashed. With yesterday's rubbish lying alongside there is a strong sense of going nowhere. No wonder the ancient mariner went mad.

When you do find the Trade Winds, sailing is mostly on a broad reach and the wind can blow from a force 2 to a 6 in the time it takes to make a cup of coffee but as long as the following seas remain regular, life is fine. Problems, and discomfort, come from seas that run across the grain. They always produce horrendous rolling but this is balanced by days and nights of easy seas and sailing down the glitter of moonshine under a star-filled sky.

Be prepared for set-backs to morale. For example, celebrating passing the halfway mark can bring home the fact that you are 1000 miles from the nearest beach. Far from arriving somewhere, you are in the middle of nowhere and not going anywhere very fast. There is a similar feeling in long-distance running. It is called the wall. The only remedy is to take a deep breath and shove the wall aside.

For those in a hurry, gennakers or cruising chutes are good sails but when you meet a mean-spirited, nasty-minded squall you need a strong crew to be absolutely confident of taking these large sails down quickly. Otherwise, you may find yourself over-canvassed and overpowered.

During the day, squalls, the bête noire of the Trades, give plenty of warning. Like Dickensian widows they dress in black with a veil of rain. The only question is will they pass ahead, astern or hit you? At night, the first you know of their arrival is the boat lurching over the ocean which, if you must carry a spinnaker or gennaker, is a good argument for changing to an easier-handled sail at sunset.

Barbados lies about 100 miles outside the main chain of Caribbean Islands. Las Palmas to St Lucia is 2670 miles. Las Palmas to Antigua is 2625 miles and to Fort de France 2645 miles.

ROUTE 3: The Trade Wind Route, Leg 5B • Las Palmas to Barbados via Mindelo (Cape Verde Islands)

Square riggers heading for the Caribbean sailed south from the Canaries 'till the butter melted' before heading west. Following this advice brings you close to the latitude of the Cape Verde Islands which is good reason for dropping in. On his first voyage Columbus worked hard to hide how near he approached the Cape Verde Islands. They were then, and for five centuries afterwards, ruled by Portugal and his presence with a Spanish fleet could have led to a diplomatic incident.

Breaking your voyage in the Cape Verde Islands has a number of attractions. It is not far off route and you do not pass this way every weekend. If you leave the Canaries before the middle of December you will be in the Cape Verde Islands in time to meet up with other boats for Christmas. Best of all, when you leave you are in the thick of the Trade Winds and the North Equatorial Current.

Route 3 Leg 5B Passage Information	
START: LAS PALMAS 27° 42´N 15° 37´W	
Time of year	November/December
Great Circle Distance	2845nm
ETE	26.6 days
Average SMG	4.5 knots
Average wind direction	065°
Average wind speed	14.3 knots (Bft F4)
Chance of calms	1.0%
Chance of gales	0.4%
Percentage sailing time beating	0%
Percentage sailing time close reaching	0%
Percentage sailing time broad reaching	24% (6 days)
Percentage sailing time running	76% (20.6 days)
Average current set/drift	263°/0.5 knots
Average wave height	5ft (1.5m)
Average sea temperature	75.6°F (24.2°C)
DESTINATION: BARBADOS 13° 01´N 59° 31´W	

Las Palmas marina. The density of the masts give some idea of the number of boats that gather here each autumn before setting off for the Caribbean. Similar numbers of boats are at anchor outside the harbour.

Running down the Trades.

TWIN JIBS

Twin jibs are a good Trade Wind rig for lightly-crewed boats. One jib can be your normal roller reefing headsail, the other any old headsail. Tack it down somewhere close to the stem head fitting and haul up on a spare halyard. Both jibs need their own poles with separate uphauls and downhauls. Balance them by rolling away the roller reefing headsail until both sails are about the same size. True decadence arrives in squalls when you roll away the genoa, letting the pole go forward until it is a few inches short of the stay so that there is no risk of chafe. When the squall is over pull the genoa out and once again you are back under twin jibs and romping along. Both operations are carried out in minutes standing in the main hatch. The ease of handling that this system provides allows you to carry both sails by day and by night.

Taking twin jibs down is a lengthy task and anyone working on deck should wear a harness and clip on.

Latitude sailing

Between the Cape Verde Islands and the Caribbean it is latitude sailing on a grand scale. Barbados is 2000 miles west but less than two hundred miles south of Mindelo. Once you find the Big Dipper, Polaris (low on the horizon) shines out like a beacon and with minimal corrections, its altitude is your latitude. Each evening you can stretch out a hand and check your latitude. It is almost as good as a fix.

On a long voyage, land always pops up when your back is turned. After days of watching rolling swells one (the one that does not move) turns out to be Barbados, a rounded whale of an island with the 329m Mount Misery its highest point. You can clear in at Port St Charles Marina six miles south of North Point. Call the marina on VHF Channel 77 on approach. Customs are found close to the arrivals berth. Alternatively, clearing in is possible in Bridgetown's Deep Water Harbour. Customs and immigration are found in the large building at the south end of the harbour. Call on VHF Channel 12 or 16 on approach. In either case when the formalities are completed, you may choose to move to Carlisle Bay, the traditional yacht anchorage in the south-west corner of the island. Motor the last few cables to your chosen spot, throw the anchor overboard and let the Trades push you back. You have arrived and are surrounded by familiar yachts. You have only two questions. Where is the bar and when is happy hour?

OPPOSITE, LEFT TO RIGHT, TOP TO BOTTOM
The Tower of Hercules marks the entrance to La Coruña harbour and the end of your Biscay crossing. There has been a lighthouse here since the Romans arrived.

Vianno do Castello is the most northerly harbour in Portugal with an exciting fiesta every August.

Spanish fiestas range from simple village fetes to major regional events, but they all manage to retain a sense of spontaneity and the impression that those taking part are doing it for fun. These occasions should not be missed.

After leaving Las Palmas, the next stop is the Caribbean. Some boats sneak away whilst others fly the flag.

chapter 20 Caribbean cruising

When you left home, crossing the Atlantic dominated your thoughts. The question of where to pass your time in the Caribbean never arose but now you have arrived, where next? It is a good question. The motto of Caribbean cruising is 'Many islands, one sea.' Each island claims to be unique and with so many, each within an easy day's sail of the next, you are spoilt for choice.

The northern boundary of the Caribbean is a line running from Cuba through the Bahamas to the Virgin Islands. The Lesser Antilles is its eastern border and it is bounded in the south and west by South America, Panama and Central America. The 100 mile wide Yucatán Channel between the Yucatán Peninsula and Cuba leads to the Gulf of Mexico, which is generally considered separately. The name Caribbean is derived from the Carib Indians inhabiting the islands when the Spanish arrived.

Caribbean geography

The Greater Antilles is geologically part of the Central and South American mountain ranges where peaks of over 2000 metres are common. The Caribbean's highest point is Pico Duarte (10 417 feet/3175 metres) in the Dominican Republic. Much of the Lesser Antilles lies on a volcanic ridge and many islands have active volcanoes. Other islands in the Lesser Antilles are coral and limestone. The highest point of the Lesser Antilles is Morne Disblotins (4747 feet/1447 metres) on Dominica. Be careful of confusing Dominica with the Dominican Republic. Elsewhere heights rarely exceed 3900 feet (1200 metres). Geologically, the ABC Islands and Trinidad are part of South America and the low-lying, coral and limestone of the Bahamas is related to the Florida peninsula.

PIRACY

Some of the remoter and less developed areas of the Caribbean carry a higher than normal risk of crime afloat or ashore. This threat seems to be greatest along the mainland coast. The offshore islands are generally regarded as no more dangerous than anywhere else. The risk of high seas piracy appear to have eased but theft from boats at anchor does occur and once ashore there are areas where the chances of being robbed increase. Some regions are politically unstable and the normal rule of law does not apply. These high-risk locations are not fixed but move about. Do not let this discourage you from visiting places like Venezuela or Columbia but the only sure way to discover the latest position is to tune into the local grapevine and radio nets and ask around. Only set out for your next port when you have done your research and know the current situation is safe.

Currents in the Caribbean are dominated by the North and South Equatorial Currents. The South Equatorial Current sweeps round the top of South America, joins the North Equatorial Current, and runs along the Venezuelan and Central American coasts towards the Yucatán Channel where it splits. Some of this current takes a tour of the Gulf of Mexico as the Loop Current before rejoining the main stream. An offshoot of the North Equatorial Current runs along the north coasts of Puerto Rico and Cuba as the Antilles Current to catch up with the main current as it rushes out through the Florida Straits as the Gulf Stream. Currents are not overly important in the Eastern Caribbean where most passages are north-south but for travelling west to east or east to west they play an important role in route-planning. The tidal range is low and except for entrances through reefs or in narrows it is usually ignored.

Marigot Bay, St Lucia.

Boats anchored in a harbour in St John, US Virgin Islands.

Where to go depends on the time available. In this part of the world there is a distinction between clock time and real time. Nearly four months seems time enough to sail everywhere and see everything. Wrong. Porto Santo's mañana philosophy may have surgically removed your sense of haste but it is only a gentle introduction to Caribbean time, a chronology that places tomorrow somewhere in the distant future and regards movement above a quiet amble with frequent stops for rest and refreshment as a cruel and unusual punishment. It is also infectious. Unless you are prepared to rush from one island to another, four months is no time at all.

Choosing where to go is not easy. For a start, there are two Caribbeans. There is the tourist brochure Caribbean and the Caribbean where real folk live. Tourism is big business. The Caribbean is the world's most popular cruise ship destination; there is a growing number of beach resorts; package tourism is growing fast; fleets of charter yachts encourage fly-and-sail holidays and ashore there are any number of attractions and tourist outings. Tourist Caribbean is not a simple backwater but a well developed, sophisticated, international leisure industry. You have the precious ability to escape the beaten track and the time to explore the hard-to-reach, out of the way corners that you discover as you meander through the islands.

The locals place bluewater sailors somewhere between back-packers and beach bums. Their attempts to persuade you to take a taxi are half-hearted for they know your natural mode of shoreside transport is the maxi-taxi and only desultory efforts are made to sell you T-shirts and other souvenirs, for they are aware that space on yachts is as limited as your purse. They accept that for a time you have come to live, not holiday, amongst them and for the most part they welcome you into their Caribbean.

A fast turnaround

If you plan to head home before the next hurricane season arrives, rule out visiting the western Caribbean. Even Venezuela is beyond reach. Once there you would not have the time to follow the winds and currents around the Caribbean. Realistically your explorations are confined to the Eastern Caribbean and even then there is not enough time to visit every island.

A favourite trip is to head from Barbados to Trinidad in time for Carnival. Carnival officially starts with J'Ouvert a street party and parade at 4.00am two days before Ash Wednesday. If you do go, make a point of stopping at Tobago on the way, for calling in is a hard slog from Trinidad on the way back. It is best to arrive early in Trinidad because berths, moorings, even space to drop an anchor, become scarce as Carnival approaches. The island fills up to the sound of steel bands and from several miles offshore their throbbing beat welcomes your arrival. Once you have recovered (nothing quite prepares you for Port of Spain during Carnival) a leisurely passage north takes you through the islands ready to position yourself for the return passage to Europe.

It is usual to make the 90-mile hop from Trinidad to Grenada an overnight passage, arriving off Grenada's south coast just after dawn and dropping into either Prickly Bay or Secret Harbour. After that everything else is an easy day-sail except perhaps the hop from Guadeloupe to Antigua. Some boats like to work their way through the islands stopping at those that have historic or cultural links to their European homeland or take in Antigua Week before heading for the Azores. Still others push further along the chain trying to balance gaining northing with losing easting before heading for Europe. The realistic limit is somewhere around St Martin.

If you wish to make your departure from the eastern seaboard of the USA you will have to make your way into the Greater Antilles then head for Florida via the Turks and Caicos and the Bahamas. It can be done but it will leave little time for sightseeing and socialising.

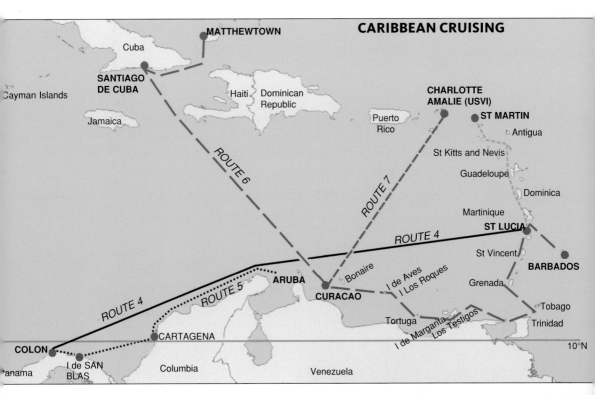

CARIBBEAN CRUISING

Cruising grounds

If you decide to spend a season or two in the Caribbean then during the hurricane season the cry is, 'South of 10°N' which is shorthand for hiding in the south coast of Grenada or in Trinidad and Tobago. Grenada is marginal. It has been trashed by passing hurricanes.

You can spend the summer refitting in Trinidad but the more adventurous spend the time in Venezuela and points west along the mainland coast. After Trinidad, Venezuela and its offshore islands, including Los Testigos, Margarita, Las Aves and Los Roques, are within easy reach and all are outside the hurricane zone. On paper, Venezuela ought to be the major all-year-round Caribbean yachting centre. It has 1100 miles of coastline, 80 offshore islands and

Catamaran moored in an idyllic spot.

the Orinoco, South America's third largest river, to explore. It has 32 national parks, 15 per cent of the world's bird species and the Angel Falls, the highest uninterrupted waterfall in the world.

Route 4: Direct to Panama • Rodney Bay (St Lucia) to Colon

Route 4 Passage Information	
START: RODNEY BAY 14° 5´N 60° 08´W	
Time of year	January/February
Great Circle Distance	1150nm
ETE	11.3 days
Average SMG	4.2 knots
Average wind direction	072°
Average wind speed	15.5 knots (Bft F4)
Chance of calms	0.3%
Chance of gales	0.7%
Percentage sailing time beating	0%
Percentage sailing time close reaching	4% (0.5 days)
Percentage sailing time broad reaching	32% (3.5 days)
Percentage sailing time running	64% (7.3 days)
Average current set/drift	299°/0.9 knots
Average wave height	5.4ft (1.7m)
Average sea temperature	79.4°F (26.3°C)
DESTINATION: COLON 9° 25´N 79° 53´W	

If your Atlantic crossing is the first leg of a circumnavigation then you may decide to hurry across to Panama. This passage would probably be made in January or February

ROUTE 5: Aruba to Colon (Panama)

Route 5 Passage Information	
START: ARUBA 12° 30´N 70° 5´W	
Time of year	November/December
Great Circle Distance	640nm
ETE	7 days
Average SMG	3.8 knots
Average wind direction	043°
Average wind speed	11.9 knots (Bft F4)
Chance of calms	2.4%
Chance of gales	0.1%
Percentage sailing time beating	0%
Percentage sailing time close reaching	26% (2 days)
Percentage sailing time broad reaching	33% (2 days)
Percentage sailing time running	41% (3 days)
Average current set/drift	062°/0.8 knots
Average wave height	4.3ft (1.3m)
Average sea temperature	82.7°F (289.2°C)
DESTINATION: COLON 9° 25´N 79° 53´W	

If you have sufficient time, then starting from Trinidad you could cruise the Venezuelan coast and once in the ABC Islands, continue westwards, visiting Cartagena and the San Blas Islands before arriving in Colon.

Boats moored in Admiralty Bay, Bequia, an island close to St Vincent and the Grenadines in the Caribbean.

ROUTE 6: Curacao to Santiago de Cuba

Route 6 Passage Information	
START: CURACAO 12° 26´N 69° 07´W	
Time of year	December/January
Great Circle Distance	610nm
ETE	4.8 days
Average SMG	5.3 knots
Average wind direction	079°
Average wind speed	13 knots (Bft F4)
Chance of calms	1.3%
Chance of gales	0.4%
Percentage sailing time beating	0%
Percentage sailing time close reaching	25% (1.2 days)
Percentage sailing time broad reaching	75% (3.6 days)
Percentage sailing time running	0%
Average current set/drift	280°/0.9 knots
Average wave height	4.6ft (1.1m)
Average sea temperature	83.1°F (28°C)
DESTINATION: SANTIAGO DE CUBA 19° 59´N 51° 23´W	

From the unmissable reefs (some boats take this literally) of Los Roques it is an easy sail to the ABC Islands, after which it is necessary to decide whether to return east towards Trinidad, continue west towards Cartagena, Colombia and the San Blas Islands and Panama or to strike north for Cuba and the Bahamas.

ROUTE 7: Curacao to Charlotte Amalie

Route 7 Passage Information	
START: CURACAO 12° 26´N 69° 07´W	
Time of year	December/January
Great Circle Distance	445nm
ETE	5.2 days
Average SMG	3.5 knots
Average wind direction	090°
Average wind speed	12.1 knots (Bft F4)
Chance of calms	2.0%
Chance of gales	0%
Percentage sailing time beating	0%
Percentage sailing time close reaching	100% (5.2 days)
Percentage sailing time broad reaching	0%
Percentage sailing time running	0%
Average current set/drift	270°/0.8 knots
Average wave height	3.3ft (1.0m)
Average sea temperature	80.1°F (26.7°C)
DESTINATION: CHARLOTTE AMALIE 18° 20´N 64° 56´W	

Heading directly for the Virgins from the ABC Islands is likely to be an uphill struggle but the south coast of the Dominican Republic is well within reach.

With the exception of going east, these options all involve long (by Caribbean standards) passages of several hundred miles before you can return to your tropical day sailing regime of wandering from island to island. Retracing your steps east along the Venezuelan coast towards Trinidad is day sailing but it means going head-to-head not only with the winds but the current. It can be done. It is possible that the winds might favour night passages and you may find an east-going counter current but it will be slow, hard work.

chapter 21 Eastward bound

Heading home laden with booty from the Caribbean, the early Spanish navigators discovered that the Trades no longer wafted them across the ocean. The benign North Equatorial Current had become the Gulf Stream and acquired a fist of steel inside its velvet glove. The route they developed, *la Carrera de Indias*, took them from Havana, staying in sight of land through the Keys, along the Florida coast, over to Bermuda and home to Spain via the Azores. It was not their secret for long. Hakluyt published his *Carrera de Indias* in the 16th century. We follow its variations today. For us there are three principal starting points:

1 North of the Lesser Antilles and the Bahamas
2 The east coast of the USA as far north as New York
3 The US and Canadian coast north of New York

Departure times

As always, catching the right weather window is everything. In 1493 Columbus headed for home on 16 January. This is too early for decent weather and he was lucky to make it; though to be fair, he made a respectable 34-day passage to the Azores. Relying on dead reckoning he had no idea where he was until he landed and asked. Another 10-day passage, in more bad weather, took him to Lisbon. He was aiming for Cape St Vincent, an error of around 100 miles in nearly 1000 miles of sailing, which is not bad, given the weather conditions.

From the first two starting points there is a narrow weather window. It opens with the end of the Northers and closes just before the start of the hurricane season. In late winter and spring cold air sweeps out from continental USA into the Atlantic as long, cold fronts that stretch from Florida to Bermuda. Ahead of these fronts are the warm trade winds and behind are strong, cold, northerlies which push out high seas for several hundred miles south. A good Norther reaches gale force and is a misery for everyone. Sometimes a front stalls and waits for the next to catch up before continuing south. They rarely make it as far as St Martin. This may tempt you to sail, but any yacht leaving the Caribbean during the Norther season is almost certain to meet bad weather.

The line of low pressure systems creating the Northers moves slowly northwards during the spring. This provides an opportunity to leave the Caribbean and sail east for Europe. This may be in mid-April or even early May which leaves almost no time at all before the hurricane season starts in June. Hurricanes can reach as far as 40°N and their associated winds and gales felt even further north. Prudent sailors aim to be in the Azores by the end of June if possible.

It is 3000 miles to the Azores; at 100 miles a day, the latest sailing date is 31 May. Delay a week and your daily average jumps to 130 miles. If you are certain that you can raise and maintain your performance by 30 per cent all is still well, otherwise you are playing catch up. Some boaters choose to extend their Caribbean cruise until early June on the grounds that the odds of a hurricane or tropical storm in June are low and that early hurricanes are unlikely to reach much beyond the latitude of Bermuda. Both assumptions have proved wrong on several occasions.

Caribbean to the Eastern seaboard of the USA

ROUTE 8: Charlotte Amalie to Miami

Some yachts prefer to leave for Europe from the east coast of the USA. There is the inevitable choice of routes to the US mainland. You can make a leisurely sail through the islands or you can hurry northwards offshore. How you get there depends on your inclination and the time you have available but most boats seem to opt for the scenic route. The route north is a reversal of the essentially day-sailing passage to the Caribbean through the Greater Antilles, the Turks and Caicos and the Bahamas, entering the USA in the area of Miami or Fort Lauderdale.

Most make their way towards Santiago de Cuba and, from there, taking the Windward Passage north, their first landfall in the Bahamas is Matthewtown on Great Inagua. This is a long day sail. The harbour at Great Inagua offers no protection from Northers and finding shelter amongst the reefs of either Great or Little Inagua requires local knowledge. The nearest sure refuge is a day's sail away in Abraham's Bay on Mayagauna where you meet up with the boats from Charlotte Amalie. Most yachts make their US landfall between Key Biscayne and North Palm Beach, after which they move north. How far north is a matter of opinion but most boats would settle for somewhere between Charleston and Chesapeake. You can take the offshore route up the coast hitching a ride on the Gulf Stream, or join the boats heading north up the Intracoastal Waterway to spend the summer in New England.

Route 8 Passage Information	
START: CHARLOTTE AMALIE 18° 20´N 64° 56´W	
Time of Year	March/April
Great Circle Distance	1200nm
ETE	10 days*
Average SMG	5.1 knots
Average wind direction	090°
Average wind speed	12.8 knots
Percentage sailing time in calms	2.1%
Percentage sailing time in gales	0%
Percentage sailing time beating	0%
Percentage sailing time close reaching	22%
Percentage sailing time broad reaching	11%
Percentage sailing time running	67%
Average current set/drift	298°/0.8 knots
Average wave height	1.13m (3.7ft)
Average sea temperature	25°C (77.4°F)
DESTINATION: MIAMI 25° 40´N 80° 15´W	

*This is misleading as most of this passage is day sailing and you can easily double this estimate.

The 16th century Castillo del Mouro guards the entrance to Santiago de Cuba.

ROUTE 9: Havana to Key West

An increasing number of yachts are visiting Cuba, most having made their way from the ABC Islands. A few cruise around Cuba and then from Cuba's north coast it is an easy 95 mile day sail to the Florida Keys with a landfall in Key West. On this route due allowance must be made for an easterly setting current of around 1.5 knots.

Non US flagged yachts do not report any unusual difficulties clearing in from Cuba and with improving relations between the two countries the same may apply to US flagged vessels but if you are concerned there may be difficulties then it is best to arrive in the USA via the Bahamas.

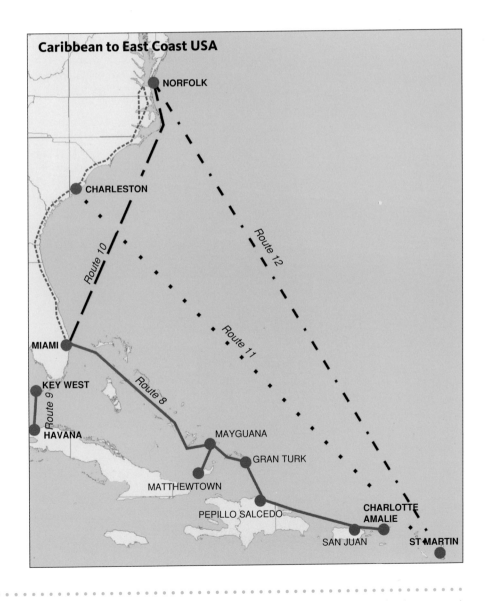

ROUTE 10: The Offshore Route • Miami to Norfolk

Route 10 Passage Information

START: MIAMI 25° 47´N 80° 10´W

Time of year	April
Great Circle Distance	740nm
ETE	5.5 days
Average SMG	6.1 knots
Average wind direction	182°
Average wind speed	14.2 knots (Bft F4)
Chance of calms	1.3%
Chance of gales	1.1%
Percentage sailing time beating	0%
Percentage sailing time close reaching	45% (2.5 days)
Percentage sailing time broad reaching	40% (2.2 days)
Percentage sailing time running	15% (0.8 days)
Average current set/drift	032°/1.6 knots
Average wave height	4.2ft (1.3m)
Average sea temperature	70°F (21.1°C)

DESTINATION: NORFOLK VIRGINIA 37°N 76° 2´W

Route 11 Passage Information

START: ST MARTIN 18°N 63° 1´W

Time of year	March/April
Great Circle Distance	1365nm
ETE	11.8 days
Average SMG	4.8 knots
Average wind direction	113°
Average wind speed	12.5 knots (Bft F4)
Chance of calms	1.9%
Chance of gales	0.4%
Percentage sailing time beating	0%
Percentage sailing time close reaching	7% (0.9 days)
Percentage sailing time broad reaching	66% (7.9 days)
Percentage sailing time running	27% (2 days)
Average current set/drift	3.6°/0.7 knots
Average wave height	4.3ft (1.3m)
Average sea temperature	75°F (23.9°C)

DESTINATION: CHARLESTON 32° 44´N 79° 51´W

This route requires good weather. The coastline is reminiscent of Portugal with harbours approached through narrow slots. In Georgia and the Carolinas, the shore is a bigger version of the Dutch and German North Sea coasts: low, sandy barrier islands protect the land with narrow tidal gaps between islands. By June the depressions that created the Northers that locked boats in the Caribbean leave the coast somewhere around the latitude of New York. Blowing over the Gulf Stream they bring seas that close harbours and are dangerous to small craft.

From Florida it is around 420 miles to Charleston. Cape Fear is another 110 miles. Cape Hatteras is 150 miles further north and there are still 115 miles to the entrance of Chesapeake Bay. It adds up to nearly 800 miles of sailing in waters that have been eating ships since the 15th century. The story goes that so many ships have been wrecked off Cape Hatteras that their remains create a local magnetic anomaly. Monitor, one of the first ironclad warships, sank hereabouts. There are few ports of refuge. It is not a voyage to be undertaken lightly. If possible, it should be planned in a series of hops that allows you to duck in and find shelter before bad weather comes.

ROUTE 11: St Martin to Charleston direct

If sailing directly from the Eastern Caribbean to ports on the Eastern Seaboard, south of Cape Hatteras, the Gulf Stream can give a welcome advantage, but if a Norther is forecast then it is prudent to sail clear of the Stream before its arrival. This avoids the high seas created by strong northerly winds blowing over a strong north-going current.

ROUTE 12: St Martin to Norfolk direct

There is little to choose either in distance or sea time between sailing from St Martin to either Charleston or Norfolk. Your decision depends on where you wish to begin the eastwards passage across the Atlantic. Breaking the passage north at Bermuda adds another 150 miles and the remaining 600 miles from Bermuda to Norfolk are hard on the wind.

Route 12 Passage Information	
START: ST MARTIN 18°N 63° 1´W	
Time of year	April
Great Circle Distance	1365nm
ETE	11.5 days
Average SMG	4.9 knots
Average wind direction	113°
Average wind speed	12.5 knots (Bft F4)
Chance of calms	2.3%
Chance of gales	0.7%
Percentage sailing time beating	0%
Percentage sailing time close reaching	0%
Percentage sailing time broad reaching	28% (3.2 days)
Percentage sailing time running	72% (8.3 days)
Average current set/drift	317°/0.7 knots
Average wave height	4.3ft (1.3m)
Average sea temperature	72°F (22.2°C)
DESTINATION: NORFOLK VIRGINIA 37°N 76° 2´W	

A hillside view of one of the most beautiful lagoons in Saint Martin, Netherlands Antilles.

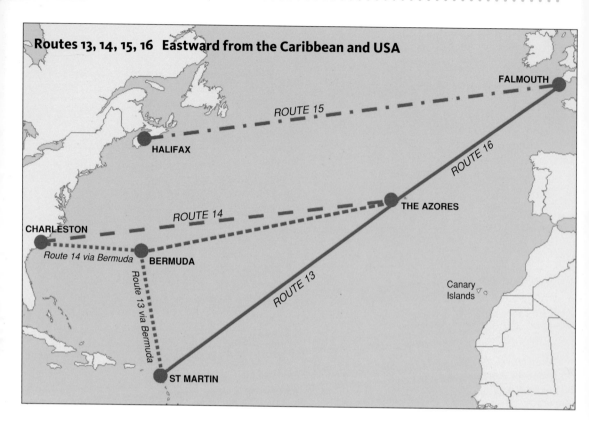

Routes 13, 14, 15, 16   Eastward from the Caribbean and USA

FALMOUTH

ROUTE 15

HALIFAX

ROUTE 16

ROUTE 14

THE AZORES

CHARLESTON

Route 14 via Bermuda   BERMUDA

Route 13 via Bermuda

ROUTE 13

Canary
Islands

ST MARTIN

Eastward routes from the Caribbean and the East coast of the USA

St Martin to the Azores

If you are sailing to Europe from the Caribbean then St Martin is a good departure point for the voyage to Europe, but wherever you start, vessels sailing from the Eastern Caribbean to Europe must adopt a circuitous course to avoid the Azores High which sits across the Great Circle route.

The first obstacle to any eastward passage is the north-east Trades. These winds, which so recently carried you across the Atlantic, are now an excellent reason for staying in the sun. If you are not stopping at Bermuda then for the first three or four hundred miles you are on a hard close-reach making as much easting as possible in the knowledge that a real sailor would be close-hauled. Either way it is several days of slap, bang, wallop and cries of 'Why me?' The squalls that ignored you on the way west pay their respects with interest now. Watching them approach, wrapped in cloaks of rain, is like going head-to-head with the school bully. Defeat appears certain but a show of defiance might delay the inevitable.

The worst squalls approach with a hem of white mist between them and the sea. They look like the gateway to the Bermuda Triangle, that twilight zone bounded by Fort Lauderdale, Puerto Rico and Bermuda where ships and men vanish, although this may have more to do with downbursts than the supernatural.

The Azores high

Around the latitude of Bermuda, the Azores High begins its rule. Tradition parks it on the Great Circle route between the Caribbean and Europe. Whether you leave from the Caribbean or the Eastern Seaboard, once out at sea your route to the Azores is a choice between power sailing and lazy days. If you wish for comfortable (as opposed to fast and rough) sailing then stay south. How far south you go is determined by the tracks the gales follow. The weather that gave rise to the Northers has moved north. By late May and June one depression after another charges out of the Hudson River to do battle with ships in the Atlantic. Crossing the warm waters of the Gulf Stream drives them berserk and they head east and north, spitting fury as they go.

The NOAA High Seas forecast gives their centre pressure and position, adding cheerful snippets, like winds 35–45 knots, seas 18 to 24 feet (5 to 7 metres) within 300 miles of centre. Try to listen to this forecast at least once a day; plot it on a laminated weather map and hatch in no-go areas. Before long you will have a fair imitation of the Berlin Wall stretching across the Atlantic and it becomes clear that, going north of 35°N, before making a decent amount of easting, means hard, rough sailing. Yachts leaving from New York or Chesapeake may wish to drop south in search of comfort. NOAA voice forecasts cover only to 38°W. Further east, Herb of Southbound 2 (he always looks two or three days ahead) and regular weatherfaxes are a good combination. See page 99.

If time or inclination does not permit sailing, then keep to the Great Circle route, and start the engine when the wind fails. If deck cargo is any indication this is a popular option. Many yachts leave the Caribbean with their decks stacked with fuel cans and looking like small, overloaded container ships.

ATLANTIS

On this side of the ocean, the Trades and Horse Latitudes are heavy with mystery. Besides the Bermuda Triangle it is, supposedly, home to Atlantis. Plato first mentioned its existence in 360BC when writing Timaeus and Critias. According to Plato, Solon, an Athenian statesman, met an ancient Egyptian priest who told him of a city state that drowned 8000 years earlier. On the strength of this umpteenth hand information of doubtful provenance Plato theorised on the size and layout of Atlantis, its ruling party (all descendants of Poseidon) and its government but lacking GPS he simply placed it west of the Pillars of Hercules which was Greek for the middle of nowhere. From all this has sprung an industrial-sized legend that has placed Atlantis in the Azores, the Aegean, the Sargasso Sea and even the Celtic Shelf off Ireland.

Columbus added his tuppence worth by claiming his compass went haywire as he came this way but he was not aware that this is one of the two places on earth where a magnetic compass points to true north.

ROUTE 13: St Martin to the Azores

Route 13 Passage Information	
START: ST MARTIN 18°N 63° 1´W	
Time of year	May
Great Circle Distance	2181nm
ETE	25 days
Average SMG	3.6 knots
Average wind direction	118°
Average wind speed	12.3 knots (Bft F4)
Chance of calms	2.5%
Chance of gales	1.0%
Percentage sailing time beating	67% (17 days)
Percentage sailing time close reaching	8% (2 days)
Percentage sailing time broad reaching	20% (5 days)
Percentage sailing time running	5% (1 day)
Average current set/drift	227°/0.5 knots
Average wave height	4.9ft (1.5m)
Average sea temperature	70.3°F (21.3°C)
DESTINATION: AZORES 38° 32´N 28° 9´W	

St Martin to the Azores via Bermuda

On both the Great Circle and the more circuitous route, many yachts choose to stop over in Bermuda. This adds nearly 600 miles but it turns a beat into a close reach, the speed made good jumps to 4.7 knots so that the passage time to the Azores, excluding stopovers, is almost the same. Juan de Bermudez was the first to see Bermuda when he was sailing home in 1503. The islands soon became an involuntary stopover for galleons running onto its reefs, making diving now one of the island's most popular tourist attractions. In 1609 Admiral Sir George Somers, on *The Sea Venture* carrying supplies for Virginia, followed the Spanish example of anchoring the hard way. Somers liked Bermuda so much he stayed. This marked the beginning of British rule and Somer's tale gave Shakespeare the idea for writing *The Tempest*.

Leaving from the Bahamas

Yachts passing through the Bahamas on their way to the eastern seaboard of the USA, and running out of time, can wander through this maze of islands until they reach the north east of the chain before making for home. The story goes that the name Bahamas is a corruption of the Spanish *baja mar*, which means low sea. It may be wrongly attributed but any cruise in the Bahamas means sailing in shallow waters that are a good test of your reef navigation skills. Deep-keeled yachts will be tempted to keep to the (very) deep water passages and hurry through the islands. About 40 of the 7000 islands in the archipelago are inhabited with most of the population crowded on to New Providence and Grand Bahama, leaving each of the remaining islands with 1500 souls or less.

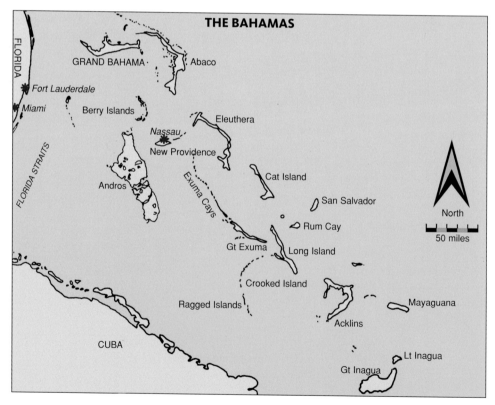

The main drawback to beginning your crossing from the Bahamas is that provisions are expensive and, in the Out Islands (just about everywhere outside of New Providence), limited in choice and quantity.

Charleston to the Azores

The Azores lie around 38°N, level with Chesapeake, a couple of degrees south of New York and five degrees north of Charleston. In terms of sea time this is not a huge difference and whereabouts on the eastern seaboard you choose to leave will depend on whether you prefer the southern comforts of Charleston over the cosy neighbourliness of Maryland. Either way the first challenge is to clear the Gulf Stream.

The Gulf Stream

Wherever you leave the eastern seaboard of the USA then the Gulf Stream lies in wait. If you think its principal task is to help east-going yachts, think again. There is no such thing as free sea miles. This is one of the world's strongest currents and part of the North Atlantic Gyre. On average it moves at between one and three knots but in the Florida Straits it can reach five knots and shift more water every second than all the world's rivers combined. Along the Florida coast it flows over an ancient coral reef called the Blake Plateau and is closest to land at Palm Beach. Hereabouts it is called the Florida Current, but by the time it has reached north Florida it is veering away from the coast. The Gulf Stream proper begins at Cape Hatteras where it falls off the Blake Plateau into the open ocean. Rachel Carson, author of *Silent Spring*, called Cape Hatteras the Mason-Dixon Line of the sea with cold water fish to the north and warm water fish to the south.

As it moves away from the coast, the warm surface water of the Gulf Stream is replaced by an up-welling of deeper, colder water from the Labrador Current. By New York, the prevailing winds have moved the surface water of the Gulf Stream far offshore and it has grown to around 300 miles wide.

The boundary between water from the Labrador Current and the Gulf Stream is the 'north wall'. This is the world's strongest oceanic front, rich in nutrients, but generating heavy winds and big waves. The rapid change in temperature between the cold, inshore slope and shelf water and the warm Gulf Stream causes primed and unstable low pressure systems coming from the USA to explode. These lows (meteorologists call them 'bombs') are most common in winter and early spring. Bomblets in the form of microbursts and downbursts can come any time.

THE SARGASSO SEA

The Sargasso Sea is a sea without a coastline, two million square miles bounded by the Gulf Stream to the west and north, where cold eddies spinning off the Stream make this one of the most energetic spots of the world's oceans. The Canary Current marks its eastern border and the North Equatorial Current the southern. It is the centre of the great gyre that circles round the North Atlantic and reaching it is uphill sailing all the way. Its waters are about a metre higher than the sea along the Florida coast.

It produces one third of the Atlantic's plankton but lacks the nutrients to attract commercial fishing, for its warm (25°C), clear blue and very salty waters (10 per cent saltier than the salty Gulf Stream) inhibit the upwelling of colder, nutrient-rich water. Instead it is famous for its sargassum weed that provides living space for tiny crabs, shrimp and octopi. Columbus saw this weed and thought he was near land when he was over the Nares Abyssal Plain. Portuguese sailors reckoned the weed (eight species have been identified) looked like the Salgazo grape and poor pronunciation did the rest.

Allied with the uncertain winds of the Horse Latitudes, the erratic swirling current in the Sargasso Sea promises poor progress. Tales of ships being trapped in the weed rank alongside the mysteries of the Bermuda Triangle or Atlantis (do not worry this is impossible) while, under your keel, eels from Europe, the Mediterranean and the Americas have come to mate, spawn and die, leaving their offspring to make the journey home by themselves. That's truly mysterious.

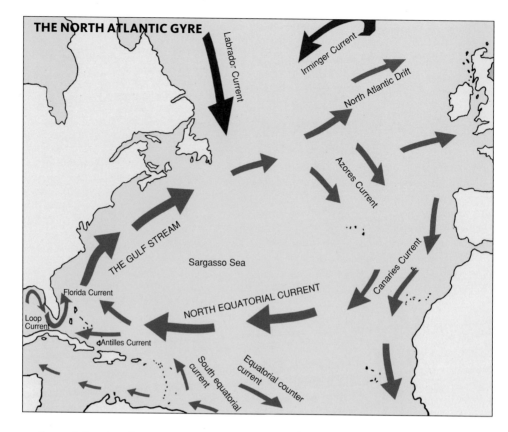

Around the Grand Banks the Stream goes head-to-head with the Labrador Current. This originates in the Arctic Ocean, flows south through the Labrador Sea and into the North Atlantic carrying a diminishing cargo of icebergs as it goes. The mixing process with the Gulf Stream produces eddies, whirlpools and advection fog, before the south-westerly winds propel the Stream north-east as the North Atlantic Drift or Current. As far as the Grand Banks, the Gulf Stream is a distinctive bright blue and very salty.

Charting the Gulf Stream

In 1769 the Board of Customs in Boston reported to the Treasury in London that mail between Falmouth and New York took two weeks longer than letters between London and Rhode Island. The Treasury regarded complaints about the mail as a matter for North America's Deputy Postmaster General, then Benjamin Franklin. He asked his cousin Timothy Folger, a Nantucket whaling captain, for help. Folger drew a chart of the Gulf Stream. Franklin sent Folger's chart to the Treasury who, if they had ever considered the matter important, now regarded it as closed. After refining Folger's chart from observations taken on transatlantic voyages, Franklin published it, but during the American War of Independence it disappeared until a copy turned up in the Bibliothèque Nationale in Paris in 1978.

Nowadays it is possible to obtain daily updates on the Stream along with the latest weather forecasts for planning your passage east. These show not a smooth arc of water advancing steadily across the Atlantic, but something resembling the irregular meanderings of a river

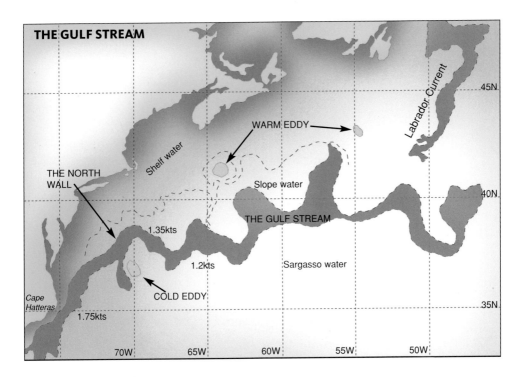

THE GULF STREAM

45N

WARM EDDY

Labrador Current

THE NORTH WALL

Shelf water

Slope water

40N

THE GULF STREAM

1.35kts

1.2kts

Sargasso water

Cape Hatteras

COLD EDDY

35N

1.75kts

70W 65W 60W 55W 50W

across a flood plain. Satellite pictures with their false colour images make the Stream look like a Chinese dragon sitting off the eastern seaboard.

A good strategy for leaving the eastern seaboard is to wait for a high-pressure ridge between low-pressure systems that lasts long enough to see you safely out of harbour and across the Gulf Stream. If this is not possible then it may be necessary to ride out to the Gulf Stream on the coat-tails of a low pressure system and use the ridge behind to escort you across. Try to avoid being caught near the Gulf Stream in a gale. Once over the Gulf Stream, the choices are exactly the same as those facing the boats that left from St Martin. Do you creep round the Azores High or motor-sail through the light winds? Stopping at Bermuda adds only 35 extra miles

Timing your departure balances the probability of meeting a gale with the chance of running into a hurricane. In April the figure for gales is 5.3%. In May it is 2.5%, dropping to 0.8% in June, but then there is the risk of an early-season hurricane.

ROUTE 14: Charleston to the Azores

Route 14 Passage Information	
START: CHARLESTON 32° 44´N 79° 51´W	
Time of year	May
Great Circle Distance	2511nm
ETE	19.9 days
Average SMG	5.3 knots
Average wind direction	228°
Average wind speed	13.6 knots (Bft F4)
Chance of calms	1.9%
Chance of gales	2.5%
Percentage sailing time beating	0%
Percentage sailing time close reaching	7% (1.4 days)
Percentage sailing time broad reaching	93% (18.5 days)
Percentage sailing time running	0%
Average current set/drift	088°/0.8 knots
Average wave height	3.8ft (1.2m)
Average sea temperature	75.5°F (24.2°C)
DESTINATION: AZORES 38° 32´N 28° 9´W	

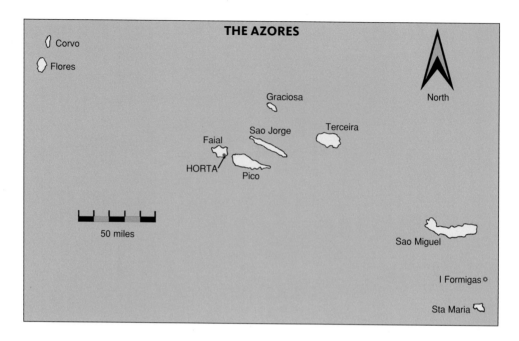

Arrival in the Azores

The most popular landfall is on the island of Faial using a waypoint to the south of the channel between Faial and Pico. If the weather is fine then Ponta do Pico (7713 feet/2351 metres and on the island of Pico), which overshadows Faial, is picked up over 50 miles away. This is bad for morale for it means that after making your landfall there is the best part of a day's sail to reach it.

After only seeing one yacht a week, boats pop up all over the horizon hurrying for the harbour at Horta, and whale watchers and fishing boats come out for the day. Suddenly it is a very crowded ocean.

It was rather different when Diego de Senill arrived in 1497. He found no evidence of any early visitors and claimed the islands for Portugal. The nine volcanic islands, volcanic seamounts made good, became famous for their flowers, fruit, vegetables, dairy produce and gentle way of life. They are divided into the Eastern Group (Sao Miguel, Santa Maria), the Central Group (Terceira, Graciosa, Sao Jorge, Pico, Faial) and Western Group (Flores and Corvo). Horta marina is well used to the seasonal crush of visitors and Café Sport accustomed to hungry and thirsty yachtsmen. They run one of the best mail drops around. If you have the opportunity to escape the delights of Horta take a trip round the island. If the sky is clear, include a visit to the Caldera which once held a lake that mysteriously drained away.

Tradition, encouraged by sellers of paints and brushes, claims it is good luck to paint your boat name on the wall. Some paintings are very colourful and some are those of old friends. Tourism is growing in Horta. Groups are taken on guided tours of the paintings. You are now a tourist attraction.

The harbour at Ponta Delgada on the island of San Miguel, Azores.

The Northern Route

ROUTE 15: The Northern Route
• Halifax to Falmouth

Yachts taking the hard, cold northern route from the New York area, and further north, ride one low-pressure system after another until they reach Europe. This is only for the best prepared, most determined yachts. The early part of their passage is over the Grand Banks where the Gulf Stream and the Labrador Current mix and fogs are common. For much of the way it is well north of the ice limits. Almost immediately after the Titanic tragedy in 1912 the US Navy began its North Atlantic ice patrol to report sightings of icebergs to shipping, and in 1914 the first Safety of Life at Sea (SOLAS) conference formally inaugurated the International Ice Patrol which continues to this day to determine the limits of all known ice (LAKI). Do not rely on radar to detect icebergs in poor visibility. The shape of the berg may reflect a

Route 15 Passage Information	
START: HALIFAX 44° 34´ N 63° 31´ W	
Time of year	June/July
Great Circle Distance	2345nm
ETE	21 days
Average SMG	4.7 knots
Average wind direction	247°
Average wind speed	14.3 knots (Bft F4)
Chance of calms	2.4%
Chance of gales	1%
Percentage sailing time beating	0%
Percentage sailing time close reaching	0%
Percentage sailing time broad reaching	25% (5 days)
Percentage sailing time running	75% (16 days)
Average current set/drift	106°/0.5 knots
Average wave height	4.7ft (1.4m)
Average sea temperature	56°F (13.3°C)
DESTINATION: FALMOUTH 50° 1´ N 5° 6´ W	

weak echo or none at all. In calm weather, bergs may be detected at ranges of 15–20 miles, but bergy bits three metres high may not be detected at ranges over three miles. In rough weather, sea clutter may hide them entirely.

There is a small window for making this passage. In May the figure for gales is 4.3%. This drops to 1.7% in June and 1.0% in July. It rises to 1.75% in August and is back to 4.2% in September.

The Azores to Falmouth

ROUTE 16: The final leg • the Azores to Falmouth

From Horta you can sail for Gibraltar and the Mediterranean, or England, Ireland, Wales, the West Coast of Scotland and Scandinavia. The expected light winds do not always materialise as you leave the Azores, but the seas will turn from blue to green to gunmetal grey. There is a tendency to regard this passage as a short sprint. In fact it is the third longest leg of an Atlantic circuit and the stable weather patterns of the tropics are far astern. Once clear of the influence of the Azores High, the weather changes its mind on a whim. You may not meet a full-blown gale but there is a good chance of meeting some prolonged unpleasant weather. In August the percentage of gales is 1.1%, rising to 2.3% in September.

The majority of boats make for the English Channel. For most of the voyage the Bay of Biscay sits to leeward with teeth bared. No wonder the square-riggers hated and feared it. Once blown into its jaws it would be hard work for them to escape. The waters grow busier. Shipping from all over the world funnels into and pours out of the English Channel.

Once in soundings, the seas shorten their stride to become the Chops of the Channel, and fishing boats weave in and out of the traffic. Tides, a nearly forgotten word, draw attention to themselves and underline the lack of an up-to-date almanac. Once past Land's End, the number of leisure craft increases. Most appear to be using the same waypoint to clear Start Point. Once that choke point is safely astern you can turn to port and head for Falmouth. You're back but it is unlikely anyone has noticed.

Falmouth was not the place that you left. Its colours are wrong. You look longingly at the boats gathering for their passage to the sun. They are about to enter the world you are leaving and you have nothing to say to each other, well, nothing either would understand. Marina life, once so seductive, has lost its charm. You miss the camaraderie of the cruising anchorage. Stopping is no longer fun. How could so many boats be so close together and be so isolated from each other?

As you slide into your home berth it is like stepping back through The Wardrobe,

Route 16 Passage Information	
START: AZORES 38° 32´N 28° 9´W	
Time of year	July
Great Circle Distance	1200nm
ETE	10.5 days
Average SMG	4.9 knots
Average wind direction	308°
Average wind speed	11.7 knots (Bft F4)
Chance of calms	2.9%
Chance of gales	0.8%
Percentage sailing time beating	0%
Percentage sailing time close reaching	15% (1.6 days)
Percentage sailing time broad reaching	79% (8.3 days)
Percentage sailing time running	6% (0.6 days)
Average current set/drift	128°/0.4 knots
Average wave height	4.1ft (1.3m)
Average sea temperature	64.6°F (18.1°C)
DESTINATION: FALMOUTH 50° 1´N 5° 6´W	

exchanging a wonderland of adventures for monochrome reality. For a year or two you have been privileged to be a member of the bluewater cruising tribe. They had welcomed you, helped you, taught you, and protected you from your greater follies. Now it is over; the world has moved on and you have fallen out of step.

Anyone taking a sabbatical must find it strange that their colleagues managed without them. Is there still a 'real' job for them to do? Do their contemporaries resent their return? Is anyone who disappears for more than a year seriously committed to work as society knows it? If returning home means joining the ranks of job-hunters, does time as a floating vagabond look good on a CV? Is it a sign of initiative, determination, with the ability to cheerfully deal with a real challenge or is it taken as evidence of being out of touch and past your sell-by date? Is it a mark of a team player or a rebel marching to their own drumbeat?

Few emerge unchanged from an Atlantic circuit. It is an experience that resonates throughout your life. Be warned, once a member of the bluewater cruising tribe, always a member. Like a reformed addict you have to live with the knowledge that to reach Narnia once more all you have to do is to cast off and head westwards.

Fair winds and good sailing.

A spectacular view of Horta, on the island of Faial in the Azores, from Monte da Guia.

Appendix

BOAT DETAILS AND CREW LIST

Clearing in and out of each country can be eased by having all the details you need to complete the paperwork ready to hand. Normally the forms are provided. Occasionally you are expected to provide your own.

Remember to include your boat name on the crew list and space for you to sign on both. Often the official forms are in Spanish and they may, or may not, give an English translation.

DETAILS OF BOAT	YOUR DETAILS
Boat name *Nombre de barco* or *Nombre de buque*	
Master's name *Nombre del capitán* You may find '*Registro bruto al mando del capitán*' which means 'under the command of captain'	
Address *Dirección*	
Owner *Proprietario* or *capitán y dueño* which means captain and owner.	
Address of owner *Dirección de proprietario*	
Last port of call *Procedencia*	
Date of arrival *Fecha de entrada*	
Time of arrival *Tiempo de entrada*	
Purpose of visit *Intención de visitar*	
Date of departure *Fecha de salida*	
Next port of call *Despachado para*	

DETAILS OF BOAT	YOUR DETAILS
Official details *Los detalles del embarcación*	
Flag *Bandera*	
Port of registry *Matricula*	
Official number *Lista*	
Type of craft *Tipo de barco*	
Hull material *Casca/casco*	
LOA *Eslora*	
Beam *Manga*	
Draft *Calado*	
Tonnage *Tonelada/tonelaje*	
Colour *Color*	
Motor *Motor*	
Horsepower *Caballos*. Also *achay pay* when spoken = HP	
Signed (Master) *Firma del capitán*	
Date *(Fecha)*	

CREWLIST

Boat name
Nombre de barco

Master's name
Nombre del capitán

Address
Dirección

Owner
Proprietario

Address
Dirección

DETAILS OF CREW

Name
Nombre

Date of birth
Fecha de nacimiento
or *nacido* = born

Place of birth
Lugar de nacimiento

Country of birth*
Pais de nacimiento
or *patria*

Country of residence
País de residencia

Nationality
Nacionalidad

Passport number
Pasaporte

Issuing authority
Expedición por

Date of issue
Fecha de expedición

Expiry date
Fecha de caducidad

Signed (Master)

Firma del capitán

Date
(Fecha)

Crew = *tripulación*
A single crew member = *uno tripulante*

Be prepared to repeat the same information on each form you

complete

Repeat for each crew member. Include everyone onboard, including the skipper. You may be asked to give everyone's position onboard: so you have mates, cooks, bosuns and deckhands

* *Britanica* = Britain
Reino Unido = UK
Estados Unidos de América = USA
Francia = France
Alemania = Germany
Los Países Bajos = Netherlands
Dinamarca = Denmark
Noruega = Norway

Index